# Understanding Social Policy

# MICHAEL HILL

# Understanding Social Policy

*Third Edition*

BASIL BLACKWELL

Copyright © Michael Hill 1980, 1983, 1988

First published 1980 by Basil Blackwell Ltd
and Martin Robertson & Co Ltd

Second Edition 1983
Reprinted 1985, 1986, 1987

Third Edition 1988

Basil Blackwell Ltd
108 Cowley Road, Oxford OX4 1JF, UK

Basil Blackwell Inc.
432 Park Avenue South, Suite 1503
New York, NY 10016, USA

*British Library Cataloguing in Publication Data*

Hill, Michael, *1937–*
    Understanding social policy. – 3rd ed.
    1. Great Britain. Government. Social
    policies
    I. Title
    361.6'1'0941

    ISBN 0-631-16225-9

*Library of Congress Cataloging in Publication Data*

Hill, Michael J. (Michael James), 1937–
    Understanding social policy/Michael Hill, – 3rd ed.
        p.    cm.
    Bibliography: p.
    Includes indexes.
    ISBN 0-631-16225-9 (pbk.)
    1. Great Britain – Social policy.   2. Welfare state.   3. Welfare
economics.   I. Title.
HN390.H52 1988                                              87-36069
361.6'1–dc19                                                      CIP

Typeset by Alan Sutton Publishing, Gloucester.
Printed in Great Britian by Page Bros (Norwich) Ltd.

# Contents

# Preface

This book is an introduction to the study of social policy. It is based on a view that those who study this subject need to consider the way in which policy is made and implemented as well as to learn about the main policies and their limitations. It has been written for people who have had no previous training in the social sciences, with the needs of social workers, health visitors and other social policy 'practitioners' very much in mind.

The preparation of the third edition of this book has involved a substantial revision. The first edition was completed just before Mrs Thatcher came to power in 1979; consequently it was necessary to produce a second edition fairly quickly to take into account the many policy changes that occurred in the early 1980s. This was done in 1983. However, the changes made to that edition were kept to the minimum necessary to ensure that it was up to date on policy details. The second edition did not reflect satisfactorily the way in which how we look at social policy in Britain was changing. Hence, the more radically revised third edition both brings the information about policies up to date and considers the ways in which the terms of the policy debate have changed. The historical chapter is no longer called 'The Growth of Social Policy' and reflects, with the benefit of hindsight, on the connections between developments in the 1970s and those of the 1980s. The chapters on policy making and implementation examine some of the new strains imposed upon the doctrine of representative government by a strong central government without the support of a substantial majority of the people but determined to curb local autonomy. The chapter on social security has been almost totally rewritten to take into account the 1986 Social Security Act. The chapters on health and social services policy look in much more depth at the 'community care' debate. The chapter on education looks at the way central government's interventions have become preoccupied with the 'three Rs' and preparation for the labour market, leaving behind the great concerns of the sixties and seventies with inequalities and socially determined under-achievement. The chapter on labour market policies shows how youth employment and long-term unemployment have undermined the preoccupation with 'active labour market policy' which characterized the Manpower Services Commission's view of the world in the 1970s. The chapter on housing policy reflects the way central distrust of local government and privatization have come to dominate the agenda. Overall, issues about public expenditure are brought into much sharper focus in the book as a whole, and not just left to the last chapter.

At this stage in the history of a textbook it becomes impossible to acknowledge satisfactorily all the people who have helped to shape the author's approach, and who have kept him up to date on developments in policy. However, a special debt should be acknowledged to two people who have been collaborators on other books, Chris Ham and Glen Bramley.

Thanks are also due to Alan and Rosemary Towers for their assistance with the preparation of the manuscript, and to Sean Magee, the third in the succession of helpful editorial staff from Blackwell who have been responsible for ensuring successful publication.

The book is dedicated to my wife Betty who, when she was a health visitor student, first helped me to identify the gap in the market, and who has taken a warm interest in the progress of the book ever since. I am happy that I have been able to share with her the fruits of its success.

# CHAPTER 1

# What is Social Policy?

## INTRODUCTION

One way to answer the question 'What is social policy?' is to provide a list of the areas of public policy included under that heading. Another way is just to try to define its scope by explaining what it is that distinguishes it from other kinds of policy. Social policy is a difficult subject to define in this way, however. Perhaps it is best just to list the policy areas to be discussed. However, because the process of declaring certain kinds of policies to be social policies, while disregarding others having a considerable impact on the well-being of our society, seems a particularly arbitrary exercise, it is necessary to look a little at the rationale for doing this. It is also necessary to examine what studying social policy implies.

Readers may be familiar with textbooks that set out to define their subject in the first chapter. These discussions are often tedious and pedantic. They frequently appear to have been written for some private academic argument rather than to inform prospective students. It is hoped that this chapter will not be dismissed as an arid academic ground-clearing exercise, since it has important things to say about the most appropriate way to approach the subject of the book.

## WHICH POLICIES?

The policy areas covered in this book are set out in the titles of chapters 5 to 10. The first three of those chapters deal with policy areas that everyone seems to include within their definition of social policy – social security, the personal social services and health. These are the policies that are the responsibility of the Secretary of State for Social Services and of his department, the Department of Health and Social Security. Whilst most people have no doubt about recognizing these as 'social services', even here the terminology causes some confusion. Notice how the secretery of state has a different title from his department. This is most confusing since, in England and Wales, there are local government departments – the social services departments – that are responsible for the personal social services but are not directly concerned with health or social security, the main concerns of the secretary of state.

Chapter 10 looks at housing policy. Most books and courses on social policy deal with housing, though with some uncertainty about the extent to which they are concerned with the private sector. There are important questions in relation to housing policy concerning the extent to which a free market can operate and the extent to which public housing authorities should act as if they were private business concerns. This chapter, together with chapter 9, on employment services, has to give particular attention to the issues, seldom far away in any discussion of social policy, of the impact of economic policy, and of the relevance of economic and commercial considerations. These are major problems in identifying, and separating off from other policies, a specific area called 'social policy'.

The other chapter on a particular area of policy deals with education. This is much less often included within social policy. The very fact that it is difficult to find reasons either for including it or for excluding it tells us something about the peculiarly arbitrary process involved in categorizing policies as 'social'. Clearly, the field of education is one in which there is a considerable amount of public expenditure upon services that contribute to public welfare. But is the hallmark of social policy expenditure its contribution to public welfare, and what does this really mean? Let us just accept that the inclusion of education within social policy is the consequence of a comparatively arbitrary decision by the author, and move on to look at the difficult problems that would have to be faced if we were to define social policy in terms of public expenditure which contributes to public welfare. We need to do this to clear out of the way, before we go any further into the study of social policy, a most misleading and widespread false assumption about the character of our subject.

T. H. Marshall, in his book on social policy,[1] has an opening chapter with the same title as this one. In it he proclaims that 'the avowed objective of twentieth-century social policy is welfare'. Readers will find a central concern about the factors that influence social welfare a characteristic of many writings on social policy. Indeed, some of the British contributions to the study of this topic assert theirs to be a distinctive academic subject, 'social administration', which has this concern as its hallmark.[2]

However, a concern to understand social policy may be distinguished from a preoccupation with the determinants of welfare. To equate this 'avowed objective' of social policy with its real objective, as Marshall seems to do, involves an acceptance of a particular ideology about the 'welfare state' that has been challenged by various writers. Moreover, to see policies as having objectives may involve confusing the character of the policies with the motives and purposes of the people who advocate, adopt and implement them.

Several recent discussions of social policy have suggested that welfare policies are promulgated not from humanitarian concerns to meet need but as responses to social unrest. Piven and Cloward, for example, argue as follows about social security policies:

> The key to an understanding of relief-giving is in the functions it serves for the larger economic and political order, for relief is a secondary and supportive institution. Historical evidence suggests that relief arrangements are initiated or expanded during the occasional outbreaks of civil disorder produced by mass unemployment, and are then abolished or contracted when political stability is restored . . . this view clearly belies the popular supposition that government social policies, including relief policies, are becoming progressively more responsible, humane and generous.[3]

Piven and Cloward are primarily concerned to explain relief policies in the United States, but they draw on British data too, and they clearly intend their analysis to apply to other countries. Other writers have analysed British policies in similar terms. In particular, Marxists have argued that advanced capitalist societies require an infrastructure of welfare policies to help maintain order, buy off working-class protest and secure a workforce with acceptable standards of health and education.[4]

Clearly, perspectives like these give a very different meaning to 'welfare'. To the Marxist 'welfare capitalism' is a perjorative term. Policies that promote welfare are explained in terms of social control; they are measures to combat disorder and crime just like police and penal policies, measures to legitimize and prop up the capitalist system. But it is not necessary to accept totally this interpretation of public policy in order to agree that there may be circumstances in which social control motives mingle with humanitarian motives in creating what we describe as 'social policies'. Moreover, the two extreme interpretations of the origins of social policies that have been mentioned do not exhaust the range of possibilities. Joan Higgins has suggested that both rest upon rational models of political action, in which actors have motives and are able to frame policies that accurately reflect their intentions.[5] Contemporary studies of both policy making and policy implementation suggest that we need to give attention to some very complex relationships between the mixed goals of those able to influence policies and the varied consequences of their interventions. Outcomes may be the unintended results of policy inputs. Most policy is incremental in character, involving marginal adjustments to what has gone before, and is motivated to correct what are seen as undesirable consequences of previous policies. Accordingly, social policy need not be interpreted in terms either of the continuous evolution of a welfare state inspired by humanitarian ideals or of a conspiracy to manipulate a powerless proletariat. Yet the rejection of these interpretations need not imply either that individuals with altruistic motives play no part in the evolution of policy, or that manipulative and social-control motivated actions are not involved in the policy process.

This discussion implies three things for the definition of social policy: first, that the policies that are identified as 'social' should not be interpreted as if they were conceived and implemented with only the welfare of the public in mind; second, that other policies, not conventionally identified as social policies, may make a comparable, or even greater, contribution to welfare; third, that public policy should be seen as a whole in which social policies are significantly interlinked with other public policies. Just because it is convenient to single out some policies for special attention, and just because there are courses on social policy that require the study of a specific and limited range of public policies, we should not therefore fall into the trap of seeing these as the main government contributions to welfare, or the 'general good'. Let us look at the implications of these arguments a little more by examining the implications, for welfare and for social policy, of policy developments in those important policy areas that no one defines as social policy: foreign and defence policy, and economic policy.

It is important to recognize that the origins of the modern nation-state lie in the achievement of a monopoly of force within a given territory. The central policy preoccupations of the government of any insecure nation are with the defence of its boundaries, the recognition of its integrity by other nations and the maintenance of order within its territories. It is only too easy for British students of public policy to lose sight of the importance of these issues. They are the daily fare of our news bulletins, but we rarely stop to think about their relevance for our own state. Incomprehension over events in Northern Ireland and a propensity to underestimate the intensity of the feelings of some people in Scotland on the issue of devolution stem from our tendency to take the integrity and security of the nation for granted. Yet without a secure nation-state the scope for development of what is conventionally identified as social policy is severely limited.

These facts have three implications for the study of social policy. First, social policy expenditure has to compete with other public expenditure dedicated to the defence of the realm. The case against heavy defence expenditure cannot rest simply on arguments that some of that money would be better spent on social policy; it is necessary to prove that some of that expenditure is inappropriate or irrelevant, or to face the argument that without it no social policy would be secure. Second, the forms of this defence expenditure have a wide range of social effects in creating employment, disrupting family life and so on. Readers may like to think about the sort of policy interactions involved by asking themselves what would be the effects upon social life and social policy of the reintroduction of a two-year period of compulsory national service. The important effects they should be able to identify will nevertheless be insignificant by comparison with the effects of mobilization for war itself. Third, while social policies do not have, except in some very marginal ways, an impact on relations with other states, it is important not to lose sight of the contribution they make to integration and harmony within the nation. It is this that has led students of social policy to draw attention to the significant impact of war upon policy. Thus Titmuss has argued: 'The aims and content of social policy, both in peace and in war, are thus determined – at least to a substantial extent – by how far the co-operation of the masses is essential to the successful prosecution of war.'[6]

The development of the role of the British state in the nineteenth and twentieth centuries is often portrayed as the establishment of 'the welfare state'. To present it in this way is to emphasize social policy developments. But it is perhaps more important to give attention to the growth of the British economy over that period, and to the role played by government in relation to that economy. Two apparently conflicting political interpretations of these events lead us to ask some broadly similar questions about the relationship between social policy and economic policy.

To the followers of the 'classical economists', who argued that the industrialized state would make the greatest possible contribution o public welfare if competition were to remain unshackled, the period between the middle of the nineteenth century and the present day has been marked by increasing government interference with the economy. Some of this interference has been seen as necessary where competition has been impossible or illogical, in the public utilities and the railways for example. Some of it has been seen as justifiable because it seeks to ensure competition and prevent monopoly. But much of it has been regarded as stemming from forces eager to interfere with and undermine the free economy, shifting the locus of decision from the market place and into the political arena.

Marxists, on the other hand, interpret the same evidence the other way round. They argue that as the industrial state has grown so the 'contradictions of capitalism' have increased. Government intervention has been prompted, therefore, by a desire to save capitalism, not from a desire to undermine it. Regulation has been introduced to prevent the logic of competition from destroying the system. State interventions to protect the working class have been designed, according to this view, to stave off revolution and help the capitalist system to survive. Late capitalist society, it is argued, experiences a form of 'welfare capitalism' in which those who originally gained so much from competitive industry are still dominant in our society.

Both of these views of the relationship between government and the economy stress the extent to which social policy should be seen as dependent upon, or even a derivative of, economic policy. The key internal political issues of our age are who controls our economy and how the rewards that stem from our industrial achievements are to be distributed. The implications for social policy are as follows: first, that the main determinants of welfare are economic; second, that the government's role in diverting resources into social policies must be seen to be closely interrelated with, even dependent upon, the role it plays in the management of the economy; third, that social policies will be determined by views about the way the economy does, or should, operate. Specific social policies need therefore to be understood in terms of their relationships to economic policies.

The following are some examples of important questions frequently asked about social policy which are essentially about the relationship between social and economic policy. Are social security policies redistributive? How far do the redistributive effects of social security operate beyond minimal insurance limits? How does any redistribution by this mechanism compare with redistribution that occurs through other economic mechanisms – the effects of competition, the impact of unemployment and the results of wage bargaining, for example? What are the effects of public housing upon the market of housing? How far are market forces in this area more influential in determining who gets what housing than state intervention?

It is important to take a wider view of social policy development relating it to economic policy. To what extent are there limits to the growth of public expenditure in a mixed economy, and therefore what impact may such limits (or the belief that there are such limits) have upon social policy expenditure? Similarly, what is the impact upon the economy, and also upon the whole political system, of the pattern of employment that has emerged as social policy has become 'big business'? Unlike those stressed above, these are questions about the impact of social policy upon economic policy rather than the other way round. Nevertheless, the key decisions about resources for the social policy sector will be regarded as economic policy decisions.

It has been suggested, then, that, while certain policy areas, subject to a few difficult boundary problems, are defined as social policy, any proper understanding of the forces that determine outcomes in these areas must rest upon considerations of other policies not social policy conventionally considered.

STUDYING SOCIAL POLICY

Social policy may be studied in a number of ways. We may merely set out to determine the main policies in the areas in which we are interested. What is our system of social security? What benefits does our health service provide? How has the government intervened in the housing market? These and similar questions need to be answered by those who want to understand social policy. They can also be related to many other points about the way the services are organized and administered. Hence the simplest approach to the study of social policy is to describe the policies and institutions that together make up the British system of social services.

Many accounts of the system of social policy include comments on the strengths and weaknesses of specific policies. They relate what there is to what, in the authors' views, there ought to be. The study of social policy, as it has developed in Britain, has been concerned to examine the extent to which the welfare state meets people's needs. Often, indeed, students of social policy go further and explicitly analyse the extent to which it contributes to social equality. In this sense an academic discipline has been built up with an explicitly political stance. Social policy is seen as concerned with the alleviation of social ills; its objectives are accepted at face value; and it is analysed in terms of its success in achieving such goals. Many who have written about social policy have done so from the standpoint of Fabian socialism, concerned with incremental social change to create a more equal society. The few who have dealt with this subject from an alternative political standpoint have mainly been liberal Conservatives, concerned to meet the needs of casualties of the social system but suspicious of the claims of the state to regulate many aspects of our lives. The writings of the late Richard Titmuss,[7] perhaps the most important British student of social policy, deals very fully with arguments between these two viewpoints, the case for his moderate socialist position against those who extol the virtues of the market.

In recent years there has been among social scientists an extensive debate about the extent to which the analysis of society and of social institutions can be 'value-free'. Broadly, there is today a consensus that there are limits to the extent to which those who study and write about society can set aside their own commitments and prejudices. Some go on to argue, however, that value-freedom within the social sciences as a whole may be achieved by the interplay of arguments and evidence, each biased in different ways but contributing to the advancement of unbiased knowledge as a whole. Others are more sceptical about the extent to which a body of systematic unbiased knowledge is built up, and they argue that the value problem is ever significant. The study of social policy has been particularly conspicuous for the specific political or value commitments of those who write about it.

The strong normative bias in the study of social policy has led at times to a greater preoccupation with criticism of policies than with attempts to discover why they take the forms they do. In fact, if one believes that policies are wrong or ineffective it is important to understand why this is so, particularly if one's objective is to change them. The view that it is sufficient to point out that policies are 'wrong' is often linked with a view of policy making in which men and women of good will are believed to be responsible and are anxious to rectify the unwitting mistakes made in the past. This approach to the understanding of the policy system was criticized above.

At this stage an author who is arguing that the study of social policy in Britain has been strong on criticism and value judgement but weak on analysis should make his own position very clear. Since he believes that students may be aided in drawing their own conclusions if writers make their own value biases explicit, it is particularly important to do this. Broadly, I am deeply concerned about the content of social policy and have contributed (particularly on social security policies and on measures to help the unemployed) to the 'Fabian' critique of policy outlined above. I should not pretend that my personal motivation in studying social policy is not linked with a commitment to non-revolutionary movement towards social equality. However, I feel increasingly strongly that a concern to influence the content of social policy must be supported by an understanding of how social policy is made. This book is, therefore, concerned with what social policy is, how it was created and how it was implemented, as well as with its weaknesses and arguments about what it should be.

An understanding of the factors that influence the character of social policy must rest upon several foundations. Some attention must be given to the social and economic conditions that create the need for social policies. This is a difficult chicken-and-egg issue. One cannot simply look at the kinds of problems thrown up by particular social structures and economic situations and analyse policies as responses to those problems, since policies themselves influence the character of the societies in which they are adopted. For example, government provision of housing may be seen as a response to the inadequacies of the market as a provider of houses, but it has also transformed the character of that market. Interactions between policies and society are complex. It is important, therefore, to draw upon economics and sociology to help with the understanding of what occurs. It is also necessary to keep in mind the historical dimensions to these issues.

But social policy making must also be seen as as a political process. It has already been stressed that social policy cannot be analysed on its own, without reference to other activities of the state. Policies must be understood as products of politics, and attention must be given to the policy creation roles of politicians, civil servants, pressure groups and the electorate. Policies must also be seen as to a considerable extent products of other policies. There is a cumulative process to be analysed in which policies create needs for other policies, opportunities for other policies and new social situations for further political responses. It will be clear that to understand social policy considerable attention must be given to the findings of political science.

An often neglected part of the study of policy is the examination of its implementation. The actual impact of any policy upon the public will depend upon how it is interpreted and put into practice by government officials. The implementation process throws light on the strengths and weaknesses of a policy, and experience at the implementation end (by junior officials and the public) gets fed back into the policy process to influence future policy change. A particular characteristic of a state in which extensive social policies have been adopted is that it is a bureaucratic state. The organizational complexity of such a state necessarily complicates the implementation process. An understanding of these issues requires the student of social policy to give some attention to organization theory and to the study of administrative law.

The portrait of the study of social policy as presented in the last few paragraphs shows that it is a subject that draws upon a number of different academic disciplines. The problem of defining the extent to which it is necessary to delve into these disciplines is like the problem discussed earlier of ascertaining the boundaries between social policy and other kinds of public policy. There is a need to make what we can of an essentially applied subject, hoping that we can gain what is required from other disciplines without going too deeply into them. The boundaries between all the social sciences are unclear. Sometimes this is a necessary feature of subjects that put some parts of the human experience under the microscope and have to abstract this from other parts. But in other cases it is a result of historical accidents in the development of the disciplines, and if the study of society were to be initiated all over again it would surely be divided rather differently. The study of social policy particularly hives off a specific area of social activity in a way that must violate subject boundaries. If it is important to understand a number of practical policies, because of a concern about their effects upon society, it is necessary to accept studies that cannot be defined in terms of a discrete intellectual discipline.

In setting out to examine what social policy is, and how it may be studied, some answers have been suggested to the question, 'Why study it?' Many who are required to study social policy are, or expect to be, involved in its implementation. That part of a social policy course that is concerned with describing policies and the institutions responsible for them has a clear face value to the social policy 'practitioner'. But equally it is important for the member of a department to understand something of the way in which it works, and the internal and external forces that shape its policies.

It may also help to understand other agencies to which that department has to relate, particularly as a great deal of policy depends, or is intended to depend, upon successful co-operation between organizations. It has been stressed that no policy area is discrete, that policies in one area affect those in others. This is particularly true of social policies, where their impact upon the public depends upon the way they interrelate. Successful treatment of the sick requires attention to their housing and income maintenance problems; the care of the neglected child depends upon co-operation between health service workers, personal social services staff and schoolteachers; the homeless often face income maintenance problems as well as housing problems; and so on – the examples are legion.

Hence the most obvious case for studying social policy is a need for the staff of the various social services to understand the system in which they operate. But that is not all. One of the characteristics of many of the people who are drawn to work in the social services is a strong commitment to those services. In this sense it is not surprising that the study of social policy has been deeply concerned with the improvement of policies. Many social services staff care considerably about the inadequacies of the policies they administer. But achieving policy change is never an easy process, particularly if one is a comparatively junior participant in a large organization. To make a contribution towards this end requires not only knowledge of alternatives and commitment to putting them into practice but also an understanding of how social policy is made and implemented.

These arguments for studying social policy have been addressed to people likely to be employed in the social services. However, they have implications for all citizens who want to influence social policy. The underlying justification for this book is that participation in policy making for a group of public services of considerable importance to us all must rest upon understanding: understanding of what the policies are, of how they are made and implemented, and of the implications of the many prevailing suggestions on how to change those policies.

SUGGESTIONS FOR FURTHER READING

This has been an introductory chapter in which it has been suggested that students do not need to delve deeply into the debate about the definition of the field of study of social policy. The essay by Carrier and Kendall (see n. 2) explores that debate, and arrives at a more positive stance on the distinctive character of the subject as an academic discipline than that suggested here.

Joan Higgins's book (see n. 5) contains a chapter on 'Social Policy and the Conspiracy Theory of Welfare', which effectively reviews the debate between the Marxist and the 'liberal' explanations of social policy. The Marxist view is argued in the writings by O'Connor and Gough (see n. 4), while Kincaid has provided a very readable descriptive and historical treatment of the development of British social policy from this perspective.[8] Richard Titmuss was the outstanding exponent of the liberal socialist standpoint on the study of social policy; indeed, he can be said to be virtually the founder of the systematic study of social policy. His main essays on social policy have recently been put together in a single volume.[9] Marshall (see n. 1) has produced the other major elementary discussion on this subject in the same tradition. Good overviews of the competing perspectives on social policy can be found in two books by Mishra.[10]

# CHAPTER 2

# The History of Social Policy

## INTRODUCTION

This chapter deals with some of the key events in the development of British social policy, relating them to social, economic and political trends in our society. It is not intended as a comprehensive potted history of the subject; it is, however, important to have a historical perspective, particularly on the relationship between social and political change, in order to understand the character of British social policy today.

At one level the story is simple. The growth of state involvement with the social welfare of its citizens can be related to the development of an industrial society, and its subsequent maturation, or perhaps decline, into what some writers have described as 'post-industrialism'.[1] Alongside this industrial development are political developments, associated with the extension of the suffrage, involving citizens more thoroughly with the activities of the state.[2] The result is a package of developments – of the state's role, the character of the economy and the nature of political processes – which those without a very dogmatic belief about the motive forces in political development find difficult to disentangle in cause–effect terms.

This version of the story of the development of the state's role in social welfare can be applied to a number of industrialized nations – to the United States, to most of the other countries of western and northern Europe and to Australasia – as much as to Britain.[3] But while these 'broad brush' features of the story must not be forgotten it is important also to try to single out characteristics of Britain's development that help to explain the particular shape of its own social policies. A proper understanding of this subject requires consideration of the general factors, which may apply to a distinct group of nations; of the special factors, which are perhaps unique to one nation; and, furthermore, of a number of factors that do not fall neatly into either of these categories. Included in this last group is, for example, the 'insurance principle' in social security, adopted in variety of ways by various governments who clearly attempted to learn from each other's experiences.[4]

## DEVELOPMENTS BEFORE THE TWENTIETH CENTURY

It is always very difficult, in dealing with the relationship between past events and contemporary policies, to know how far back to go in time. To understand British social policies some consideration of the history of the poor law, with its roots in Elizabethan legislation, is necessary. The Tudor age saw considerable population movements, with changes in agriculture, the growth of towns and some rudimentary developments in manufacturing. The government found it necessary to try to impose a centrally determined framework on what had hitherto been entirely local, and often monastic, charitable initiatives. It placed responsibility for the poor upon each parish, with the requirement, under the Acts of Settlement, that the itinerant poor should be returned, if necessary, to their parishes of origin. The parishes were required to levy rates to provide for the relief of the poor.

The history of the poor law between the sixteenth and twentieth centuries was one of attempts to make this formula work – for local initiative with broad guidelines laid down centrally – despite social changes. As Britain became industrialized and urbanized a strictly local system of administration came under strain. Population movements graduallly rendered the Acts of Settlement obsolete. The tasks of the poor law became more complex as parishes had to cope with, for example, trade recessions and outbreaks of infectious diseases, each affecting large numbers of people in the new towns and cities. By the middle of the nineteenth century developments in medicine offered a new challenge to the parish 'guardian', who had previously provided only the most rudimentary care to the sick.

The most significant nineteenth-century attempt to modernize the poor law was the Poor Law Amendment Act of 1834. This set up a national Poor Law Commission to superintend the system, and formed the parishes into groups known as poor law unions. This important step towards the development of a national system was only a limited success. However, its main contributions to the development of policy were the 'workhouse test' and the doctrine of 'less eligibility'. The aims of these were to curb indiscriminate outdoor relief; if the poor were not sufficiently desperate to enter the workhouse they could not be really in need. The system was intended to ensure that those who received help were worse off ('less eligible') than the poorest people in work. In practice many poor law unions did not strictly enforce the workhouse test, and as the years passed the elderly and the sick were increasingly given outdoor relief. Nevertheless the elimination of the workhouse, and the abolition of the means test adopted to confine relief-giving, became an important preoccupation of twentieth-century critics of the poor law. The principle of less eligibility has continued to influence decisions about relief until the present day.

While the basic nineteenth-century response to poverty was to try to strengthen older institutions, some of the consequences of urbanization and industrialization posed problems for which entirely new responses were necessary. Measures were taken to curb the hours worked by women and children in factories, and to improve safety and working conditions. This significant development in state intervention in the economy seems to have come about as a result of a mixture of growing humanitarian concern and embryonic working-class pressure. The enforcement of this legislation was put into the hands of a central government inspectorate, the first of a number of such inspectorates to be set up in the nineteenth century and to operate, according to Roberts,[5] as an important source of pressure for further social reform.

The rapid spread of infection in areas where people were crowded together was, like the exploitation of child labour, not a new phenomenon. But in an increasingly urbanized society it took new forms more apparent to political opinion and more threatening to life and industry; and there were very many more large populous areas devoid of the most elementary arrangements for disposing of waste or supplying pure water. Furthermore, it was only during this period that scientific advance identified the main links between insanitary conditions and disease. In a few areas local government agencies took some steps to tackle this problem, but real progress did not come until central government gave local authorities powers to act effectively, and also required them to take such action.

Here, then, was an important area of government intervention, pushing local authorities to tackle some of the problems of their own areas. The local government system of the time had been given some shape by the Municipal Corporations Act of 1835, but it was not until the end of the century that it acquired a structure that would enable it to take on the range of functions it has today. In the nineteenth century, therefore, some reforms required local authorities to take action and to employ professional staff, such as the medical officers of health required by an Act of 1871. Others, however, set up *ad hoc* authorities to take on functions delegated by central government.

The evolution of state education during the nineteenth century provides a good example of a series of *ad hoc* responses. Religious societies had begun to become involved in the provision of cheap basic education for the children of the poor early in the century. By 1833 they had persuaded the government to provide a small grant towards this work. In 1839 the government set up an inspectorate to further central supervision of the way the growing state aid was being spent. It was not until 1870, however, that the government moved really forcefully into the provision of primary education. Motivated, it is widely believed, by a concern about the illiteracy of the growing electorate (the franchise had been considerably widened in 1867), but also undoubtedly by a recognition of a need for a better educated workforce, Parliament provided that school boards, to set up state-financed schools, could be established where there was a clear educational need and the voluntary schools were insufficoient in number. In 1880 a further Education Act made schooling compulsory for children between five and ten, and in the 1890s it was established that most elementary education should be free. During the last years of the century some of the school boards even became involved in secondary education, producing a confused pattern of educational growth that was to prompt government action at the beginning of the twentieth century.

Reference has already been made to the way in which developments in medicine began, in the late ninetenth century, to render inadequate the traditional poor law approach to the care of the sick. Alongside the development of poor law hospitals many voluntary hospitals, assisted by charitable funds that enabled them to provide cheap or free services to the poor, were founded or grew in strength from their earlier origins. The local authorities were also given powers to establish hospitals to fulfil their duties to contain infectious diseases and to care for the mentally ill. Medical care outside the hospitals grew in importance in the second half of the century, becoming more than the prerogative of the rich. This was partly a poor law development, partly the extension of the services of the voluntary hospitals, and partly an aspect of the growth of insurance against misfortune widely practised by the more prosperous of the working classes. In all, a very mixed package of health care measures was evolving. This complex mixture, dominated by a powerful medical profession firmly established during the nineteenth century, posed problems for subsequent attempts to rationalize the health services, and therefore influenced the shape the national health service eventually achieved.

At the end of the nineteenth century the verdict of the legal philosopher Dicey was that *laissez-faire* had given way to collectivism; that government had begun to assume a role in society that had taken Britain well on the way to becoming a socialist state.[6] The factory legislation and the government intervention in the cause of health and safety implied important changes in the role of the state. The educatio- nal system at the primary (or, as it was known then, the elementary) level had received a crucial injection of public enterprise. The poor law, on the other hand, had been changed but little. A need for new policies in that area was just beginning to become apparent at the end of the century, as scientific surveys and journalistic investigations charted the existence of severe problems of poverty caused by factors, in particular sickness and old age, largely outside individual control.[7]

It was suggested earlier that the agencies set up during the nineteenth century to implement social policies were often *ad hoc* bodies. While local government was responsible for public health, and for the rudimentary planning, housing and hospital functions required to help achieve more sanitary urban areas, education was made the responsibility of separately elected school boards. The poor law, of course, came under yet another kind of authority, the boards of guardians, descendants of the former parish officials. However, legislation late in the century provided a new local government structure much better able to take on a wide range of functions. Local government Acts in 1888 and 1894 set up a system of local authorities that was to remain almost unchanged until the 1970s. They gave a shape to local government, with a split between the highly urbanized areas and the rest of the country, that dominates local politics to this day. The less-urbanized areas acquired a two-tier system of county government, accompanied by lower-tier urban and rural districts. In many urban areas county boroughs were set up as single all-purpose authorities. London acquired a special two-tier system of its own.

It is very convenient, for the presentation of historical accounts, when a specific date can be identified as a watershed. It further adds neatness when that date is the beginning of a century. While there is always an arbitrary aspect to the choice of such dates, particularly in social history, the dividing point between the nineteenth and twentieth centuries seems a particularly significant one. At this time the large working-class element added to the electorate in 1885 was just beginning to influence political thinking. The Labour Representation Committee was set up in 1899 to try to get more working men elected to Parliament. This body was to turn itself into the Labour Party in 1906. The major political parties, the Conservatives and the Liberals, were increasingly aware of the need to compete for working-class support. For the Conservatives the formula was an interesting blend of imperialism and social reform.[8] The Liberals had a radical wing, temporarily disadvantaged by the jingoism of the Boer War but ready to push the party towards acceptance of a package of new social measures.

Late in the nineteenth century Britain had begun to discover that an advanced industrial nation is vulnerable to alarming economic fluctuations, owing to the uncoordinated nature of much business decision making and the international complications of the trade cycle. New competitors had also emerged as other nations – Germany, France, the United States – industrialized rapidly. The Empire still looked secure, but the competition for new trading outlets was increasing dramatically. At the same time as doubts were beginning to be felt about Britain's economic vulnerability, the working people were increasingly organizing in trade unions to try to secure, or guarantee, their share of the progress. The political price of economic failure was being raised. New initiatives to preserve the unity of the nation were required.

1900 TO 1914

The period immediately before the First World War was dominated by a series of reforms adopted by the Liberal government after 1906. However, before those reforms are considered two earlier events require comment. In 1902 the Conservatives enacted an important Education Act. This passed the responsibility for state education from the school boards to the county and county borough councils, and devised a formula for the comprehensive financial support of the church schools that preserved a measure of voluntary control. The other important feature of this Act was that it legitimized expenditure on secondary and technical schools, and thereby stimulated the growth of this element of state education.

The other significant event was the Boer War. This rather inglorious episode in British imperial history had a considerable significance for social policy. In general it led to a concern to examine what was wrong with Great Britain that it should have been unable to fight effectively against apparently fragile opposition. In particular, politicians sought to examine why so many volunteers to fight had been found to be unfit to do so. Hence as Fraser argues:

> In that bizarre way which again and again seemed to link imperialism and social reform (sometimes as allies, sometimes as competitors), it seemed to some that Britain would only be able to sustain its Empire if she ensured that the new generation of children, tomorrow's Imperial Army, was properly nourished.[9]

An Interdepartmental Committee on Physical Deterioration was set up. It reported in 1904, urging the establishment of a school medical service and the provision of school meals within the public education system. Both these measures were adopted by the Liberals and implemented soon after they came to power.

Before they lost office the Conservatives also responded to the growing evidence on the extent of poverty, and the inadequacies of existing measures, by setting up a Royal Commission on the Poor Laws in 1905. The report of this body, which did not appear until 1909, contains a most thorough discussion of British social policy at that time. There was both a majority and a minority report, and the latter provided a well argued critique of the system. However, without waiting for the Royal Commission the Liberal Government decided to promote two pieces of legislation that significantly modified the role of the poor law in the provision of social security, the Old Age Pensions Act of 1908 and the National Insurance Act of 1911.

These two pieces of legislation provide interesting contrasts in approaches to the provision of social security. The old-age pension was non-contributory and based upon a simple test of means. It was an extension of the outdoor relief given by some boards of guardians, but its means test was a personal and not a family one. The national insurance scheme, on the other hand, was contributory but not means-tested. It provided cover against sickness and unemployment for some, initially limited, categories of workers. The contribution was to come jointly from the employee, the employer and the state. The sickness scheme provided not just cash benefits but also medical treatment, from a 'panel' doctor who was remunerated on a 'capitation basis' in terms of the number of patients he accepted on his panel. The Friendly Societies and insurance companies, who were already involved in the provision of sickness cover for many working people, were allowed to participate as agents for the scheme and providers of additional benefits. The scheme protected only employees themselves and not any members of their families.

The National Insurance Act is most important for introducing the 'insurance principle' into British social security legislation. A number of European countries had adopted state or municipal insurance schemes during the last years of the nineteenth century. The British policy makers were particularly aware of the German scheme. Heclo provides, in the following passage, an interesting account of the role played by Beveridge, one of the architects of the new scheme, in introducing insurance ideas:

> In his first column for the *Morning Post*, February 16, 1906, he had dismissed contributory social insurance on the German pattern, as had all British investigating committees, with the standard view that it would require an 'un-British' amount of regulation of the individual. Beveridge, however, studied the German experiment more closely during the next year and concluded that the contributory insurance principle could not only reduce costs; it could also eliminate reliance on means tests.[10]

This adoption of the insurance principle had important consequences for the development of social policy. In various measures after 1911 governments extended benefits in ways that undermined the *true insurance* basis of the scheme; but the contributory principle remained an important political symbol, and from time to time attempts were made to return the scheme closer to its roots. It is always difficult to combine the hard-headed actuarial principles of insurance with a concern for effective and comprehensive social security; yet, as Beveridge recognized, when the only viable political alternative is means-testing the contributory principle has a great appeal. Beveridge was to play an important part in the 1940s in maintaining the insurance approach to social security.

The 1911 National Insurance Act had implications for more than social security policy, in two ways. The provision of medical services under the sickness benefit scheme used a model for the state payment of general practitioners that has continued in the National Health Service to the present day. Abel-Smith has pointed out that before 1911 the doctors were in conflict with the Friendly Societies about the conditions under which they were hired to care for members.[11] Hence they were predisposed to secure contracts under the state scheme which preserved their freedom. This right to operate as independent contractors rather than as salaried servants of the state has been zealously preserved by general practitioners.

It is also important to perceive the National Insurance Act as the sort of response to the problem of unemployment that has remained dominant in Britain. The earlier years of the twentieth century saw a number of small experiments in combating unemployment by providing publicly subsidized work. Yet these did not achieve any great scale, perhaps because of suspicions of their implications for state involvement in the economy. There was, however, one measure, adopted in 1908, the Labour Exchange Act, that came to assume importance. The National Insurance Act gave the newly set up exchanges the role of administering the system of unemployment benefit. This was the activity with which they came to be most closely identified in the first fifty years of their existence. The hallmark of the British response to defects in the working of the labour market became the provision of relief to the unemployed, and not either the creation of special work programmes or measures to facilitate movements of workers between jobs.[12] Not until the 1970s was this emphasis really challenged.

The Liberal government could, of course, have developed its social security measures as direct measures of redistributing incomes without either means tests or contributions. Neither the Liberal measures nor any of the social security measures that have succeeded them have involved the wholesale redistribution of resources. However, both of the early measures required quite large subventions from taxation. It is important, therefore, to bear in mind the significance of the budget that

Lloyd George introduced in 1909 to finance both social welfare reforms and increased government expenditure on other matters such as defence, by increasing taxation and making it more redistributive. This seems to have been the first occasion on which a British government's annual budget was presented, or perceived, as an instrument for the redistribution of income. This in itself is of note. Lloyd George, whose penchant for the rhetoric of class warfare gives a misleading impression of his readiness for the reality of such conflict, described the budget as follows: 'This is a war budget. It is for raising money to wage implacable warfare against poverty and squalidness.'[13] The most controversial part of the budget was a group of measures to tax land. Lloyd George defended them by an aggressive verbal attack on the privileges of landowners:

> The ownership of land is not merely an enjoyment, it is a stewardship. It has been reckoned as such in the past, and if the landowners cease to discharge these funtions, the time will come to reconsider the conditions under which land is held in this country. No country, however rich, can permanently afford to have quartered upon its revenue a class which declined to do the duty which it was called upon to perform.[14]

Such was the populist rhetoric of the time. It did not usher in a revolution, but it helped to change the tenor of British politics. Inside Parliament the working-class interest was advanced by a comparatively cautious radical Liberal group, supported by an equally cautious small caucus of Labour MPs. Outside, Marxist socialism was beginning to be given attention by orators, and syndicalist trade unionists were beginning to flex their industrial muscles. Against all this the landowning interests – not, it must be noted, the industrialists – fought a rearguard action. The House of Lords threw out Lloyd George's budget. The consequence was a Parliament Act, with which the Lords eventually aquiesced after two general elections and the threat of mass creation of peers, which curbed the power of the Lords to block Commons legislation.

The events of 1909–11 have been given comparatively lengthy attention. The political balance in Britain tipped quite markedly at that time, with important implications for social policy. Such was the ferment of the times throughout Europe, and such was the rising volume of political controversy within Britain (bear in mind also the Suffragette agitation and the conflict over the future of Ireland), that a more dramatic tipping of the balance than actually occurred in the next few years might have been expected. Certainly many new social policies were shortly to come, but these did little to disrupt the status quo; indeed, many must be seen as designed to preserve it.

1914 TO 1939

It is important not to regard the development of social policy in Britain as simply involving two dramatic jumps forward in the periods 1906–11 and 1944–9. Between these a great deal happened to influence policies and to give them a character they often retain.

In the First World War Britain experienced conscription for the first time, and the mobilization not only of the whole workforce but also of many women, hitherto not in employment, to assist the war effort. The war* economy produced many domestic shortages. Initially the government was reluctant to impose controls and rationing, but its desire to curb wage rises and industrial unrest forced it to intervene. In general, then, the 'collectivist state' advanced considerably during this period. Civil servants learnt to carry out, and members of the public came to expect, government policies in areas of life never before influenced by state action. This was the general impact of war upon public policy. Its specific impact upon social policy was more limited. The imposition of controls upon private rents was a rare, but significant, example of social policy innovation in this period.

However, during and at the end of the war the government made many promises for a better future. Even before the war ended an Education Act was passed which recognized the case for state support for free education up to the age of fourteen. At the end of the war Lloyd George promised 'homes fit for heroes', and one of the first pieces of postwar legislation was a Housing Act that provided government subsidies to local authorities to build houses for the working classes. This Act, known as the Addison Act after its sponsor the minister of health, while not the first legislation to allow local authority house building, was the first to subsidize it. It effectively initiated a programme of council-house building that has continued, albeit subject to regular modification as governments have changed the subsidy arrangements, until the present day. After the Addison Act both of the minority Labour governments, in power in 1924 and in 1929–31, extended the local authority house-building programme by means of further subsidies. In the 1930s there was a shift in housing policy, with the government encouraging local authorities to put their emphasis in house provision upon clearing the slums. The strict rent control, introduced in the war to protect private tenants, was partly lifted during the interwar period. But with this, as with council-house building, no real attempt was made to turn back the clock on processes that were ultimately totally to transform the character of Britain's housing market.

The evolution of relief policies for the unemployed in the interwar years is an interesting story. Unemployment was a recurrent problem throughout this period. Immediately after the war the government mismanaged the discharge of servicemen back into civilian life, and unemployment rose rapidly. Then the economy picked up and the problem abated. But this proved to be a temporary respite, and by 1921 registered unemployment was over 2 million. It remained over a million throughout the period, falling back a bit in the middle twenties but then rising steeply in 1930. By 1931 it was over 2.5 million, and it did not fall below 2 million until 1936.

The 1911 National Insurance Act provided unemployment benefit only for workers in a limited number of trades, ones at that time not liable to extensive and prolonged unemployment. It also contained strict rules to protect the insurance fund. Benefits were dependent upon past contributions, and the duration of weekly payments to individuals was limited. The scheme was not designed to provide widespread relief in a period of mass unemployment. Gilbert, in his detailed study of social policy in this period, has shown that politicians were alarmed by the reports they received of unrest and agitation among the ranks of the unemployed.[15] They were particularly conscious of the expectation among ex-soldiers that they would receive generous treatment from the government. Hence the government faced a dilemma, which it resolved by breaching the strict insurance principles and extending the scope of the unemployment benefit scheme.

It would be inappropriate here to set out all the convolutions in public policy on relief for the unemployed. What a whole succession of ministers and official committees had to try to resolve was the conflict between the demand for economy in government expenditure and the rising cost of an insurance benefit scheme no longer entirely restrained by insurance rules. Broadly, the compromise reached was extended but not unlimited insurance benefits, the operation of strict and quite unrealistic tests to ensure that people were 'genuinely seeking work',[16] the use of additional means-tested benefits known then as 'doles', and acceptance that the poor law authorities would give extensive 'outdoor' relief to the unemployed. Eventually rationalization came in 1934 when a unified national means-test scheme for benefits additional to insurance benefits was devised, to be administered by the Unemployment Assistance Board (UAB). This new organization was the forerunner of the National Assistance Board set up in 1948, and therefore of the Supplementary Benefits Commission that operated until 1980. The UAB provided a model that enabled central government to take over the functions of the poor law agencies. It transferred responsibility for means-tested benefits for the unemployed to this national organization in 1934, added similar benefits for the elderly to its responsibilities in 1940, and added most other cash aid in 1941. By 1948, when it was finally killed, the poor law was all but dead already.

The demise of the poor law was also assisted by another piece of legislation in this period, the Local Government Act of 1929. This handed over responsibility for the poor law from the boards of guardians to the local authorities. As far as the administration of relief was concerned, this made little difference; the public assistance committees of the local authorities could be regarded as broadly the guardians under another name. However, the handover of powers brought the institutions that had evolved from the old workhouses into the hands of authorities that could more effectively bring them up to date. This was particularly important for the hospitals, since now a unified public service could be provided. This was an important step towards a national health service, though in practice few authorities did much to modernize their facilities. Instead, the transformation of the hospital service awaited the special arrangements that were made to co-ordinate their activities with those of the voluntary hospitals during the Second World War.

While little attempt was made to alter the character of the patchwork of health services available in the interwar period, all the parties that were to be involved in their transformation in the 1940s were beginning to examine the weaknesses of the existing provision and to formulate alternatives. In view of the importance of medical acqiescence in the system eventually adopted, it was probably necessary for many doctors to become aware of the need for change.

Education services similarly went through a phase of detailed examination of their weaknesses and future potential during the interwar period. Here, however, the roles given to the local authorities by the Acts of 1902 and 1918 left scope for innovation where money allowed. The teaching profession grew in strength at this time, developing a formal system of training to replace the nineteenth-century pupil-teacher system. Education beyond the primary stage grew in various ways, and this part of the system was ready for rationalization by the end of the 1930s.

This section has described the interwar period as a period of consolidation in social policy. But at least one really significant innovation occurred, the development of a public housing sector, and the inroads made into poor law were of considerable significance for the future. One other element of this that deserves a brief outline was the adoption in 1925 of a contributory pension scheme to run alongside the non-contributory one. This period is often thought of as a failure in British politics, of failure to cope with the rise of Hitler and Mussolini abroad and a failure to deal with unemployment at home. It was, however, also a period when complete adult suffrage was achieved, and in which a political consensus was built up that enabled the Labour Party to establish itself alongside the older parties, so that an element of working-class power developed without turning into a revolutionary force. The key Conservative politicians of that age, Baldwin and Chamberlain, were very much men of the 'consensus', eager to promote cautious innovation in social policy. The key Labour politician, Ramsay MacDonald, was equally eager to occupy the middle ground. Some readers will no doubt regard this consensus politics as another of the failures of this age, urging that the compromises by the Left prevented radical change from occurring. Its significance for social policies, however, was that it created a platform for changes to occur in the 1940s, changes that secured very widespread social and political acceptance.

THE 1940s

The government was very much more ready to mobilize all the nation's resources in the Second World War than it had been in the First. Regulation and rationing were not adopted reluctantly but as measures essential to the war effort. Politically, at least after Churchill replaced Chamberlain as prime minister in 1940, the nation was more totally united. The Labour Party regained its self-confidence, lost after it had been deserted by its leaders, who formed a National government and then heavily defeated it in a general election in 1931. It regarded attention to social policies as one of the conditions of its involvement in a wartime coalition government. Although Churchill sometimes appeared to be unhappy about it, planning for the peace was widely accepted as a legitimate political task during the war. But before looking at the two most important examples of planning for peace, the Beveridge Report and the Butler Educaton Act of 1944, it is important to note a number of ways in which peacetime policy changes were foreshadowed by *ad hoc* wartime measures. In the last section reference was made to the way in which the Unemployment Assistance Board, which was renamed the Assistance Board in 1940, took over various functions from the public assistance committees in the early part of the war. Mention was also made of the integration of the hospital services during the war, under the Emergency Hospital Scheme. The evacuation of children called for the development of special services, foreshadowing developments in child care practice after the war. Rents were again strictly controlled, and empty houses were requisitioned. The wartime state had many of the characteristics of the 'welfare state', which is popularly regarded as having been created after the war.

The Beveridge Report was the report of a committee on Social Insurance and Allied Services, published in 1942. This recommended the adoption of a contributory social security system which improved on the existing system by protecting all citizens in sickness, unemployment and old age. The new system should, it was argued, include family allowances, maternity benefits and provision for widows. The contribution principles should be insurance ones, involving the employee, the employer and the state as before, but the coverage of the scheme should be universal and therefore involve a national pooling of risks. There was, in the arrangements for dependants and widows, inevitably built into the scheme certain assumptions about the male breadwinner and his relationship to the family unit, which have left a difficult legacy for attempts to balance the interests of men and women in our own age. Otherwise it is still possible to evaluate the British system of social security in terms of the extent to which it matches up to the model outlined by Beveridge in 1942.

Beveridge argued that other social policies were necessary to underpin his insurance scheme. Support for children would be necessary through a universal 'family allowance' scheme. A system of means-tested assistance would be necessary as a 'safety-net' for the minority whose needs were not adequately covered by the scheme. The maintenance of full employment would be essential to enable social insurance to work properly. A national health service should take over the provision for medical care in the old insurance scheme and effectively underpin the new one.

Beveridge's insurance scheme was broadly put into legislation. Family allowances were provided by one of the last measures of the coalition government. The rest was enacted by the postwar Labour government, though there was one crucial departure from the insurance principle in that the qualifying period for full pension was very short. This deviation from Beveridge's plan made the scheme expensive to general taxation, and probably tended to prevent the adoption of benefit levels sufficient to provide subsistence incomes to those with no other resources and to inhibit subsequent increases to keep up with the cost of living.

The Education Act passed in 1944 and often identified by the name of the minister responsible, R. A. Butler, provided the framework for the education system we have today. The Butler Act provided for universal free state secondary education, but did not specify the form it should take or rule on whether or not there should be selective schools.

At the end of the war the coalition broke up. In the ensuing general election both parties promised substantial social policy reforms, but the electorate swung strongly towards the Labour Party, rejecting the old war leader Churchill in favour of that party's clearer commitment to a vision of the 'welfare state'. The social security reforms embodied by the Labour Party in the National Insurance Act of 1946 and the National Assistance Act of 1948 have already been mentioned. With the adoption of these measures came the abolition of the poor law, its income maintenance responsibilities going to the National Assistance Board and its responsibilities for residential care and other welfare services going to local authority welfare departments.

In 1946 the creation of the National Health Service provided another crucial innovation in social policy. General practitioner and hospital services were provided free for everyone, in a complex structure designed to unify the hospital sector while leaving general practitioners as independant contractors and other community services in the control of the local authorities. This structure was achieved after hard bargaining between the minister, Aneurin Bevan, and the doctors, who were deeply suspicious of state medicine.[17] The scheme was funded out of general taxation, though an element of payment for the health service remained in the national insurance contribution, creating a confusing illusion that this was what paid for the service. The notion of a totally free service did not last for long. Very soon chancellors of the Exchequer, exploiting concern that demand for services was much greater than expected, secured first small payments for spectacles and dental treatment, and then prescription charges, as ways of raising revenue.

In among these widely publicized social policy reforms came another measure, with much less impact upon the general public but nevertheless with important implications: the Children Act of 1948. The origins of this reform of the services for deprived children seem to have been in a child care scandal, the O'Neill case, which led to the setting up of the Curtis Committee to investigate contemporary practice.[18] The Children Act consolidated the existing child care legislation, and created departments in which professional social work practice would develop in child care, and in due course in work with families.

The Labour government of 1945–51 did not alter the system of subsidizing local authority housing developed in the interwar period, but it did, by the Housing Act of 1949, substantially extend the subsidies available. The Act formally removed the limitation confining local authority provision to housing for the 'working classes'. The government's concern throughout the late 1940s was to stimulate building to make up the deficiencies in housing stock arising from bomb damage and the wartime standstill in house building. However, postwar shortages of materials made it difficult to accelerate new building. The Labour government laid its emphasis upon local authority housing rather than on private building for sale. It also involved itself, as no government ever had before, in an attempt to secure effective land use planning and to curb land speculation. The Town and Country Planning Act of 1947 provided a grand design for this purpose, though one of limited success, which was subsequently dismantled by the Conservatives. Another crucial planning innovation, with major implications for the provision of public housing, was the New Towns Act of 1946. This provided jobs and houses in new communities for people from overcrowded cities and run-down industrial areas.

Government involvement in the planning of the use of national resources, which had been one of the necessities of wartime, was continued by the Labour government as a matter of principle. This in itself was important in enlarging the involvement of government with many aspects of life in Britain. There was a commitment to the maintenance of full employment, with the Keynesian doctrine that budgetary mannagement could achieve this now a matter of economic orthodoxy.[19] In the 1940s such economic management was slightly inflationary, but this was broadly seen as a reasonable price to pay for full employment and economic growth. In retrospect it is hard to judge the extent to which the success of this policy (and, for all the worries it caused at the time, it was a success by comparison with the economy management disasters of the 1960s and 1970s) was due to good management, and the extent to which it was due to external and internal economic factors outside government control, in particular to the postwar recovery and the stimulus provided by the continuing military activity of the 'cold war'.

The 1940s were, in both war and peace, crucial years for the building of the system of social policy Britain has today. But it has been shown that few of the innovations of this period were without precedent in the policies of earlier years, and that much of the crucial thinking about the form these new institutions should take had been done in the interwar period. Continuity is also evident in the behaviour of the two major political parties. The Butler Education Act and the Family Allowances Act were both measures of the Conservative-dominated wartime coalition. Preliminary work had also been done during the war on the ideas for the social security scheme, and plans had begun to be drafted for a national health service.

The political continuity is also apparent in the fact that the Conservatives did comparatively little, on returning to power in 1951, to dismantle the 'welfare state'. The Labour Party policies that they did contest, and partly reverse, were nationalization policies not social welfare ones. Otherwise, they shifted the house-building emphasis from public to private building but by no means eliminated a substantial public element from their enlarged building programme; they were marginally more ready to increase health service charges; and they were, perhaps, rather slow to raise social security benefits. In the later 1950s they encouraged education services to flourish; and some local authorities began to innovate in this policy area in ways that in due course came to be regarded as radical and politically contentious.

## SINCE THE 1940s

The presentation of policies in this section will be sketchy because they are generally covered more fully in the appropriate detailed chapter later in the book. The aim here is to give the flavour of the key developments in this period as part of the history of social policy.

Broadly the period 1951–87 can be divided into four parts: 1951–64, a period of comparatively little social policy innovation which may be regarded as a time of consolidation or stagnation, according to one's political viewpoint; 1964–74, a period of fairly intense policy change stimulated by both political parties, in which considerable difficulties were experienced in translating aspirations into practice; 1974–78, a period in which rapid inflation and government by the Labour party without a parliamentary majority administered a severe shock to the political and social system, and to all who believed that there was still a need for developments in social policy; and 1979–87, when much more explicitly anti-welfare state Conservative administrations reinforced that shock by deliberately treating inflation as more deserving of its attention than unemployment, attacking public services which were seen as inhibiting economic recovery and seeking ways to 'privatize' public services. Bearing these points in mind let us look at developments in each of the main policy areas over the whole period.

The period 1951–64 was a boom period for house building, both private and public. It was during this time that two kinds of tenure began to dominate in Britain, owner-occupation and local authority tenancy. The decline in the size of the privately rented sector was rapid, and towards the later part of this period it was accelerated by slum clearance. In 1957 the government, believing that the private renting market could be revived if rent controls were removed, passed a Rent Act that allowed some decontrol. The main impact of this measure was that many landlords used the freedom to evict allowed under decontrol to sell previously let properties into owner-occupation. In the 1960s the Labour government legislated to restore security of tenure and to allow rent levels to rise only to levels that fell short of market prices.

When Labour returned to power they were committed to reversing the emphasis upon building for owner occupation within the building boom, but otherwise they wanted to produce even more houses per annum. The use of restraints upon building investment as an economic regulator to prevent excess domestic demand made it difficult for them to achieve their targets. By the end of the 1970s the additions to the housing stock had been so considerable that arguments were increasingly heard that Britain had enough houses. What complicated this debate was the question of whether there were enough houses of the right kind in the right places. Certainly some of the earlier building activity may have been misplaced effort. In particular, many local authorities has acquired high-rise flats which were hard to let.

Another of Labour's policy commitments was to try again, like their predecessors in 1946, to do something to rationalize planning and curb the activities of the land speculators. While the central problem here was the unrestrained inner-city office and commercial development, the concern about this issue also had implications for owner-occupied housing. Politicians of both parties have become increasingly concerned in the last twenty years about the problems of house-buyers, in the face of spiralling land and building costs and high rates of mortgage interest.

When they came to power in 1970 the Conservatives decided that public expenditure on local authority housing needed to be curbed. Their Housing Finance Act of 1972 set out to adapt the 'fair-rent' principle, which Labour had applied to private rents in the 1960s, to the local authority sector. They linked this with a national rent rebate scheme, rationalizing the variety of local schemes that had been set up over the previous decade, to offset the costs to the poorer tenants. This Act was designed to reduce the general subsidy to council tenants; it was linked to changes in the system of national subsidies to local authorities designed to phase out indiscriminate help of this kind in due course. Labour opposed this measure and limited its impact, but on returning to power in 1979 the Conservatives, by reducing new expenditure on public housing, modifying the subsidy formula and encouraging rents to rise, set out to eliminate most subsidies to public housing. At the time of writing this.goal is quite close to achievement. In addition legislation enacted in 1980 to give local authority tenants a 'right to buy' has also made extensive inroads into the system of public housing. At the time of writing, after the Conservatives under Mrs Thatcher have returned to power for a third term, further legislation is being considered which could completely dismantle the system of local authority owned public housing. It would be replaced by a mixture of housing associations, tenants' co-ownership schemes and further individual ownership.

The Conservatives did little to change the social security system in the period 1951–64. Towards the end of the period the two parties began to produce competing plans to superimpose an earnings-related pensions scheme on top of the inadequate flat rate system. In 1959 the Conservatives introduced a very limited graduated pension scheme. In 1964 the Labour Party came to power committed to a much more comprehensive scheme. However, they failed to complete the preparation of this before they lost office in 1970. The Conservatives then took the idea up in a slightly more limited way, but Labour returned to power to put their own scheme on the statute book in 1975. This scheme provided for a mixed system of public and private pensions, with many of the better paid and more secure groups of workers able to 'contract out' into private schemes so long as they were at least as good as the State Earnings Related Pensions Scheme (SERPS). Conservative legislation in 1986 has extended the scope for contracting out, allowing schemes which do not necessarily compete favourably with the state scheme and also reducing the benefits available under SERPS.

In the early 1960s a number of academic studies were published showing that the 'welfare state' had by no means abolished poverty.[20] This 'rediscovery of poverty' would seem to be a function of an academic and political interest that had emerged, concerned to look at the adequacy of social policies. Indeed, it can be said to be a consequence, but also a cause, of the growth of the academic subject with which this book is concerned. It was not, at that time at least, a consequence of any particular social or economic change between the late 1940s and the early 1960s, except inasmuch as increased affluence for many heightened the 'relative poverty'[21] of those left behind. The emphasis upon the weaknesses of existing social security policies for the relief of poverty led to a reappraisal of those policies. The Labour government of 1964–70 made a number of changes, therefore. Some of the changes raised some people's incomes, and there were a number of increases in benefit rates. Inflation was, however, increasing, and public resources were, as ever, limited and in great demand for a wide range of policy objectives.

The main social security policy changes in this period were the introduction in 1965 of earnings-related supplements to sickness and unemployment benefits and of a redundancy payments scheme. Also, in 1966 'national assistance' was replaced by 'supplementary benefit'. This reform was designed to remove the stigma of assistance by making rights to these means-tested benefits much clearer, particularly for pensioners.

One particular focus of attention in the debate about poverty was family poverty, and particularly the problems faced by the low wage-earner. The principle, adopted in 1834, that wages should not be subsidized had been carried forward in social security legislation, but the margin between the income of those in work and those out of work sometimes made the principle of 'less eligibility' appear under threat. The Child Poverty Action Group, a pressure group set up in the 1960s, urged governments to deal with this problem by increasing family allowances. These had fallen in value, in real terms, since little effort had been made to update them properly. However, the conventional political view was that family allowances were an unpopular and indiscriminate handout. The 'poverty lobby' sought to persuade the government that family allowances could be increased at the expense of child tax allowances. This approach was gradually accepted, though not before inflation had reduced the tax threshold so low that most poor wage-earners were also benefiting from the tax allowances. In the 1970s the Conservatives floated an alternative approach, a form of negative income tax called 'tax credits',[22] and implemented a means-tested benefit for poor wage-earners, 'family income supplement'. Labour, on return to power, decided to press on with the development of a new family alllowance scheme, called 'child benefit', designed to replace the older allowance, extended it to the first child in each family, and offset it against the abolition of tax allowances.

On first returning to power in 1979 the Conservatives set out to make piecemeal adjustments to the social security system. They reduced the value of contributory benefits by altering the procedure for inflation-related increases, and by extending the taxation of benefits. They shifted the responsibility for provision for sickness absence for the first twenty-eight weeks from the national insurance scheme to a statutory sick pay scheme to be run by employers. They attempted also to rationalize the burgeoning supplementary benefit scheme by developing a stronger rule-based structure, and introduced a housing benefit scheme.

However, in 1983 they decided more radical reform of social security was necessary. It was an element in public expenditure which they were finding very hard to control, not surprisingly in the face of an ageing population, rapidly rising unemployment and government measures designed to shift the subsidy of housing on to the social security scheme. Proclaiming themselves to be engaged in the most radical review of social security since Beveridge, they set up a number of ministerially dominated committees to explore options for reform.[23] The eventual outcome was the 1986 Social Security Act. This legislation modified SERPS (in the way outlined above), replaced supplementary benefit by 'income support' and family income supplement by 'family credit'. These two new schemes operate with much simpler rule structures than had supplementary benefit. Housing benefit was altered to bring it in line with these other two benefits. Some anomalies which had been arising as a result of the previous piecemeal evolution of means-tested benefit were eliminated. The maternity grant and the death grant, two benefits initiated in the Beveridge era but not properly updated in line with inflation, were abolished, to be replaced by means test-related benefits for the very poor. The system of single payments available to help people on supplementary benefit with specific needs was replaced by a much more limited system, in which all most people could get were loans. Overall the 1986 Act made many detailed changes, it extended and rationalized means tests, but it did not take social security in the radical new direction that 'negative income tax' or 'social dividend' advocates were suggesting.

In the period 1951–64, of all the policy areas with which this book is concerned, it was probably education that saw the most innovation. The Butler Act had, as was stressed, laid the foundation for the creation of a sound secondary education system. At that time the orthodox view was that such a system should be selective and tripartite, with children routed at eleven-plus into grammar, technical or secondary modern schools according to their aptitudes and abilities. However, as time passed this doctrine was increasingly questioned and an alternative, non-selective, comprehensive model was championed. Various local authorities began to introduce comprehensive schools in the 1950s, motivated sometimes by political and educational ideology but sometimes, particularly in rural areas, by a recognition that such schools were a more realistic response to local needs. It was not until the 1960s that battle-lines began to be drawn, with Labour in favour of comprehensivization and the Conservatives against; and even then the Conservatives in central government were not hard-line opponents of this policy in the way that, by the end of the decade, Labour had become hard-line advocates. Nevertheless Labour legislation requiring local authorities to introduce comprehensivization schemes, enacted in 1976, was repealed by the Conservatives in 1980.

In a variety of other ways the Conservative governments of the period 1951–64 rapidly increased the resources available to state education. In many respects this was a necessary response to the child population 'bulge' created by the 'baby boom' of the immediate postwar years. This in itself created a need for new schools and teachers, and therefore provided a platform for educational innovation. But clearly governments were ready to encourage innovatory thinking. Advisory groups were created to look at various educational issues. These produced a memorable series of reports: on early leaving;[24] on education between fifteen and eighteen;[25] on the education of less academic children;[26] on higher education;[27] and on primary education.[28] The crucial policy changes influenced by all this committee activity were the rapid expansion of higher education in the 1960s, the raising of the school-leaving age to sixteen in 1973 (after delays in implementing a change first announced in 1964), and a distinct shift away from streaming and selectivity at all stages before the teenage years. But it was the change in amounts of public money spent on education that was most important. By the mid-1970s the 'bulge' had nearly worked its way through the system, and this, together with disillusion with innovation in education, brought to an end the role of the education service as an expenditure growth-leader among the public services.

This reversal was extended in the 1980s to some extent, particularly in the case of higher education, in advance of the fall in the size of the relevant generation. At the same time education-based expenditure on meals, milk and transport came under attack.

The late 1970s also saw the initiation of the questioning of the value of educational growth. Controversy grew about some of the bolder experiments in egalitarian education, and it was increasingly alleged that basic education, the 'three Rs', was being neglected. Some people put some of the responsibility for the growing youth unemployment on educational inadequacies, giving sustenance to the Manpower Services Commission's bid to control low-level post-school education. Once the Conservatives came to power in 1979 the unrest began to be translated into policy form. The completion of the comprehensivization programme was arrested, and new opportunities were created for state-financed places at private schools. The 1980 Education Act, which extended parental choice of schools, was seen as creating pressures for the raising of academic standards. At the time of writing the Conservatives are taking these developments much further; they plan for a centrally determined basic curriculum, with obviously a strong emphasis on the three Rs, a system of testing at various stages in the educational process, and the development of centrally funded schools removed from local authority control.

In the 1950s the principal government concern about the health service was the difficulties in controlling costs. No substantial changes resulted from this preoccupation. The relationship of the doctors to the government was, and remains, a sensitive area. A great deal of attention was given to their terms of service and remuneration.

The only major item of legislation in the health field between 1951 and 1970 was the Mental Health Act of 1959 which altered the procedures for the compulsory admission and retention of the mentally ill in hospital, abolishing the old 'certification' procedure. The treatment of mental illness was advancing considerably at that time, and it probably contributed more than the legislative change to reducing both the use of compulsory procedures and the incidence of long stays in hospital.

In the 1960s, as part of the wholesale review of the institutions of central and local government, proposals were introduced for the reorganization of the National Health Service. Two green papers were produced, suggesting different ways of doing this.[29] Eventually the change was effected by the Conservatives in 1974. This change created a new structure, with the former local authority health services integrated with the rest of the service. Lay participation in the running of the service was reduced; in its place community health councils were created to represent the public. The new structure was criticized as over-elaborate – with its three tiers of regions, areas and districts – almost as soon as it was created. Discontent over the operation of the new service was one of the factors that led the Labour government to set up a Royal Commission on the National Health Service in 1976. This reported in 1979,[30] recommending the removal of a tier; the government responded, by eliminating areas but enlarging some districts, in 1982.

Two important stimuli to the search for the right structure for the NHS throughout this period were a concern about effective policy control in the face of professional domination, and anxiety about the extent of inequalities in health between social classes and between regions. These two concerns were brought together during the 1970s with the development of a system for the allocation of resources between regions and districts based upon health indices (RAWP, see chapter 7). They, and particularly the former, also fuelled a concern to strengthen management. In the Griffiths Report,[31] published in 1983, a hierarchy of general managers was advocated for the NHS, weakening the influence of the nominated regional and district 'authorities'. This proposal was enacted.

The development of the personal social services between the 1940s and the 1970s is a story of steady consolidation and one important structural change. At the end of the 1940s local authorities organized these services within two or three departments. Children's services were the responsibility of one department, required by statute. Children's departments built up a body of social work expertise, and gradually extended their activities, from work to deal with the acute child care problems into work designed to prevent child neglect and abuse and work with delinquent children. Two Children and Young Persons Acts, in 1963 and 1969, legitimized and encouraged these changes in emphasis.

The other local authority welfare services, or personal social services, were organized by welfare departments and by health departments (or by departments that combined these two functions). A social work career was developed in connection with this work, but not so effectively as was the case in the children's departments. A government report in 1959 made recommendations that influenced developments in the training of social work staff of this kind.[32] But the activities of these departments were growing in other ways, too. Their legacy from the poor law was a stock of homes, for the elderly and disabled, that were ex-workhouses. A central task, therefore, was to phase out these institutions, replacing them by smaller, more welcoming and civilized homes, and also to seek to develop ways of caring for people within the community. Developments in day care, the home help service and other domiciliary services were the currency of growth in these departments. In 1970 the Chronically Sick and Disabled Persons Act placed obligations upon the local authorities to identify and help the disabled. But progress in this area of policy should not necessarily be measured by statutes. Earlier, permissive legislation had already enabled some authorities to innovate in services for the disabled.

The important structural change for all these local authority services was an Act passed in 1970, on the recommendations of the Seebohm Committee,[33] which created integrated 'social services' departments in authorities in England and Wales. In Scotland the Social Work (Scotland) Act of 1968 had already created integrated 'social work departments', in that case including the probation officers, who remained in a separate service independent of local government in England and Wales. The structural change in England and Wales was accompanied by a change in central government organization, whereby the Home Office's responsibility for children's services was passed over to the Department of Health and Social Security, which was already responsible for other welfare services. These changes represent another example of the statutory creation of a 'platform for growth'. This duly occurred, but by the 1980s had been checked.

With that check came renewed questioning about the balance between services provided by the social services departments and the many forms of family, neighbourhood and commercially purchased care that they supplemented. Within social work the quest continued for the best way to organize a service that could be responsive to community need.[34] From outside social work doubts were increasingly raised about the adequacies of that profession, particularly in the face of a growing number of child abuse 'scandals'.

During the period 1950–87 the local government structure, within which many of the social services are based, came under review. In 1972 the Local Government Act made the first major change in the local government system of England and Wales (apart from the restructuring in London, which took place in 1963), since the nineteenth century. This reform created a new two-tier system of local government. In the metropolitan areas the model, like the earlier one adopted in London, was of lower-tier authorities for most purposes and of top-tier counties responsible primarily for structural planning. Outside the metropolitan areas the division of the social policy functions was more even: the counties acquired responsibility for education and social services, while the districts were made responsible for housing. Similar changes followed in Scotland soon afterwards. Then, in 1986 the Thatcher government abolished the metropolitan counties. Their functions were either devolved to the districts or given to *ad hoc* joint boards.

An accompanying central government preoccupation about local government in this period was the fact that it was becoming an increasing spender (not surprisingly, in the light of central government's expectations of it in areas like education, personal social services and housing). In the period up to the middle 1970s central government steadily increased its contribution to local expenditure. It also struggled, rather fruitlessly, to find ways wholly or partly to replace the system of local taxation, the rates assessed on property. In the last year of the Callaghan government the central contribution to local expenditure began to be cut. The Thatcher government continued this process, much more zealously, developing a formula which deliberately penalized those authorities it deemed to be over-spenders. Then, in addition, it decided it must limit local authorities' powers to go on increasing local rates. It developed a power which enabled it to 'rate cap' a group of authorities whom it deemed to be high spenders. Finally, at the time of writing, it is abolishing rates and replacing them by a poll tax known as the 'community charge'. Scottish legislation to do this is already on the statute book, and legislation for England and Wales is before Parliament.[35]

This section has described policy developments in a period in which the Conservatives and Labour alternated in power. Thirteen years of Conservative rule was followed by nearly seven years of Labour rule. Then there was an episode of nearly four years of Conservative government. After that Labour 'enjoyed' a period of four years in government in which continuance in office depended upon the support of the Liberals. Then, in 1979 the Conservatives won a clear majority. They won a second term of office in 1983, and a third term in 1987.

In the first edition of this book it was argued that levels of controversy over social policies since 1951 had not been particularly high. Conservative ideologists had had much to say about the case for bringing market conditions more effectively to bear upon the distribution of social services, but only in the housing field had Conservative governments taken steps that represented major responses to this viewpoint. Labour had disappointed many of its supporters, who closely identified the party with the advancement of the welfare state. A succession of economic crises had limited the money available for new social policies. Yet both parties had considerably advanced public expenditure, particularly on social policies, to the point where some economists had argued that this kind of expenditure had become an inflationary force, limiting the scope for new wealth-creating private investment. This is a view both parties had taken very seriously. The most staggering growth had been in public employment and in social security transfer payments, two forms of growth politicians find very hard to limit.

However, political dominance since 1979 by a Conservative government much more openly hostile to the welfare state has changed the political atmosphere. Today the welfare state is to some extent 'under siege'.[36] Hence the title of this chapter has been changed from the positive word 'growth' used in the two earlier editions of the book to the more neutral word 'history'. In fact, however, as is shown in some detail in chapter 11, while the Conservatives have been very committed to public 'expenditure restraint and have stopped the growth of public employment, they too have found social policty expenditure hard to curb.

Public sector housing expenditure has experienced severe cuts. Education expenditure has been cut a little. Health and personal social services expenditure trends are harder to interpret. The figures suggest slight growth, but needs and costs have grown faster and some decline has been experienced. Nevertheless social policy expenditure as a whole has grown, driven upwards by the considerable growth in its major component, the social security budget.

Undoubtedly the political and economic climate for social policy growth has chilled. In the 1950s Keynesian economic management techniques were employed to try to retain full employment without inflation. Critics of policies of that period like Samuel Brittan have suggested that chancellors found it difficult to time their uses of the economic 'brake' or 'accelerator' properly,[37] and that the 'stop–go' pattern that emerged provided a poor economic environment for investment decisions, and thus inhibited British growth. The particular motivation for some fairly panicky use of the 'brake' was a concern with Britain's tendency to run into balance of payments problems, importing more than it was exporting. However, during this period a rate of growth was achieved that was good by the standards of the mid-1970s, full employment was maintained, and inflation, while ever present, was never so high as to cause alarm.

In the 1960s, despite an increasing commitment to economic planning, the cyclical pattern got worse. Inflation increased, balance of payments crises forced the application of strong restraints to public expenditure and private incomes on a number of occasions, and, at the depressed point of the cycle, quite marked increases in unemployment occurred. In the mid-1970s Britain faced a more severe crisis, in which very high inflation, a balance of payments problem and continuing high unemployment occurred all at tha same time. Measures to cope with the first two by traditional means worsened the third. At a time when governments seemed to have learnt a great deal about economic management they found it increasingly difficult to practise it. In fact, the rise in economic management problems can be correlated with the dramatic increase in the number of economists in the civil service!

Different schools of economists have preached different solutions to these problems. On the Right the 'monetarist' school of thought has become increasingly influential, arguing that governments must control the money supply and let economic forces bring the system under control.[38] This viewpoint was put partly into practice in the 1970s, but politicians were reluctant to let bankruptcies and redundancies occur on a sufficient scale to really test the monetarist hypothesis. More influential, and more in conformity with Keynesian orthodoxy, were those economists who argued that income restraint was necessary to bring unemployment and inflation into balance, and to prevent Britain's balance of payments getting out of hand as rising wages led us to import goods we could ill afford while making it more difficult to sell things. As far as they were concerned, what happened was that wage bargaining was no longer restrained by the social and political forces that hitherto limited rises to figures that would not disrupt the economy. Incomes policies were seen as crucial to help solve our problems, yet over and over again governments found that political pressures made these very difficult to sustain for any length of time. The whole picture was, however, complicated by changes in the pattern of trade in the world, and particularly by rises in prices of primary commodities.

After 1979 the 'monetarist' theory was more boldly put into practice. The government treated the money supply and particularly the public sector borrowing rate as the key phenomena to keep under control. It was prepared to let unemployment rise rapidly in the cause of the war against inflation. It abandoned incomes policy in the private sector, seeking only to keep pay increases to public employees tightly under control. Initially it found the removal of pay controls and its own taxation adustments produced severely inflationary effects. But then it was successful in bringing inflation under control, but achieved that at the expense of a rapid increase in unemployment. Numbers registered as out of work rose from just over a million in 1979 to over 3 million in 1983. They have remained close to the latter level ever since.

In chapter 9, one of the issues which will be examined will be whether social policy measures can help to cope with unemployment or whether it is primarily an economic problem. While one school of economists, broadly on the Left, see a way forward toward economic stability and growth in employment through protection against imports, doubts are inceasingly raised about how such measures can counter a developing trend towards lower job opportunities. There is evidence that the character of demand for labour is changing, and that new investment is essentially capital-intensive and therefore unable to absorb much labour. Analysis of the issue is complicated by questions about the changing composition of the labour force, which large numbers of married women have joined since the war, and about the extent to which the unemployed lack the skills and capacity now required by industry.

Early in this chapter it was pointed out that at the beginning of the century British governments adopted an approach of relief of unemployment that largely ruled out the creation of specific employment opportunities. In the early 1970s interest was awakened in Britain in the case for the development of 'active labour market policies' of the kind adopted in Sweden.[39] These involved such things as assisting labour mobility, expanding training when unemployment rises, and creating special work projects for the unemployed. Their appeal was that they were conceived in Keynesian terms as helping to reduce the extent to which measures to alleviate unemployment, in a largely fully employed economy, created inflation.

Their adoption in Britain occurred at a time of high unemployment. Accordingly instead of serving the economic function for which they were originally advocated they have been modified to serve the political function of reducing the number of unemployed whilst minimizing intervention in the economy as a whole. There has been a particular concentration on measures for young people to the extent that many who leave school at sixteen can expect up to two years in government schemes which combine work experience with training.

These reflections upon some of the problematic relationships today between economic and social policies conclude this chapter on the development of social policy in Britain. It has been hard to decide what should be given attention, and how much detail should be included. It was important to sketch in some of the history of developments in social policy. In our complex society so many of the peculiarities of our institutions and policies can be explained only by what has gone before. It is also necessary not to view policies in a static way; they have been built up slowly over a long period and they are still changing. The factors that helped to build them will be examined further in the next two chapters by looking at the forces that influence the making and implementation of social policy. After that we will be ready to look at specific policies in more detail.

SUGGESTIONS FOR FURTHER READING

Such is the wealth of historical literature that it has been difficult to decide what to give in notes in this chapter. References have been confined to some of the more significant primary sources and to secondary sources that readers may find particularly interesting or readable. Some of the major historical works upon which the author has depended have not been cited.

Derek Fraser's *The Evolution of the British Welfare State* (see n. 9) is a good general historical textbook but is stronger on the nineteenth than the twentieth century. Pat Thane's *The Foundation of the Welfare State*, deals with the period from 1870 onward.[40] The interwar period is well covered in Gilbert's book (see n. 15). A number of recent books deal with the 1945–51 Labour government. Amongst these K. O. Morgan's *Labour in Power* is recommended.[41] Historical accounts of the more recent period are, generally speaking, still to be written, as is an overall review of social policy development since the Second World War. However, Nicolas Deakin's *The Politics of Welfare* provides the rudiments of such an account.[42]

# CHAPTER 3

# The Making of Social Policy

## INTRODUCTION

This chapter deals with the social policy-making system, introducing the key institutions involved in the process in Britain. The next chapter looks at the implementation of social policy. The two chapters must be considered together; dividing the policy processes between 'making' and 'implementation' is, in various respects, difficult. It is hard to identify a dividing line at which making can be said to be completed and implementation to start. There is also a considerable amount of feedback from implementation which influences further policy making, and many policies are so skeletal that their real impact depends upon the way they are interpreted at the implementation stage.

The starting-point in the chapter is the ideal to which the British system of government is presumed to correspond, in which policy making is seen as the responsibility of our representatives in Parliament, who answer to the people at the general election for their stewardship of the public interest. The chapter will first look at the features of the system that correspond to this model, and at the institutions that are reputedly responsible for the policy-making process. It will also look at the implications of the presence of lower-tier organs of government, at local levels, and at the way in which representative government seems to be expected to work within them.

After this, the discussion will turn to consider the various ways in which the model of representative government is modified, or perhaps even undermined, in practice. It will consider how the people's will is translated into political action. It will look at the part played by pressure groups in the system, and it will examine the case that has been made for regarding democracy as significantly undermined by 'political elites'. The relationship between government and Parliament will be scrutinized, together with its parallels in local government. Attention will be given to the role played by the machinery of government, by the civil service and by local government officers in the policy-making process, and some general points will be made about what we mean by that 'process'. These later issues will lead naturally into the examination of the implementation process in the next chapter.


## THE REPRESENTATIVE GOVERNMENT MODEL

When the systems of government in Britain, the United States, most of Western Europe and much of the Commonwealth are claimed to be democratic, that rests upon a view that a form of representation of the people prevails in their governmental systems. Clearly, these systems do not involve direct democracy since in complex societies large numbers of decisions are taken by small numbers of representatives. Some countries seek to involve the people more directly, from time to time, by the use of plebiscites.

There is a further sense in which representative government is indirect. A distinction is often made between representatives and delegates. Delegates are regarded as mandated by those who elect them to support specific policies and to return to explain their subsequent decisions. British politicians have persistently rejected the view that they should be regarded as delegates, arguing instead that their duty is to make judgements for themselves in terms of their understanding of their constituents' best interests, while recognizing that they may, of course, be rejected at the next election if they become seriously out of touch with the people they represent. In this sense they claim to be concerned with the interests of all their constituents, and not just those who voted for them. This doctrine was first expounded by Edmund Burke in the late eighteenth century. Today, of course, the importance of political parties makes it difficult for members of Parliament to claim to represent all their constituents; but equally makes it difficult for them to assume delegate roles. The presence in Parliament, and in the local councils, of party groups exerts an influence in favour of party programmes and away from a direct relationship between member and constituency. The modern modification of representative democracy is therefore to see the public as being allowed to choose from time to time between two or more broad political programmes, and being able to reject a party that has failed to carry out its promises.[1]

If this model of democracy prevails, social policies may be expected to be determined by the commitments of the political parties, and proposals for policy changes will be set out in election manifestos. The growth of the welfare state will be clearly relatable to the growth of democracy, with the people *choosing* to see their society change in this way. The limitations of this view of the policy-making process will be explored, but first there is a need to identify more explicitly the institutions of government to which such an analysis must relate. Those who have previously done courses on the British constitution may wish to skip the next two sections.

## THE CENTRAL GOVERNMENT SYSTEM

The curious feature of the British constitution is that Britain has democratized institutions that were created in an undemocratic age. Most countries have systems of government that are relatively modern creations, either designed after cataclysmic political events which required the setting up of entirely new institutions, or set up to meet the needs of newly created or newly independent states. The governments of France and Germany, for example, fall into the first of these categories, and those of the United States and the Commonwealth countries into the second. The British pride themselves on having developed a system of government that has been a model for the rest of the world. The truth is that, while certainly many constitutional ideas *have* been borrowed from Britain, the British system contains features that no one designing a system of government today would conceivably want to adopt.

The monarchy and the House of Lords are the two most significant British 'anomalies'. Formally, neither has much influence on the policy-making process. Monarchs have relinquished their rights to interfere; the House of Lords has been largely stripped of its rights by successive parliamentary Acts since 1911. This discussion need not go into the residual rights and responsibilities of these two.

The House of Commons is elected from over 600 constituencies (an exact number has not been quoted as regular constituency boundary changes alter it), each of which returns the person with a simple majority of votes at each election. After a general election the monarch has the formal responsibility to ask the leader of the majority party to form a government. On most occasions the Monarch's duty is clear, but situations in which there is no party with a clear majority may complicate the task. Broadly, the expectation is that the Monarch will not have to take a decision that will then prove to be a violation of the democratic process, because it will be up to whoever agrees to form a government in these circumstances to prove that he or she has adequate parliamentary support. In other words, the position of a minority government can be made untenable if all the other parties combine against it. There are, however, ambiguities in such a situation, as the lives of minority governments may be perpetuated more by a reluctance to force them to resign than by any positive commitment to their support.

The newly appointed prime mimister will then form a government, giving a hundred or more governmental offices to his or her supporters. Again, the normal assumption is that these will be members of his or her own party, but exceptionally a coalition may be formed in which government offices go to other parties. All those given office will normally be, or will be expected to become, members of either the Commons or the Lords. Most will be members of the Commons (known as 'members of Parliament'). The choice of members of the government rests significantly upon the preferences of the prime minister. However he or she cannot disregard interests and factions within his or her own party, and will obviously give some attention to the competence of those appointed.

The most important prime ministerial appointments will be those of the members of Cabinet. The normal practice is to appoint a Cabinet of fifteen to twenty-five members. It will include the main departments of government together with some members who do not have departmental responsibilities who may be given political or co-ordinating roles. The Cabinet, chaired by the prime minister, is the key decision-making body within the government. New policy departures of any significance and new legislation will need Cabinet approval, and conflicts of interests between departments will have to be fought out in the Cabinet or its committees. Each Cabinet sets up a number of committees to do more detailed work. Some of these will draw on the help of non-Cabinet ministers.

The government departments to which attention must be given in the discussion of social policy in England (the different situation in the other component countries of the United Kingdom is outlined later) are the Treasury, the Department of Health and Social Security, the Department of the Environment, the Department of Education and Science and the Department of Employment. Two other departments, the Cabinet Office and the Home Office, also play a small part. Readers must be warned that it has been the practice of governments in recent years to alter the departmental structure from time to time, ostensibly in an effort to find the best possible framework for policy co-ordination, but – it may be suggested – with less elevated political motives in mind too. Accordingly, it may be the case that by the time this book is in your hands departments may have new names and policy responsibilities may have been moved from one department to another. Had this book been written in 1964, for example, the responsibilities of the Department of Health and Social Security would have been described as coming under the Ministry of Health, the Ministry of Pensions and National Insurance, and the National Assistance Board.

The prime minister is technically the First Lord of the Treasury. This archaic title serves to remind us that, while today we regard the chancellor of the Exchequer as the senior Treasury minister, the prime minister is, above all, bound to be involved in major decisions on expenditure, taxation and the management of the economy. The importance of this aspect of policy is so great that there are often other Treasury ministers in the Cabinet, such as the chief secretary to the Treasury and the paymaster general. These may be expected to play important roles in relation to decisions on public expenditure.

Each of the departments listed above has its senior minister, the secretary of state, in the Cabinet. Again, the prime minister may choose to have other ministers from specific departments as Cabinet members. Under the last Labour government, the minister of state in the Department of Health and Social Security who took particular responsibility for social security, Mr Stanley Orme, was a Cabinet minister. Each department head has the support of several junior ministers, known as ministers of state or under-secretaries, who may take on particular responsibilities for specific policy areas. The recent trend towards 'super-ministries' taking on several different but related areas of policy has made this political division of labour particularly important.

The role of the minister who is also a Cabinet member involves a quite considerable conflict between a position as a member of the central policy co-ordinating team within the government and responsibility for the protection and advancement of the interests of a department. In his *Diaries of a Cabinet Minister* the late Richard Crossman gave considerable attention to this problem.[2] It is personally difficult for any individual to give wholehearted attention both to departmental issues and to the main political strategy problems arising outside his or her own responsibilities. There is likewise a crucial problem for a rational approach to government in which strategic questions may not be best resolved by bargaining between a group of individuals all of whom have conflicting, 'tunnel vision' images dictated by departmental needs and priorities. Clearly, the members of the Cabinet without departmental responsibilities are expected to help to resolve this problem, but they often suffer from a sense of being outsiders without the detailed departmental briefs possessed by their colleagues.[3] The creation of a group of special civil servants, including individuals recruited from outside the public service for their expertise or political connections, has been seen as a further desire to strengthen strategic thinking in government. There would seem, however, to be a continuing and inevitable conflict here.

As far as his or her departmental duties are concerned a minister's work will fall into roughly four categories. First, he or she may be responsible for putting forward new legislation. Clearly this is something the ambitious politician will want to do. He or she will hope to secure a job that involves the initiation of policies from the party's programme. Second, he or she will have a large amount of day-to-day administration to oversee. Much of this will involve the formulation of new policies that do not require legislation, or the determination of responses to new crises within the department. It is in this kind of work that the distinction between policy making and implementation becomes so unclear. In many respects any issue that a department regards as requiring a ministerial decision is likely to be describable as a 'policy issue'. Third, he or she will have to deal with questions from members of Parliament about the policies and activities of the department. While this may be seen primarily as a defensive kind of action, involving much routine work by civil servants who are required to produce the information needed for parliamentary answers, it may also provide opportunities for publicizing new policy initiatives. Indeed, many questions are planted by friendly MPs, from the back benches on the minister's own side, to enable activities to be advertised. Fourth, the minister has a wide public relations role beyond Parliament. This will involve a programme of speeches, meetings and visits relating the department's activities to the world outside.

Several references have already been made to the support of ministers by civil servants. It is self-evident that civil servants have an important role to play in implementing policy. What also needs to be emphasized is that civil servants are also heavily involved in making policy. Until recent changes in the structure of the civil service, designed to reduce barriers between the various grades and to stress the importance of many of the managerial roles played in connection with policy implementation, it was possible to draw a fairly clear distinction between the 'administrative class', containing the 'higher' civil servants responsible for policy, and the rest of the civil service. Now, the policy-making group is a little more difficult to define. Each major department has at its headquarters a group of 100 or so civil servants, from the grade of 'principal' up to 'permanent secretary', who are concerned with decisions of a 'policy' kind, many of which require ministerial approval. The theory of representative government clearly requires that they be called the *servants* of the minister, providing information and evidence on policy alternatives but not taking policy desisions.

The British system of government involves more than a network of departments headed by ministers. Responsibility for various specific public services is hived off to a range of special agencies, though in each case ultimate responsibility for policy lies with one of the central departments. Again, these subordinate bodies might be described as being concerned with implementation and not with policy making. But, while this is broadly true, many do this within only general guidelines and have therefore an important, if subordinate, policy-making role. Students of social policy will come across a number of important examples of bodies of this kind with a nationwide remit. In the field of manpower policy the Manpower Services Commission, containing representatives from both sides of industry, has been delegated extensive responsibilities by the Department of Employment. This is an example of government efforts to foster new initiatives by creating an agency outside of direct central political control. There are others at regional and local levels, particularly in the health service, which will be mentioned later.

The discussion in this section has moved from the consideration of the composition of Parliament, and the nature of the relationship of government to Parliament, to a more detailed account of the agencies concerned with policy making. There is a need, however, to look a little more at the role of Parliament. It has been shown that about 100 of the 600 members elected to Parliament become involved in specific government jobs. What role do the rest play in policy making?

Primary policy making involves the promulgation of Acts of Parliament. The overwhelming majority of these are promoted by government, and thus the initial 'Bills' are prepared by civil servants within the departments. Bills then go through four stages in each House: a 'first reading', which simply involves the formal presentation of the Bill; a 'second reading', at which there is likely to be a large-scale debate on the basic principles of the Bill; a 'committee stage', when the legislation is examined in detail (normally by a small 'standing committee' and not by the whole House); and a 'report stage' and 'third reading', at which the Bill that emerges from the committee is approved, but may be re-amended to undo some of the actions of the committee. Clearly, members without ministerial office may participate in all of these stages, and Opposition members will take particular care to scrutinize and attack government action. The leading Opposition party organizes a 'shadow cabinet' to provide for a considered and specialized response to the activities of the government.

Back-bench MPs may be able to promote new policies through 'private members' Bills'. These cannot have direct financial implications for the government, and they have little chance of becoming law without government support. Occasionally governments assist private members with their Bills, particularly by allowing extra parliamentary time. Some significant social policy measures have become law in this way. The Abortion Act of 1967, for example, was promoted by a Liberal MP, David Steel, and became law because many key ministers were sympathetic. In this case the Bill concerned an issue of conscience on which many felt it would be inappropriate for Parliament to divide on party lines. The abolition of capital punishment and reform of the law on homosexuality came about in a similar way. In the 1970s the Labour government supported a private member's Bill which took over an item which would have been included in its own programme if there had been sufficient parliamentary time. This curious reversal of roles may have owed something to the agreement of the Liberals to support a government without a clear majority; the legislation was the Housing (Homeless Persons) Act of 1977 promoted by a Liberal, Stephen Ross.

In addition to Acts of Parliament both Houses have to deal with a great deal of what is known as 'subordinate' or 'delegated' legislation. Many Acts allow governments to promote subsequent changes and new regulations. It is important to recognize that many policy changes pass through Parliament in this way. It would be an extravagant use of parliamentary time to require new legislation for changes of this kind. Controversy arises, however, over the extent of the use of delegated legislation, since some Acts convey very wide scope for this kind of ministerial action. To promote subordinate legislation the government has to publish a 'statutory instrument' which is open to scrutiny by MPs. Some of these require parliamentary approval; others may be annulled if a negative resolution is passed by either House within forty days of their initial publication. Hence back-benchers may intervene to prevent subordinate legislation. A joint committee of the Commons and the Lords has been set up to scrutinize statutory instruments, and therefore to facilitate parliamentary review of subordinate legislation. They have, however, a mammoth task and only give detailed attention to a limited number of the statutory instruments that are put before Parliament.

Readers will find a good example of legislation for which statutory instruments are important in the 1986 Social Security Act. They will look in vain for detailed information on, for example, the housing benefit scheme or the 'social fund' in the Act: this is contained in subsequent regulations. In particular actual benefit rates are not included in such legislation but set out in regulations which are regularly updated and amended

Reference has already been made to parliamentary questions as providing an opportunity for back-bench scrutiny of government actions. Members put down initial questions in advance. Many questions are answered in writing, but those that receive oral answers may be followed up by supplementary questions. In addition to the powers to ask questions, various parliamentary procedures provide scope for MPs to promote short debates on topics that concern them. The main Opposition party is extended more specific facilities of this kind, so there are days allocated for debates on topics of its own choice.

One peculiar characteristic of the British Parliament that distinguishes it from many legislatures in other countries, and particularly from the United

States Congress, is the slight use made of specialized committees. This is also a difference between the central government system and the local government system in Britain. The committees that consider Bills are in no way specialized; they consider new legislation in rotation regardless of subject and do not do any separate investigatory work.

There is also, however, a system of select committees. Perhaps the most important of these is the Public Accounts Committee, concerned to look at the way in which public money has been spent. Then there are select committees on the work of the Parliamentary Commissioner for Administration (the 'Ombudsman'), on Statutory Instruments and on European Legislation. In 1979 fourteen committees were set up to concern themselves with the work of specific (or in some cases two specific) government departments. *Ad hoc* committees may also be set up to investigate specific subjects. However, such is the power of the executive in our system that it is doubtful whether these new committees can do other than play a rather superior pressure-group role. They investigate specific topics, with the aid of specialist advisers, and have issued some influential reports. But, as stressed above, they have no role with regard to legislation.

This account of the institutions of British central government has shown that elected representatives have a wide range of parliamentary duties. If they belong to the party that wins power they may well take on a government office of some kind. If they do not achieve office they are still in a special relationship to government in which, while some advantages may accrue from being a member of the ruling party and having many colleagues and friends in office, there may also be disadvantages in that party allegiance implies a duty to support the governnment. Some of the scope for the criticism of policy that comes to Opposition members is denied to government supporters. On the other hand opposition, in a Parliament organized strictly on party lines, implies a situation in which it is very hard to secure majority support for your own ideas.

REGIONAL AND LOCAL GOVERNMENT

The term 'regional government' is used here to cover two phenomena: the government of Scotland, Wales and Northern Ireland, and the organization of the government of specific services on a regional basis.

Northern Ireland had a devolved system of government between 1922 and 1972. The Government of Ireland Act of 1920 conferred a considerable measure of self-government upon Northern Ireland. All social policy legislation was the responsibility of the Northern Ireland government, and revenue was raised partly by local taxes and partly by the United Kingdom taxation system. In practice legislation at Stormont, the Northern Ireland Parliament, tended to follow legislation at Westminster quite closely but often a few years behind. The people of the province were represented both at Stormont and at Westminster. The British government possessed reserve powers, so that it could interfere in the government if it so wished. Until the 'troubles' of the late 1960s it studiously refused to do so. However, in 1972 the Northern Ireland (Temporary Provisions) Act suspended Stormont and imposed direct rule from Westminster. In 1974 an attempt to begin to restore self-government through a new Northern Ireland Executive, elected by proportional representation to try to provide for the involvement of the Catholic minority in government, was brought to an end after a strike by Protestant workers. In 1982 a further, very limited, form of political participation was started. Government of Northern Ireland is through a secretary of state for Northern Ireland at Westminster who heads a Northern Ireland Office. Within Northern Ireland itself the former separate departments operate but all are technically under the jurisdiction of the Northern Ireland Office. The various junior ministers in the Northern Ireland Office share the 'ministerial' responsibilities for these departments. Naturally, the Northern Ireland departments operate on the basis of legislation passed before the demise of Stormont. This is supplemented by special legislation from Westminster where appropriate.

Scotland's affairs are conducted from Westminster by way of a secretary of state for Scotland and a separate Scottish Office, which is split into several departments. Much Scottish legislation is already separate. Those social services that come under local government – housing, personal social services and education – have their control devolved to the Scottish Office and are regulated by separate legislation. The health service in Scotland has a slightly different structure and its own separate laws, but here the centralizing tendency for control from London has been very strong. The social security system is, on the other hand, that obtaining throughout Great Britain. Within Parliament there is a convention that only Scottish MPs participate in debates on Scottish matters. Since the 1987 general election the ranks of Conservative MPs have been reduced to a very small number. This is likely to bring the arrangements for Scottish legislation under strain and increase the pressure for political devolution.

Devolution to Wales is not so extensive. Whilst there is a separate Welsh Office, most legislation deals jointly with England and Wales. After the 1987 election Mrs Thatcher appointed an Englishman, representing an English parliamentary seat, to head the Welsh Office and represent it in Cabinet. In many respects the Welsh Office is little more than an integrated 'regional office' bringing together, in a way not present in the English regions, concerns about health, personal social services, education and housing.

Acts were passed in 1978 allowing for devolution of most of these administrative powers to elected assemblies in Scotland and Wales. These were subject to acceptance by the people of those countries, who were consulted by referenda early in 1979. The people of Wales conclusively rejected the proposals. In Scotland there was a majority in favour of devolution but it fell short of the 40 per cent of the electorate required by the statute.

The Channel Islands and the Isle of Man have substantially more independent systems of government, and do not send MPs to Westminster. In view of their small size, however, it does not seem appropriate to say anything more about them.

In the context both of the discussion of devolution to Scotland and Wales and of the consideration of the reorganization of local government, some attention has been given to the case for regional government in England. While it seems unlikely that any regional system will be developed, it is important to note that most government departments with responsibilities for local services have systems of regional offices. These regional structures appear to have comparatively little significance for policy making, with perhaps one exception of some importance for social policy. This is that the National Health Service is administered through regional health authorities, consisting of a small body of people appointed by the secretary of state. This is an important tier within the complicated government structure set up for the health service, with responsibilities for the allocation of resources and for strategic planning.

Local government in England and Wales is organized into two distinctive systems. In the metropolitan areas of London, West Midlands, South Yorkshire, Greater Manchester, Merseyside and Tyne and Wear there has been, since the abolition of the Metropolitan Counties (see p. 35) a one-tier system of metropolitan districts responsible for personal social services, education and housing. There are *ad hoc* bodies dealing with some of the functions of the former counties, but these need not detain us as their tasks do not fall within the main concerns of this book. In the inner area of London, however, one special *ad hoc* body remains, which was in fact created when the London reforms of 1963 were enacted: the Inner London Education Authority. This Labour-controlled body is not popular with the Thatcher government. New legislation may allow inner London boroughs to take over education, perhaps on a piecemeal basis.

In the rest of England and Wales there are county authorities which are responsible for education and personal social services, but also a lower tier of districts which include housing amongst their responsibilities. In autumn 1978 the Labour government announced a commitment to give social services responsibilities, and perhaps those of the education service, to the largest of the district councils. The Conservative administration, whose party members do not often control these large urban authorities, has shown no interest in this matter. Planning responsibilities are shared between the two tiers. There is also a third tier of parish councils, with minimal powers. Whilst many of these are old parishes, others are towns that previously had significant powers of their own, some retaining mayors and calling themselves town councils. In Wales these third-tier authorities are known as community councils. None of these third-tier authorities have significant social policy responsibilities, so they will not be examined further here.

In Scotland there is a two-tier system very similar to that operating in the non-metropolitan areas of England and Wales. The top-tier authorities are there known as regions, a more appropriate title perhaps, as one of them, Strathclyde, contains half the population of Scotland. There are great variations in population size between the regions, a probably inevitable consequence of the uneven way population is distributed in Scotland. In those parts of Scotland that are most isolated (Orkney and Shetland and the Western Isles), there are single unitary authorities that deal with all local government functions.

Local government in Northern Ireland has been stripped of almost all its significant powers. It had previously been notorious in some areas for the manipulation of electoral boundaries and for the practice of religious discrimination. Health services and personal social services come under four appointed boards. Education is the responsibility of three separate education and libraries boards. Public housing is the concern of the Northern Ireland Housing Executive.

The health service, outside Northern Ireland, has its own separate system of regions and districts. The local authorities are represented on the district authorities, and health districts have been partly designed to facilitate liaison with local authorities.

The field of social policy that does not have an even partly devolved structure below the national level is social security. The Department of Health and Social Security is itself responsible for the delivery of social security benefits, and maintains its own regional structure and a system of local offices for this purpose. There is, however, a separate system for Northern Ireland.

National legislation defines the powers of local authorities, and may set limits to those powers. It also imposes upon local government a range of duties. The relationship between central and local government in Britain is a complex one. Local government is not autonomous, but neither is it merely local administration. Some statutes impose fairly clear tasks for local authorities. But many give powers, and indicate ways in which those powers should be used, without undermining the scope for local initiative. Other Acts of Parliament merely grant local authorities powers, which they may choose whether or not to use. Exceptionally, a local authority may itself promote a 'private' Act to secure powers to undertake new ventures. Local authorities are therefore able to make or elaborate policies and are not merely implementing agencies.

However, the relationship between central and local government involves both partnership and conflict. Central government seeks to impose its will not merely through legislation but also through the communication of large amounts of guidance. This may be embodied in circulars, regularly sent from central departments to local authorities, or through less formal communications from ministers, administrators and professional advisers. Central intervention will be justified in terms of national political commitments, to ensure that central policies have an impact upon all localities. There is an inherent conflict between the demands of local autonomy and the principle of 'territorial justice', requiring that citizens in different geographical areas secure comparable treatment.

Central government also justifies its interventions in local government in terms of its concern with national economic management. It is its financial control over local government that tends to weaken its claim that the central–local relationship is a partnership. The problem is compounded by lack of a satisfactory way for local government to raise its own revenue. Local authorities have three major sources of income: rates, payments for the provisions of services and government grants. Rates are local taxes imposed upon property. They are unpopular since they are regressive and are poorly related to income. As local services grew, therefore, government grants have become an increasingly important source of income. By 1977–8 about 61 per cent of all local authority income in England and Wales came from government grants. Since that time central government has taken steps to reduce the proportion of local expenditure it funds. By 1985–6 it had brought it back to just below 50 per cent. While, theoretically, local authorities may spend their own incomes in ways they themselves choose, the government, in calculating local government grants, increasingly indicates how it expects the authorities to allocate funds between priorities. In the determination of its grant to local authorities the government uses a complex formula which tries to take into account the extent of need for the various services.

In chapter 2 it was pointed out that the Thatcher goverment had made strong efforts to curb overall local government expenditure. It has attempted to be very explicit about what it considers to be unnecessary local expenditure. As far as the central grant is concerned, it has developed a technique that enables it to cut the money given to some authorities which it considers to be over-spenders by an amount equal to or more than any expenditure increase. As far as rates are concerned, it has imposed 'rate caps' on a selection of local authorities, which prevent or put limits upon any rate increase. It is important to note that most of the authorities which have experienced the more punitive forms of grant limitation and all but one of the authorities which have experienced rate capping have been Labour controlled. Many of these have also been authorities with substantial areas of inner-urban deprivation within their boundaries. Not surprisingly these measures have been controversial, and a central–local battle has developed with a strong party political character.[4]

In early 1986 the government took its concern to influence the financing of local government a stage further. In a Green Paper, *Paying for Local Government*, it proposed the abolition of domestic rates; the setting of non-domestic rates by central government and their distribution to authorities by way of a pooling system; and simplification of the grants system.[5] In 1987 it embraced these proposals in an Act to apply to Scotland, to come into force in the financial year 1989. A Bill before Parliament at the time of writing will extend this measure to England and Wales in 1990. The abolition of domestic rates involves their replacement by a flat rate 'community charge', widely called a 'poll tax', which every adult must pay. Some low income people may have reductions, as they do now with rates, probably through housing benefit. But the government intends everyone should pay some amount.

The community charge will have dramatic redistributive effects – to put it simply, away from small numbers of adults in high valued homes towards larger numbers in lower valued ones. It is therefore likely to be more regressive than rates. It will be administratively complex because it will bring many more people into the local taxation net. It is seen by the government as a measure which makes more people pay directly for local services and which will increase local accountability. The effects upon the services with which this book is concerned and upon the behaviour of local government are hard to predict at this stage.

This has been a rather large digression from the main concerns of this chapter, but it is important to bear in mind this important change, which appears likely to occur very soon.

Central government also maintains control over local authority borrowing. The trend, in recent years, has been away from a system of strict, item by item controls to broad limitations upon total borrowing. The system is currently a complex combination of these two approaches to control, which will not be examined in detail here.

Policy making in local government is the responsibility of elected members. These represent districts, or wards, within each authority in much the same way as MPs represent constituencies. Today a great deal of local politics is arranged along party lines, and most councillors represent the political parties that are also found at Westminster.

Local authority members each belong to a number of committees. Most business in transacted in these committees, so that the meetings of the full councils are largely rubber-stamping affairs, affording opportunities for the making of political points. The committee structures are primarily related to the various functional responsibilities of the authority. Many local authorities operate 'policy committees', which aim to co-ordinate the activities of the authority as a whole. In most authorities the parties are represented on the committees in proportion to their distribution on the whole council. Often the majority party will assume the chairmanship of each of the committees, and occasionally the policy committee is used as a one-party cabinet. The increasing politicization of local government is intensifying the conflict between central and local government, and particularly between radical Labour authorities and the current Conservative administration.

THE VOICE OF THE PEOPLE?

It has already been noted that in the British system of government MPs and councillors are elected in individual constituencies on the basis of a procedure in which the candidate with a simple majority is the winner. It is generally the case that the voter has to choose between two to four candidates, each of whom is the representative of a specific political party. In this way electoral choice is peculiarly structured. Voters have to make their decision on the basis of assessments of particular people, with their own special policy commitments, in relation to the more general political biases and policy commitments of their parties. The parties' intentions are perhaps of more importance than individuals' commitments. However, what the parties offer are broad packages of policies, within which voters may like some items while disliking others.

Hence the individual voter's starting-point in trying to influence policy through the electoral process is a situation of very limited choice in which it is general policy biases, or even more general considerations, often described as 'party images', that must govern his or her selection of an MP. Moreover, his or her vote will be taken together with large numbers of other votes, perhaps motivated by very different policy preferences. Hence, one person's voting choice may be influenced by a party's commitment to raise pensions, which leads him or her to support it despite its commitment to other policies – say increasing educational expenditure – with which he or she disagrees. But others who vote for the same party may be motivated by directly opposite considerations – a strong commitment to education, say, but no concern about pensions. Furthermore the candidate for this party in one constituency may stress a commitment to education, while colleagues in other constituencies may make the pensions increase the central plank in their programme.

The above example was chosen to illustrate the basic underlying problem about the use of choices between representatives as a means of settling policy priorities. The reality is that party platforms are considerably more complex, with choices between desirable ends deliberately obscured. No party presents the electorate with explicit choices between widely desired ends; they generally seek to convince it that they can bring a little more of everything that is wanted. Voters are forced to discriminate between the parties in terms of their general ideologies, value biases and images.

Furthermore, most voters do not really make electoral *choices*. Many vote for the same party every time they vote, and probably give little attention to the personalities or policies of specific candidates. Voters behave in ways that, as far as the collective pattern of choices is concerned, political scientists are largely able to predict from their occupations, social origins and personalities. Only a minority of the electorate changes sides between elections. Indeed, many of the changes that alter the balance in power in Parliament are no more than changes between voting and non-voting, or vice versa. Research findings suggest, moreover, that the people most likely to change their votes – the floating voters – are generally the least informed within the electorate, and are thus not people who can be said to be making careful choices between policies. It is suggested, instead, that political *images* are particularly significant – the personalities of the leaders, their projections of competence and of their capacities to deal with the nation's problems. An important consideration at a general election is the success or failure of the government in power in coping with the economic situation. In this sense a verdict may be given on its policies, but only in a very general way.

Clearly, therefore, electors are not normally provided with the opportunities to make clear choices about social policies, or between social policy options. There are certainly general characteristics of the parties' approach to social policies that may help people to decide between them; and at particular elections (such as, for example, the general election of 1945) one's social policy commitments may be particularly clear. But at other times it may be very difficult to single out policy issues that divide the parties. In 1970 the Child Poverty Action Group attacked the Labour government's failure to deal effectively with family poverty and secured a pledge from the Conservatives that family allowances would be increased. The Conservatives did not increase these allowances, but it is doubtful whether many voters were influenced to change their allegiances on this issue. Those who studied the parties' platforms carefully would have had to relate the Labour Party's generally stronger commitment to universal social security policies to the Conservatives' specific pledge. It may be suggested that what the Child Poverty Action Group expected, and wanted, was a new Labour government returned to power, chastened by criticism of its family policies, and not a Conservative government.

Another characteristic of social policies is that, while some involve broad responses to popular needs and wishes, many are specific measures to assist quite small disadvantaged groups in the population. Policies to assist disabled drivers, for example, may be viewed as generally desirable, and in that sense may have electoral appeal; but the people they benefit directly or indirectly is a very small minority in the population. Disabled drivers may be a relatively 'popular' minority group; but what about policies to help the long-term unemployed, rehabilitate criminals or provide facilities for vagrant alcoholics, for example? If there were a direct relationship between the pursuit of electoral popularity and the determination of social policies, surely minority causes would receive much less attention than they do now, and unpopular minority causes would receive no attention at all (or even more punitive responses). Opinion polls suggest that a variety of social reforms carried out in Britain in the last few years – the abolition of capital punishment and the liberalization of the law relating to homosexuality, for example – were enacted in the face of popular opposition.

Other survey evidence suggests, moreover, that a majority of the population has little sympathy towards those most in need of help from the welfare state.[7] This suggests the presence of a political mood that is electorally exploitable. The problem, however, in understanding the popular impact upon social policies is in explaining the fact that governments seem peculiarly restrained in translating such opinion into policies.

At a time when the British electorate has elected a Conservative government for the third time on the basis of a minority of the votes cast it is additionally important to add to this examination of the impact of 'the voice of the people' upon social policy determination the observation that our 'first past the post' electoral system can convey a very ambiguous message. After the 1987 election Mrs Thatcher can claim to have a very clear mandate. But her opponents can point to the majority vote against her, split, largely speaking, between the Labour Party and the Liberal/SDP Alliance. Similarly, as has already been suggested with reference to Scotland, in our very centralized political system it can be shown that government support is very low in some regions. Yet, of course, the introduction of some kind of proportional representation system would not necessarily solve this 'political arithmetic' problem, for policy priorities would then be influenced by the way negotiations between potential coalition parties developed.

## PRESSURE GROUPS AND POLITICAL ELITES

Much of the detailed analysis of the role of pressure groups in the policy-making process has been carried out in the United States. There the political system has several characteristics that particularly facilitate the mobilization of small groups of people to influence decisions. First, power within the system is very fragmented – between President and the two Houses of Congress, between the federal government and the states, and between the state government and local government. Second, in that vast and diverse country political choices are much more dictated by local interests than they are in Britain. Hence the relationship between members of the Congress and their local electorate is much less affected by national party considerations. Third, at federal level the parties are accordingly much less unified by political ideologies. Political actors are therefore readily influenced by small groups which can effectively threaten to have an electoral impact.

In Britain pressure groups are probably just as much in evidence as they are in the United States. A number of studies have dispelled the notion that they are of no importance in the British system.[8] But there is a need to beware of the assumption that they have as direct an impact upon the political system as they do in the United States. Their importance in the politics of that country has led political scientists to propound a modification of the theory of representative government in which the weakness of the individual voter, discussed on pages 54–7, is seen as compensated by his or her membership of interest groups.[9] Democracy is thus seen as 'pluralist' in character with politicians engaged in continuing processes of compromise with multiple groups. Such a theory is then seen as explaining the deference of politicians to the interests of minorities; and a new and perhaps superior version of democratic theory is presented which has as its hallmark the achievement of a political consensus in which minority interests are protected.

This theory has, however, come under fire in the United States. It has been pointed out that there are biases in the system that make it much easier for some interests to be heard than others, and much easier for modifications to the status quo to be vetoed than to be supported.[10]

These general points about the plurality of pressure groups are worthy of our attention since they suggest important questions about the way the British system operates. The contrasts made above between the political systems on the two sides of the Atlantic suggest that it may be much more difficult for British pressure groups to identify points at which the political system is particularly open to influence. In individual constituencies grievances with the established political parties have to be very deeply felt, and very widely shared, to upset the normal national electoral swings. Direct interventions in elections motivated by local issues are rare, except in the areas where nationalist parties can have an impact. Outside Scotland and Wales politicians have often been able to be singularly insensitive to local issues. And the current three or more party system further distorts the picture.

There are similar problems for a national pressure group in persuading political parties that disregard of its case carries electoral dangers. Furthermore, any interest group able to threaten in this way probably has a special relationship with a major political party, and is acknowledged as important in that sense. Many of the most powerful of the British pressure groups tend to have an established relationship with one or other political party. The trade unions are, of course, the clearest example of this phenomenon. They played a key role in the original establishment of the Labour Party, and provide a large proportion of the party's funds today. Correspondingly the other side of industry is an important paymaster for the Conservative Party. It is unlikely that the major elements in either of these groups will actually change sides, but it may be threatening to the parties if they are lukewarm in their support. However, there are ambiguities even in these power relationships. While it is arguable that the Labour Party dances to the trade unions' tune, it is also the case that the special relationship facilitates bargaining. By contrast, the danger of union opposition to the Conservatives is that the strike weapon may be used to resist policies. Similarly, the Labour Party has to face, when in power, a commercial and financial establishment that can de-stabilize the economy through speculation and the movement of currency.

These reflections lead us to an alternative view of pressure group power in Britain: that the strongest weapons are forms of direct action and not the manipulation of electoral choice. If this is correct, it gives a very different emphasis to political pluralism, one that makes democracy through the ballot box of much less importance. Attention must be given to ways in which pressure groups secure or resist policies through their power to take actions that directly affect either the success of policies or the stability of the political system. This suggests the need to examine the power of groups whose co-operation is needed to implement new policies, and the influence of agencies that are expected to play a crucial part in the policy process. What, for example, is the basis for the influential role doctors have been able to play in health service policies? To what extent does the increasing militancy of other civil servants influence policy making? Why does government give attention to the views of the associations that represent the various groups of local authorities? What is the significance of organized resistance to rent or rate increases? The threat of direct action seems to put a very different complexion upon political bargaining processes, transforming the view of the significance of pressure groups. Yet in the 1980s the capacity of a determined government to 'sit out' forms of direct action – most obviously in the case of the 1984–5 miners' strike – raises doubts even about this form of pressure-group action.

It is important to look more closely at the ways in which, regardless of the possession of a direct capacity to disrupt the political system, particular groups enjoy an institutionalized relationship to the political system. In particular, it is necessary to go beyond the examples of close relationships to political parties to consider whether the positions some groups enjoy in relation to the political system owe nothing to particular party allegiances. Indeed, there are groups whose very power in Britain might be jeopardized if they were seen as identified with specific political parties.

The power of some pressure groups can only be explained in terms of what may be called an 'insider' status within the policy-making system. This implies a further deviation from democratic theory, a system within which some individuals and groups have special statuses. A number of political scientists have suggested that societies possess a political 'elite', that decision makers are drawn from a narrow spectrum within a society.[11] Marxist analyses of the social structure suggest that the political system is dominated by representatives of the bourgeoisie, the capitalist class. But other political theories, notably those of Pareto and Mosca, suggest that there is a ruling elite that is not necessarily characterized by the possession of economic resources.

Modern interpretation of elite theories seek to show either that key policy offices are held by people from a narrow spectrum of social origins, or that a limited number of people, characterized by close links with one another, dominate decision-making roles. For Britain it has been shown that Cabinet ministers, senior civil servants, members of key advisory bodies and the heads of prestigious organizations tend to be drawn from a relatively narrow social class group, characterized by education at public schools and Oxbridge and by having had parents in a similarly narrow range of upper-middle-class occupations. The picture is, however, not simple, and there is some evidence that the backgrounds of top decision makers have changed to embrace a slightly wider range of social origins in recent years. While certainly it seems plausible to suggest that, if there are people from similar social or educational backgrounds in a number of key roles, the relationships between those people will facilitate the sharing of ideas and opinions, the processes involved cannot necessarily be explained as simply as this. Beware of the argument by inference: since X went to the same school as Y, is it inevitable that he is able to influence his decisions?

What is more important to explain the place of some of the pressure groups in Britain in relation to the structure of power is to examine the sense in which the policy-making power is perceived as involving assumptions that some interests should be consulted. Such assumptions rest upon several foundations. One of them is that expertise conveys the ability to help with public decision making. This is the technocratic view, that experts' opinions carry a greater weight than other people's. It is the basis upon which academics sometimes secure a measure of influence in government. Similarly, some pressure groups secure attention because of their expert knowledge. In the educational and medical fields such 'heavyweight' pressure groups abound.

Another foundation upon which pressure groups may secure influence is their association with traditional elite groups. Voluntary organizations benefit by royal sponsorship and by the acquisition of prestigious figures as vice-presidents and supporters. Such sponsorship is not always easily earned. It is clearly helpful to have a cause that readily attracts the sympathy of influential people. It may also be important to behave in ways that are deemed respectable. This is a curious feature of this kind of pressure group activity; to some extent the power of groups depends upon their ability to forswear the more direct weapons in the pressure group armoury, to avoid mounting vociferous opinion-forming campaigns or threatening forms of direct action. The supposition, here, is based upon a belief that there is an underlying elitist approach to government in Britain. A fairly narrow range of people are responsible for key decisions; some of these attain such positions through democratic representational procedures, but they co-opt others to their ranks. These other people may be individuals of shared social backgrounds, but the process of co-optation may be more haphazard. Individuals from pressure groups, or at least representing specific interests, secure entry into the ranks of those who exercise power by virtue not only of expertise but also of personal qualities, such as persistence and charm, which enable them to persuade that they have something to contribute to public decision making. They also generally have to establish that they understand some of the unspoken rules relating to public participation: that they don't embarrass their sponsors by the use of direct tactics or indiscreet communications with the press or unseemly behaviour in committee situations. In so doing they join that list of people who have been called upon over and over again to sit on public committees and advisory bodies.

This argument, then, is that political influence may be secured in Britain without the aid of independent power. The system co-opts others to join its ranks, and pays attention to some citizens very much more readily than others. In this day and age people are rightly cynical about propositions concerning the power of ideas. They look around for other explanations and ulterior motives. But in the study of social policy, the importance of individuals should not be wholly underestimated. There are examples of people who, through the strength of their commitments and the power of their attention to detail, have secured a place in the policy-making process. In the first half of this century William Beveridge was such an individual.[12] More recently Richard Titmuss seems to have played an important role.[13] There are many lesser examples around, of people whose influence upon policy making owes nothing either to any notion of representative government or to the cruder theories about pressure-group activity

A great deal of pressure group activity is, of course, concerned with 'good causes'. Again, a theory of the policy-making process needs to find room for 'good causes' as well as for 'good people'. There are important questions that should not be brushed aside about the place of altruism in policy making. It is not naive to argue that politicians, or if you prefer *some politicians*, have commitments to ideals. It is certainly important to recognize that many politicians want to be seen as supporters of 'good causes'. Hence, pressure groups for the disabled, the old, neglected children and so on will exert influence out of proportion to their naked power. For them the skilful use of mass media may be important, and key contacts in positions of power will be a great help.

No account of social policy making should disregard the potential influence of these 'good causes', however much there may be scope for controversy about their real power in situations where interests are in conflict. Indeed one of the frustrating phenomena many pressure groups of this kind experience is continuing assertions by politicians that they do matter, which is accompanied by minimal concrete action. It is very hard to predict the political circumstances that will favour interests of this kind, but manifestly many have secured benefits without the use of any perceptible political 'muscle'. It is perhaps useful here to bear in mind the distinction often made in the study of pressure groups between 'interest' groups and 'cause' groups, though in the tactical struggle for influence each may seek to co-opt the support of the other. Interests seek to be recognized as 'good causes', and causes try to enlist the backing of more powerful 'interests'.

It has been suggested in this section that pressure groups provide a crucial qualification to the notion of a simple relationship between electors and elected. Some writers have suggested that they solve the problem of the powerlessness of the individual in relation to the political machine.[14] While there are many circumstances in which that is true, it seems important to acknowledge that the political system contains biases that make it much easier for some groups to secure influence than others. In addition, in Britain there is the peculiar phenomenon of the exercise of influence by groups that, according to the crude calculations of political arithmetic, do not seem to have a power base at all. This must lead us to look at the shortcomings of the 'how many divisions has the Pope'[15] approach to the estimation of political influence. It implies, however, a recognition that the minority who occupy powerful positions in British society are able to make choices, based neither upon notions of democracy nor upon calculations about who has power, about whom they will listen to or consult.

## MINISTERIAL POWER. THE ROLE OF OFFICIALS AND THE INFLUENCE OF OUTSIDE GROUPS

In *The Sociology of Public Administration* the author developed a typology of local government styles to try to elucidate different characteristics of politician/official relationships in different political situations.[16] The emphasis was upon local government because it was felt that it was easier to develop a comparative analysis drawing upon the considerable number of studies of local decision making in Britain and the United States. However, the typology was intended to have a more general relevence and provides a useful starting-point for this discussion. Three types of political system were identified: 'ideological politics', 'administrative politics' and 'bargaining politics'.

A system of 'ideological politics' relates most clearly to the model of 'representative government'. It is one in which the traditional distinction between politics and administration is most easily made. Political parties compete to win elections by submitting distinct programmes from which the electorate can choose. Politicians instruct administrators to frame policies compatible with their mandates and commitments. The Thatcher governments have stood out as examples of this phenomenon.

'Administrative politics' describes a contrasting system in which full-time officials are much more clearly dominant. The 'politics' are organizational rather than public, and many of the key conflicts are between departments. Ministers in central government, while formally possessing the key decision-making powers, in fact find themselves involved primarily in expounding views and defending policies generated within their departments. Politicians of the majority party without ministerial office find themselves frustratingly shut out from a decision-making process into which they are given few insights. In British local government the committee system provides scope for the wider use of elected representatives in an administrator-dominated context, though here such involvement may further undermine representative government since it will depend primarily upon personal characteristics. J. M. Lee has described such a situation admirably:

> It is misleading to think of the County Council primarily as a body of elected representatives who make decisions of policy and then order officials to execute them. Although such a view constitutes the theory, the reality is vastly different. It is better to regard the system of county government as a body of professional people placed together in a large office at County Hall, who can call upon the representatives from all places throughout the area which they administer. Some of these representatives by sheer ability and drive make themselves indispensable to the successful working of the machine; others merely represent points of view which come into conflict with it.[17]

The concept of 'bargaining politics' was derived from examination of accounts of local politics in the United States. In recent years, partly as a result of exposure to the American literature and partly because of a desire to adopt a tough-minded approach towards power, British social and political scientists have increasingly been on the look out for signs of a similar system in Britain. In such a system political outcomes are seen to depend upon inputs of resources of power. Those who hold elected positions are not 'representatives' so much as 'brokers' bringing together coalitions of interests. Their desire for re-election forces them to adopt strategies in which they are highly sensitive to pressure groups. Some reservations about this view have already been suggested, but it was acknowledged that elements of bargaining are by no means absent from the British scene. Bargaining politics implies a clear role for politicians which may suggest that officials will occupy subordinate positions. While this is true inasmuch as political futures are at stake, it has been suggested that in Britain deals with quite explicit electoral implications are rare. Bargaining may therefore be more concerned with the maintenance of specific policies or particular organizational arrangements. If this is the case, it may be that officials have more to lose, or have more explicit commitments, than the politicians. Key conflicts concern relationships between departments and the outside world; ministers are expected to help defend departmental interests.

It is not suggested that the individual types fit any specific political system. British central government must be noted as a context where conflicts often appear to be of an ideological nature and where the representative model is treated as of some importance. Yet a key theme in discussions of relationships between ministers and their departments has been the extent to which politicians enter with apparent policy commitments but become socialized into roles determined by the permanent administrator and particularly by the need for 'policy maintenance' within their department. Furthermore, a related theme to the ministerial discovery that cherished policy innovations are not administratively feasible is the recognition that vested interests and pressure groups carry a political 'clout' that had not been realized when policies were planned outside government. Policy-making outcomes may be determined by the interaction of three forces: political input (ideological politics), organizational considerations within departments (administrative politics) and external pressures (bargaining politics). Some decision-making processes are influenced more by some factors than by others; thus it is probably appropriate to stress the importance of political input in British central government, of organizational considerations in British local government and of bargaining with external forces in American government.

Beyond these generalizations, the more detailed study of the factors influencing the way that policy is made needs to take various considerations into account. First, what are the kinds of policies involved? This raises the question so far evaded in this chapter: What is policy? Writers on policy analysis are agreed that a policy is something more than a decision. Friend and his colleagues suggest that 'policy is essentially a *stance* which, once articulated, contributes to the context within which a succession of future decisions will be made'.[18] Jenkins similarly stresses the notion of interrelated decisions concerned with the selection of goals and the adoption of a course of action.[19] Smith suggests that 'the concept of policy denotes . . . deliberate choice of action or inaction, rather than the effects of interrelating forces': he emphasizes 'inaction' and reminds us that 'attention should not focus exclusively on decisions which produce change, but must also be sensitive to those which resist change and are difficult to observe because they are not represented in the policy-making process by legislative enactment'.[20]

Policies are thus not easy to define. It is doubtful whether much can be gained by trying to achieve any greater precision than that suggested in the definitions above. It is more fruitful to look in a concrete way at the relevance of policies for the activity of a minister and his department. On appointment to office a new minister will take over responsibility for many departmental policies. The overwhelming majority of these will be just existing ways of doing things. A good many will be enshrined in Acts of Parliament. But these will be accompanied by organizational arrangements, systems of administration and working conventions which will also help to define policy. There is a distinction to be made between policy and arrangements made for its implementation. This will be explored further in the next chapter; here it must be stressed that these arrangements will in many cases have a quite fundamental impact upon the character of the policy and may thus be deemed to be part of the policy.

It is this existence of policies determining most everyday practice in a department that provides the most crucial group of constraints for a new minister. Existing policies keep most people occupied most of the time. Innovations depend upon finding opportunities for staff to work on developing new policies. They may also depend upon getting people from within the department to work to change old policies which have hitherto been regarded as quite satisfactory. Clearly an innovating minister has to find ways to get a vast operational organization to change its ways.

What is perhaps more significant is that a new minister will also find that his department is developing new policies. These are not necessarily merely the left-over business from a previous administration. Many of them will derive from weaknesses in existing policies that have been recognized within the department, and that administrators are striving to correct. Some, moreover, will have their roots in changes in the world upon which existing policies operate, changes that are making those policies unsuccessful or irrelevant. This group of policies or 'would-be policies' is important. New ministers may find that their own, or the party's, policy aspirations mesh with the policy issues upon which the department is working. In such circumstances they may find it comparatively easy to become, or to be seen as, innovators. But they may have to face the fact that their own view of his department's policy needs are irrelevant to the main problem being tackled within it, or even that their own commitments lead in quite opposite directions to the ones being taken by those concerned with policy innovation in the department. Popular discussions of the success or failure of ministers are often carried out in terms of their personalities and their experience. Of course it is often possible to distinguish 'strong' and 'weak' ministers; but it must not be forgotten that the comparatively temporary incumbent of the top position of a large organization may be just lucky or unlucky – in arriving when key advisers are likely to agree that exciting innovations are necessary, or conversely in finding that the consolidation of existing policies, or the confronting of unpleasant realities, is more important than the policy changes he or she cherishes.

There are various kinds of policy initiatives. Some policies may be enacted by the passing of a law. Reform of criminal law, for example, may have no administrative implications. A second category of policies with only indirect consequences for the minister's own department are those whose enactment and implementation depend upon another agency. Legislation giving powers, and even sometimes duties, to local government comes into this category. The Chronically Sick and Disabled Persons Act of 1970 is a classic example in this category. While it seems to involve the development of a national policy for the disabled, in practice its dependence upon local government makes it a gesture in which central government involvement is comparatively slight. This measure arose as the result of an initiative by a private member, Alf Morris. A new piece of legislation on this issue, the Disabled Persons Act 1986, seems to have similar characteristics. Individuals and voluntary organizations are likely to have to work hard to make local government implement it. Clearly it is easier for a minister to accept this sort of legislation than to develop a policy that effectively changes the direction of a great deal of work going on *within* the department. In the above case the policy making may be more 'symbolic' than real; ministers may hope to derive kudos without really enacting innovations.

Once a minister seeks to enact policies that require the expenditure of 'new money' he or she becomes engaged in what is inevitably a more difficult political exercise. Formally the approval of the Treasury is required, probably together with the support of the Cabinet in one of its priority-setting exercises, where the minister is involved in competition with colleagues who have alternative expenditure aspirations. What this implies for the minister's relationship with civil servants is altogether more complex. The specific expenditure commitment will be by no means the only one the department might undertake. Hence there will be an intra-organizational battle about the case for that particular innovation. What the outside world sees as a minister promoting a particular project is probably the end of a long process in which different groups of civil servants within the department have argued about the case for that venture as opposed to other ventures. A minister who says 'I want to do X' will have to face civil servants who argue 'but we need money for Y, Z' and so on. The political negotiations between a minister and the Treasury ministers will be matched by much more elaborate negotiations between civil servants. A case that is comparatively weak when argued within the department will come up against further problems in this tough forum, and a minister who successfully overrides objections within his or her own department may well lose in this wider battle. Students of government have, moreover, raised questions about the extent to which civil servants will fight effectively for their minister against the Treasury, in view of the prestige and power of the latter within the civil service as a whole.[21]

In differentiating various kinds of policies, and in interpreting their implications for ministerial power, it must be recognized that some policies have implications for more than one department. A new approach to assistance with housing costs, for example, may have to be considered both by DHSS, with concern for social security policy, and DOE, with its responsibility for housing policy. In addition, local government is likely to be involved. This adds a form of complexity that greatly enhances the significance of negotiations between civil servants, and the related tendency for the maintenance of the status quo. Such policies place strains upon the unity of the political group involved. Two key aspects of government emphasized in the Crossman diaries are the difficulties facing a minister with departmental responsibilities who tries to take an overall view of government policies as a whole, and the related tendency for ministers to take narrowly departmental views which sabotage interdepartmental co-operation.

This discussion has distinguished between policies that ministers can enact with relatively slight implications for their own departments and those that require elaborate departmental involvement. It has implied that where ideological commitments are involved a distinction may be made between relatively easy gestures and hard administrative battles. Yet it may also be the case that some difficult aspects of 'bargaining politics' are involved where policy success depends upon the response of other organizations.

It is, of course, outside the field of social policy, in industrial relations, that the best examples are found of the undermining of policy innovations by groups outside government. The 1964–70 Labour government found that its alliance with the trade unions limited scope for action in this field. The Thatcher government has found some of its ideas for tax and social security reform affected by the reservations of small business about new tasks for government. Within social policy, however, the power of the doctors provides related examples. In this case the problem comes, if not exactly within the secretary of state's own department, at least from within a public agency. More important, however, for the analysis of social policy is the interplay between central government and those other organs of government, particularly local government, which have a crucial role to play in the implementation of policy, but are also themselves in certain respects policy makers.

A new minister with an overall responsibility for the health and personal social services within the Department of Health and Social Security, or for education, or for housing policy (together with local government in general) within the Department of the Environment will find an 'established' relationship between the department and local government or the health service with certain key characteristics. There will be a body of enacted legislation, a pattern of grants from central government, a range of procedures relating to the sanctioning of new initiatives including the taking up of loans for new capital expenditure, perhaps a pattern of inspection or policy review, and a variety of policy expectations enshrined in circulars and related messages from the centre. In a few cases the obligations of the local authorities will be quite clear. In a rather larger number of situations the authorities will have quite explicit duties but will not have been given detailed guidance on how to carry them out. In yet other important cases the local authorities will regard themselves as the key policy-makers; the central requirements will have been specified in such general terms that the decisions that really dictate the quality of the service given to the public are made locally. Then there will be some situations in which central government has made it very clear that the policy initiative rests with the local agency, by *permitting* activities if they so wish. Finally, there will be a few situations in which local authorities have been almost entirely the innovators, in which they have sought to promote local acts through Parliament or in which they have interpreted general powers given to them in quite novel ways.

The new minister who wants to introduce changes into this pattern has a variety of options open, but each may involve complications wherever there is resistance to new ideas. New policies are expressed as much in ministerial statements, White Papers and circulars to the local authorities as in new statutes. In each case the minister may be able to back up a recommendation with indirect weapons: by control over loans and other powers to permit or limit activities, by co-operation or its refusal in situations in which joint central–local action is necessary. In the National Health Service the control over funding also facilitates policy change from the centre.

The local authorities often fight hard to try to protect their independence. They may be unresponsive to ministerial suggestions, and they may make this opposition very clear through the local authority associations. The threat of non-co-operation from the local authorities may make the minister think again. The most publicized cases of such non-co-operation have occurred where some authorities have stood out against the minister on a highly political issue. It may be suspected that issues on which there would be widespread local resistance, but where a party political split is not clearly in evidence, rarely hit the news headlines because they are quietly negotiated in private discussions between the minister, or civil servants, and the local authority associations. The public conflicts of recent years have involved confrontations between different policical ideologies: the resistance from the Clay Cross Urban District to the Conservative Housing Finance Act; the rejection by Merthyr County Borough of the Conservatives' withdrawal of free milk for schoolchildren; the resistance of a number of Conservative education authorities to the Labour commitment to the introduction of comprehensive secondary education; the resistance of Labour local authorities to the Conservative government's legislation on the sale of council houses; and the forms of creative accounting developed in the mid-1980s by some local authorities to evade expenditure restraints. The evidence suggests that a determined central government, generally backed by the courts, has (at least since 1979) been able to impose its will in most central–local battles.

Although the local authorities are themselves, as has been suggested, policy makers, the force of influence for policy change is not just one-way. Just as the new ministers encounter groups of civil servants within their departments with policy concerns that conflict with their own, so too they encounter local authorities keen to take new initiatives. These will be eager to protect their own autonomy, but may also seek to convince ministers that their local initiatives should be enshrined in national policy.

Hence, as a source of local initiatives local government may be as important as central government. The example of comprehensive education is again interesting. Before the 1964–70 Labour government made it Department of Education and Science policy, a number of local authorities had already set up comprehensive schools. It is significant that, while in some areas, such as London, this development was motivated by a political commitment, in other places, for example rural Devon, it was educational administrators who had convinced councils, of a broadly Conservative persuasion, that the development of such schools was the most appropriate policy.

In this section the discussion has ranged over many of the influences upon policy. Using the notion that is particularly associated with representative government, of a new minister with explicit policy commitments, attention has been given to the pressures that frustrate such commitments, or replace them by commitments derived from other sources. It has been stressed that there are strong forces in favour of the maintenance of existing policy, and that many new initiatives are in fact derived from concerns not so much to innovate as to correct the imperfections of existing policies. Policy analysis needs to be concerned with a flow of interrelated policies, with abrupt changes of direction a comparatively rare occurrence.

Hence, it is interesting that, while the historical account of social policy tended to stress a variety of significant contributions to policy, building constructively on the past – the 1911 National Insurance Act, the 1944 Education Act, the 1946 National Health Service Act – perhaps a key theme in modern writings on the policy process is the absence of rational forward planning but in its place a phenomenon that has been called 'disjointed incrementalism'.[22] Is there a conflict of approaches here?

Braybrooke and Lindblom, the theorists who drew attention to the significance of 'incrementalism', were particularly concerned to attack that portrayal of the policy process which perceived it as, or able to become, a rational appraisal of all the alternative consequences of alternative policies followed by the choice of the best available. If incrementalism is perceived in these terms there is little difficulty in understanding its applicability to social policy. As the historical chapter showed, the development of social policy has been very much a process of piling new initiatives on top of older policies, without ever clearing the ground to facilitate a fresh start. Then, as this piling-up process has proceeded, it has created new interests which future developments have to take into account. Since political values have often been at stake in conflicts over social policy, the very character of the ideological issue has precluded a cool appraisal of all the policy options.

If the choices are between understanding policy making as a pure exercise in rational decision making, as the putting into practice of ideologies, or as a quite incoherent process of bargaining and muddling-through, it is sensible to reject each alternative. It is a compromise between all three, with perhaps the first least apparent and the third most in evidence.

## SUGGESTIONS FOR FURTHER READING

Like the previous chapter, this one has drawn upon a vast literature, this time largely from the discipline of political science. Reference notes have largely been chosen to include some of the classic works that expounded particular theoretical viewpoints together with textbooks that most clearly interpret theories and issues for British audiences. The following suggestions for further reading will be primarily in the latter category.

For those who require a basic textbook on British government Hanson and Walles's *Governing Britain* is recommended.[23] An alternative with a strong constitutional law bias is Hartley and Griffith's *Government and Law*.[24] Jowell and Oliver's *The Changing Constitution* reviews some emergent issues of importance.[25]

An account of the local government system is provided by Tony Byrne.[26] Gyford's book provides a review of the evidence on the nature of British local politics, drawing on a large and growing literature.[27] Travers's *The Politics of Local Government Finance* (see n. 35 in chapter 2) and Loughlin's *Local Government in the Modern State* (see n. 4 in this chapter) explain the development of the central/local government conflict discussed in this chapter.

Valuable discussions of the policy-making process in social policy are found in Hall et al.'s *Change, Choice and Conflict in Social Policy*,[28] in Banting's *Poverty, Politics and Policy*,[29] and in Ham's article 'Approaches to the Study of Social Policy Making'.[30] Chris Ham and the present author's *The Policy Process in the Modern Capitalist State* explores many of the theoretical issues about the study of policy making.[31]

# CHAPTER 4

# Implementation

## INTRODUCTION

Why devote a chapter in a book on social policy to the study of policy implementation? What is the significance of this issue for our subject? There are several reasons why it is important. First, the discussion of policy making in the later part of the last chapter suggested that many new initiatives stem from the recognition that older policies are failing to meet desired goals. This may be because these goals have changed, but it may equally be because the social world for which the original policies were designed has changed. This is an implementation problem. It may also be because there were weaknesses in the older policies, many of which became apparent once policies were implemented. In this sense it is important to scrutinize the implementation process with some care.

Second, this concern with the ineffectiveness of policies is now recognized as requiring the asking not only of questions about the character of policy but also about what is wrong with the implementation process and the organizations responsible for implementation. It may be that the policies are at fault, or it may be that corrective action is most appropriately applied to the implementing agencies. This is the central concern for what we may call the 'top–down' approach to the study of implementation: why don't those who are expected to carry out policies do what is required of them?

Third, and finally, while it is true that the impact of all policies must be subjected to careful scrutiny, it is clearly particularly important to give attention to what it feels like to be on the receiving end of social policy. This may be described as a concern with 'impact' rather than with 'implementation'. However, it is this concern that has led students of social policy to give increasing attention in recent years to the activities of that group of public servants who may be called 'street-level bureaucrats', to ask questions about what actually happens in the exchanges between these people and the public.

Before, therefore, exploring any further the phenomenon of policy implementation, a brief account of the main groups of people responsible for social policy implementation in Britain is appropriate. An examination of the wide range of people involved, of the many different roles they play and of their varying involvement in or distance from the policy-making process will help to stress the importance of giving attention to implementation and to introduce the more theoretical discussion that is to follow.

Social security benefits are calculated and paid to the public by a very large number of Department of Health and Social Security staff based in regional and local offices throughout the country. Over 90 per cent of the staff of DHSS, the government department with the largest complement of non-industrial civil servants, is based in local offices. Those responsible for contributory benefits are concerned with the paying out of amounts determined by a largely computerized central system. Until the implementation of the 1986 Social Security Act the largest group of local office staff was concerned with the administration of the supplementary benefits system, interpreting a complex system of rules largely without the use of new technology. The introduction of the new 'income support' and 'family credit' schemes involves the adaptation of most of these people to a more routine computerized system. However, a minority of them are concerned with the highly discretionary 'social fund'.

There is only one other large group of people defined in Britain as civil servants that is concerned with the implementation of the social policies discussed in this book, and that is those involved in the employment services. Otherwise field-level social policy implementation is the responsibility of National Health Service and local authority officials, who, since they are not employees of the central government departments, are not regarded as 'civil servants'.

At the time of writing employment and training services are the responsibility of the Manpower Services Commission, a quasi-autonomous public body which operates under the overall surveillance of the Department of Employment. But the government has just announced that this staff concerned with employment advice will move back into the Department of Employment, to ensure that their work is more integrated with that of the staff paying benefits to the unemployed. The exact details of these changes are not yet clear. It is presumed that staff concerned with training and with the operation of special work creation schemes will remain with the Manpower Services Commission.

There is also a small band of people with employment responsibilities for young people, who work for local education authorities: the careers officers.

The implementation of health policy is devolved by DHSS to regional and district health authorities (DHAs). The latter are concerned with field-level policy. The important feature of this system for policy implementation is that the districts have both policy-making and implementation responsibilities. While, since the changes recommended by Griffiths, there is a key managerial cadre in district health authorities, health remains an area of social policy in which professionals – particularly doctors and nurses – have extensive degrees of autonomy. It is often difficult to make the policy implementation distinction with reference to a service operated by professionals. Day-to-day service provision decisions may actually determine, or pre-empt, priorities. In this sense they can be described as policy decisions. This may seem to violate the definition of policy making as involving more than isolated decisions, yet individual professional judgements of this kind may cluster or have similarities that suggest implicit if not explicit policy decisions that are being made at the operational level.

In addition to the regional health authorities there are other regional organizations with relevance for several of the other services with which this book is concerned. The social security network is organized into regions under the supervision of a regional office. The Department of the Environment has a system of regional offices that handle many aspects of relationships with the local authorities. The DHSS has regional social work inspectors who help the department to relate to the local social services departments. In all these cases these regional organizations are likely to have an impact upon policy implementation. But the peculiar feature of the health service organization is that the regional links in the chain, the regional health authorities, are semi-autonomous organizations, standing between DHSS and another rather similar set of organizations, the district health authorities.

Primary responsibility for the implementation of education policy lies with local authorities in England and Wales. As suggested in the last chapter, there has been a considerable amount of conflict in recent years about the autonomy of these authorities as 'policy makers'. To some extent the implementation issues in this service concern the relationship between the authorities and the schools. While the chain image is not entirely appropriate, since varying responsibilities and degrees of autonomy are involved, and individuals in the chain may be bypassed, it is important to acknowledge that implementation may depend upon the following series of links: education committee, chief education officer and his or her administrative staff, local authority inspectors, school governors and managers, head teachers, departmental heads within the schools, and class teachers. The examination of policy implementation in the education service raises a number of interesting questions about local authority autonomy, the role of school management and the place of professional discretion.

Higher education in Britain has required special forms of organization designed to take into account the fact that many colleges serve more that the local authority area in which they are based, and to acknowledge the special claims to autonomy of the universities. For the university sector a special intermediary body exists, the University Grants Committee, and, apart from local authority representation on university governing bodies, there is no link with local government. For the rest of higher education – the polytechnics and colleges of higher education – the involvement, in most areas, of more than one local authority has been acknowledged through special arrangements to share management and pool costs. These may, from time to time, make policy formulation and implementatioin a complicated business.

At the time of writing the education control system is undergoing changes. The government proposes to set up a network of secondary schools under direct central control. It is also tightening its mandatory requirements of the local education system, particularly in respect of the curriculum. In higher education a new central body is proposed, to take control over polytechnics out of the hands of local authorities. The universities are also experiencing much more direct government intervention, now to be exerted through the Universities Funding Council. It will be interesting to observe the extent to which this increased centralization runs into implementation control problems.

The personal social services are the responsibility, inasmuch as they are under public rather than voluntary control, of social services departments within local authorities. While professional discretion and autonomy is also to some extent an issue in this service, implementation is not complicated by either a multi-tiered structure like that of the health service, or by powerful institutions like the schools and colleges. While many directors and senior staff in social services departments are professionally qualified social workers, a relatively small proportion of the staff is engaged in social work. Other key workers include home helps, residential care staff and occupational therapists. Policy implementation is often influenced by the character of co-operation between these different occupational groups. It may also be heavily dependent upon voluntary effort, much of which is only loosely co-ordinated and is marginally subsidized by the public departments.

While for education there is a major department of state, the Department of Education and Science, which is responsible for national policy and the relationship between the centre and the local authorities, the personal social services is only the smallest of the three policy concerns of the Department of Health and Social Security. One implementation problem here is that the main central department responsible for local government is the Department of the Environment. This department, together with the Treasury, deals with the main financial and legal links with local government, but has no responsibility for education or social services. This exacerbates a tension, at the local level, between the demands of an integrated and corporate approach to local government and the separable service interests of two large, heavy-spending departments, of education and social services. For social services the link with DHSS encourages the giving of attention to relationships with the health service, and to a lesser extent with social security. DHSS has been engaged on seeking to co-ordinate the planning of health and social services. This is a development of some importance for the evolution of integrated caring services in the community. A special device, developed recently, that cuts across the link between social services and the rest of local government but strengthens that with health, has been the 'joint financing' of social services ventures with health service money.

Local authority housing is the responsibility of the lower-tier local authorities. In Northern Ireland protests about discrimination by local authorities led to the creation of a provincewide Housing Executive; and in Scotland there is an important nationwide public housing authority to supplement the work of the local authorities. There is also in England and Wales a Housing Corporation, responsible for the provision of funds for housing associations. In the New Towns special development corporations provide public housing. A feature of recent government policy has been a quest for new ways of managing and financing housing. This is increasing the importance of bodies like the housing associations, financed by public money or by a combination of public and private money.

The implementation of housing policy is fragmented not only because of the mixture of kinds of housing authorities; this is an area of social policy in which many significant decisions are made by private agencies. Since there are four main types of housing tenure – renting from a local authority, owner-occupation, renting from a private landlord and renting from a housing association – and the government intervenes, or has intervened, to try to influence the quality and cost of each type, policy implementation is often a very complex matter. In studying it, attention has to be given not only to the relationship between government and the local authorities, but also to government attempts to influence the behaviour of building societies and landlords. There are also some other public–private interactions of some significance for housing policy. For example, there have been government efforts to influence the price of land and to curb land speculation, government intervention in the money market, and government manipulation of the costs and benefits of various statuses in the housing market by means of taxation and social security policy.

Finally, it is misleading to suggest that these relationships between government and the various private sectors are of no concern to the local housing authorities. The latter increasingly seek to influence housing opportunities of all kinds in their areas, and to give advice to those they do not house themselves. Moreover the housing authorities, of course, have a significant interest in land prices, and have planning responsibilities to relate housing activities to other kinds of development in their areas. Housing policy implementation has many dimensions.

## THE RELATIONSHIP BETWEEN POLICY AND ITS IMPLEMENTATION

In the previous chapter it was suggested that policies are complex phenomena which are hard to define with any precision. This obviously makes for difficulties in distinguishing policy making and implementation, and for identifying implementation issues and problems. The distinction between policy making and implementation seems to need to rest upon the identification of decision points at which a policy is deemed to be made and ready for implementation, like a commodity that is manufactured and ready for selling. This is not, though, to imply two separable processes. The difficulty, however, with this analogy is that policy-making and implementation merge. The policy-making process is like the design of a building for a specific occupant by an architect; the implementation process affects policy design quite early on and will continue to influence some details of it even after implementation has begun, just as modifications are made to buildings after occupancy.

Policies have characteristics that must affect the nature of the implementation process. Many policies will be complex, setting out to achieve objectives $x$, $x_1$, $x_2$ . . . under conditions $y$, $y_1$, $y_2$. . . . These complexities may very well complicate the implementation process. Others will involve vague and ambiguous specifications of objectives and conditions. These will tend to become more specific during the implementation process.

Constraints are not merely contained within new policies themselves. While it is possible, in the abstract, to treat policies in isolation from other policies, in practice any new policy will be adopted in a context in which there are already many other policies. Some of these other policies will supply precedents for the new policy, others will supply conditions, and some may be in conflict with it. The process of inaugurating new policies will continue after the adoption of the policy and will then further affect implementation.

Another general constraint that must not be overlooked is, of course, the fact that the scarcity and control of public finance frequently sets limits to policy development. In some cases these limits are quite explicitly set by central government. Perhaps they arise because the government does not recognize the true costs of its new policies, or perhaps because of a resistance to making a particular policy effective which comes from within the central government machine. In other cases the split between central government as a policy initiator and local government in the role of implementer produces a situation in which central intentions appear to be thwarted by local scarcities. Hence the Chronically Sick and Disabled Persons Act of 1970 expects local authorities to provide a range and scale of services that in practice they rarely can. However, since central government in Britain is the dominant influence upon the availability of local finance, there is a certain political duplicity here in legislation which requires local agencies to provide benefits that the centre knows they are unlikely to be able to afford.

Policy goals are often specified, as has been pointed out, in general or unclear terms. We may identify a number of different reasons for this lack of clarity. Firstly, it may be simply that policy makers are far from clear what they really want. The lack of clarity may be so total that it is comparatively meaningless to seek to identify a policy or to study its implementation. Some of the 'policies' of this kind derive from political aspirations to demonstrate a popularly desirable commitment. It was suggested in the last chapter that some so-called 'policies' may be merely symbolic.

Second, it is important to take account of the extent to which a lack of clarity about policy stems from a lack of potential consensus. Policies emerge that are not merely compromises but also remain obscure on key points of implementation. Where this occurs it is likely that there will be a lack of consensus among the implementers, too. Hence wide variations in practice may emerge, together with a range of conflicts surrounding the implementation process. The 1977 Housing (Homeless Persons) Act provides examples of implementation problems – concerning the definition of priority groups, the extent of the duty to provide help and advice, and the identification of the responsible authority – that would seem to have emerged from the conflict during the legislation process. In the same way, the author has elsewhere suggested that some of the difficult 'value' problems faced by the former National Assistance Board (NAB) staff stemmed from the ambivalence of legislation:

> The traditional attitude to the poor had been to regard them, in the absence of unambiguous evidence to the contrary, as undeserving individuals on whom public money should be spent most sparingly. The National Assistance Act seemed to turn its back on this doctrine, yet it failed to jettison the view entirely and it failed to provide financial resources sufficient to enable the Board to avoid having to distinguish between the claims made by applicants, particularly as regards their more unusual needs. Consequently the onus of

distinguishing between the 'deserving' and the 'undeserving' poor tended to fall upon the officer dealing with the applicant in the field, just as it had fallen upon the relieving officer in the past. While the politicians and administrators who framed the Act would not have wished to have espoused the notion of the 'undeserving poor', they felt unwilling to risk the public criticism that would have resulted from an approach to poverty that involved ignoring the potential waste on the 'work-shy' and the fraudulent application in order adequately to meet the needs of the majority of applicants.[1]

This has continued to be true of many aspects of social security policy.

This source of implementation problems is closely related to another of some importance. Sometimes the political ambivalence about a policy is reflected not so much in the policy itself as in the constraints that are set upon the implementation process. The simplest form of constraint here is, of course, the failure to provide the means, in money and staff, to enable a policy to be implemented properly.

Another example of a quite deliberately imposed implementation problem is the adoption of administrative procedures that are explicitly designed to affect the impact of a policy. Thus Deacon has shown how 'the genuinely seeking work test' was manipulated in the 1920s to make it difficult for unemployed people to establish their claim to benefit.[2] He describes it as imposed as a quite explicit deterrent, without reference to the actual availability of work.

It is important, while acknowledging that many policies are made complex and ambiguous by the conflicts within the policy-making process, to recognize that it is intrinsically difficult to specify some policy goals in terms that will render the implementation process quite clear and unambiguous. This is one important source of discretion for implementers. Jowell has drawn attention to examples where the concern of policy is with 'standards' that are not susceptible to precise factual definition.[3] He argues that standards may be rendered more precise by 'criteria', facts that are to be taken into account, but that 'the feature of standards that distinguishes them from rules is their flexibility and susceptibility to change over time'. Questions about adequate levels of safety on the roads or in factories, or about purity in food, are of this kind. So are many of the issues about need in social policy. Discretionary judgement is likely to be required by policy, alongside the more precise rules that it is possible to promulgate.

If a policy is a complex and ambiguous phenomenon, with aspects that go 'too far' for some people and 'not far enough' for others, it is important to acknowledge that the dissensus that attends its 'birth' will continue to affect its implementation. It may therefore provide opportunities for some implementing agencies to develop new initiatives that were perhaps not originally envisaged. However, policies also often contain 'footholds' for those who are opposed to their general thrust, or who wish to divert them to serve their own ends. Bardach has developed an extensive analysis of the various 'implementation games' that may be played by those who perceive ways in which policies may be delayed, altered or deflected.[4] While some policies contain few features that their opponents can interfere with – laying down, for example, a clear duty to provide a particular service or benefit – others, such as the DHSS commitment to the development of community care for the mentally ill, depend heavily upon the commitments of implementers, and are relatively easily diverted in other directions or even rendered ineffective.

It is important to raise questions about the ways in which policies are expressed, and the evidence required to establish the extent of implementation. Policies may be conveyed to local implementers in a range of ways from, at one extreme, the explicit imposition of duties and responsibilities to, at the other end of the continuum, the very loose granting of powers which may or may not be used. We can contrast, for example, the comparatively strict ways in which regulations under the 1986 Social Security Act instruct local authorities in the administration of housing rebates, with powers given (originally in the 1963 Children and Young Persons Act, now in the 1980 Child Care Act) to local authorities to make money payments, in exceptional circumstances to prevent children being taken into care, where no attempt has been made to prescribe how this should be done.

In this discussion it has been hard to draw the line between issues that are essentially 'characteristics of policy' that affect implementation, and points that are really observations about the characteristics of either the relationships between central policy makers and local implementers, or of the organization of the implementing agencies. While it is helpful to make a distinction between 'policies' on the one hand and the implementation process on the other, this must raise problems at the margin. Policies are formulated with the implementation process in mind, and often it is more realistic to see policies as *products* of implementation rather than as 'top–down' inputs into the process.

## THE 'CENTRE-PERIPHERY' RELATIONSHIP

It is possible to some degree to distinguish between those implementation issues that arise essentially from the 'distance' between what we may describe as 'centre' and 'periphery' and those that are facets of other aspects of relationships within complex organizations. The latter, which will be discussed in the section after this, are of course considerably complicated by the problem of 'distance', particularly when two or more separate organizations are involved.

In British public administration the 'centre' will generally have been involved in the policy-making process. But where implementation is delegated to other organizations the 'centre' generally maintains an interest in the implementation process. Equally, the 'periphery' has an interest in policy making and can be expected to contribute to a feedback process from implementation into policy elaboration. However, there are several different kinds of centre–periphery relationships that significantly influence the implementation process. The simplest model is clearly that in which the centre and the periphery belong to the same organization. The most complex occurs where policy implementation depends upon co-operation between separate autonomous organizations, and particularly where responsibility at the periphery is (a) delegated to several organizations with separate territories and (b) dependent upon co-ordinated action between two or more local organizations.

Even the more straightforward implementation systems tend to involve a complex organizational structure. The DHSS has, at headquarters, a Regional Directorate to channel policy directives on social security matters to the regions and local offices. This was set up in 1972 to cope with the fact that, in the words of the director of the regional organization,

> More and more instructions, more and more complex in their nature descended more and more frequently upon local offices, but without any adequately effective co-ordination at the Headquarters level to ensure that those in the outfield had a clear enough idea of what their order of priorities should be as they became less and less able to deal effectively with the totality of their responsibilities.[5]

Previously when bottlenecks arose in the benefit delivery system regional or local decisions had to be made that might affect implementation; now there is a central 'directorate' which is likely to be involved in the examination of policy feasibility and which plays an important part in determining how policy is implemented. Crucial as this innovation may have been for co-ordination, it has contributed to an increased sense of 'distance' between policy makers and implementers in a policy system that operates primarily in a unified, top–down, manner.

Recognition that there may be issues to consider about 'levels', even in the social security system, emphasizes the importance of this dimension for the study of implementation where separate organizations are involved. It is clearly important to identify not merely the issue of the relationship between different levels of elected government but also the existence of a variety of organizations whose relationships to either central or local government, or both, is often ambiguous: the health authorities, the Manpower Services Commission, the University Grants Committee and the universities, the New Town Corporations and so on.

It is important to bear in mind the wide range of inter-agency linkages that may be necessary, without reference to the subject matter of those linkages. Pressman and Wildavsky have made a tentative attempt to draw attention to what may loosely be described as the mathematics of implementation, the way in which the mere quantity of agreements necessary may, even when all parties are committed to a policy, undermine or delay effective action.[6] Hence it is necessary to give attention to the following issues about centre–periphery relations:

1   the relationship will be likely to involve two or more organizations at either the 'centre' or the 'periphery' or both. Effective implementation may depend upon co-operatoion not merely between the two 'levels' but also between different organizations at the same level;
2   the centre–periphery relationship may be mediated through one or more intermediary or regional body;
3   relationships between agencies will in practice involve a number of different issues, and the symmetry that it is possible to draw in an abstract model will not be the same for each issue.

In reality any organization will be involved in a web of relationships, which vary in character and intensity according to the issue. Hence, local authorities have to deal with a number of different central government departments, but the extent to which this is the case varies from issue to issue. Equally, some activities require considerable co-operation between 'peripheral' agencies while others require very little. However, it may be misleading to lose sight of the overall pattern since the outcome of one relationship will affect responses to another. Relationships are ongoing; each will have a history that conditions reactions to any new issues. Equally, each organization will have developed its own sense of its task, mission and role in relation to others. These will affect its response to anything new.

One issue deserving of attention, if only because of the importance it assumes in the United States implementation literature, is the 'special' agency set up to concern itself with policy making and implementation in a specifically limited policy field. Schon has described government agencies as 'memorials to old problems'.[7] It has long been recognized in the United States that there are difficulties in getting old agencies to implement new policies. A crucial innovation strategy has therefore involved the creation of new agencies for this purpose. However, students of this process have pointed out that these new organizations then face problems about there relationships to older agencies.[8] While new organizations may possess a strong commitment to a new policy, and may have powers that enable it to bring together the resources for its implementation that were not possessed by any single previous organization, it still has to relate to a world in which other agencies have a great deal of power to influence its success.

One of the crucial issues, to which the creation of *ad hoc* agencies in the United States is a response, is the problem, at all levels but particularly at local level, of 'overlapping governments'. There are so many ways in which different government agencies can veto or neutralize other agencies' initiatives that a new agency, with more precisely defined policies, is seen as offering, perhaps in desperation, a new way to 'get something done'. While it would be foolish to suggest that a comparable problem does not exist at all in Britain, it is important to recognize that ours is a more simple system in which individual agencies have more clearly defined powers and more definite boundaries to their responsibilities and sphere of influence. Only rarely, therefore, can we identify examples of agencies set up explicitly to circumvent problems of this kind. Moreover, when they do occur they are more often allowed to operate in territories (in both a spatial and a policy sense) in which others' intervention is limited.

The New Towns are examples of successful British innovations in this sense. What is interesting about them is that, while the development corporations acquired powers that gave them a great deal of autonomy within their own territories, there is today a variety of questions to be raised about the extent to which their 'success' was secured at the expense of other policies to which they 'ought' to have related. While the New Towns often built up relatively successful and prosperous new communities, they have done little to relieve the problems of the least priveleged in the old communities from which they drew, and hence, while by providing for 'overspill' they have helped to solve some inner-city problems, they have exacerbated others.

While the use of the New Town device is now being discontinued, British governments continue to experiment with approaches to urban renewal which bypass existing agencies. The Urban Development Corporations are the latest such devices, spawned by a central government which sees the local authorities as likely obstacles to local economic development.

Three motives can perhaps be identified for the creation of special agencies in Britain, although there are of course dangers in taking ostensible motives as real ones: to create an effective separate and accountable 'management system', to reduce political 'interference' and to provide for the direct representation of special interests. The development of a separate manpower policy agency seems to have been carried out with all these motives in mind. The University Grants Committee has been seen as serving the second and third purposes.

Doubts are being expressed about whether its successor, the Universities Funding Council, will do this. Clearly, the special character of the National Health Service structure owes a great deal to the strength of special interests, though its reorganization in the 1970s owed much to 'managerial' thinking. It is also interesting as perhaps the key example of a special system designed to minimize political influence at the local level, since local authority involvement is only indirect and slight.

Two of the three 'motives' outlined above are of special importance to the study of implementation, since the removal of some aspects of policy making from direct political influence and deference to special interests both introduce complications that make it particularly difficult to distinguish policy making from implementation. These agencies may be seen alternatively as implementers that affect the the character of policy or as independent creators of policy forever in a relationship of tension with the 'centre'. It is this tension that can then sometimes be seen as leading to central efforts to curb the independence of agencies whose initial feedom was provided by government. All three of the agencies mentioned in the last paragraph have recently been the subject of central limitations to their activities or curbs upon their freedom!

## THE ORGANIZATIONAL CHARACTERISTIC OF IMPLEMENTING AGENCIES

In the study of agencies concerned with policy implementation two significant bodies of literature can be drawn upon. There are studies by organizational sociologists that suggest the limitations upon the formal control of subordinates by means of rules,[9] and the behavioural studies of law enforcement, which have emphasized the significance of bargaining and discretion in the activities of the police and other rule-enforcers.[10] Both suggest that there are finite limits upon the prescription of subordinate behaviour. Very detailed rule-making is a difficult and time-consuming activity. If it has to be backed up by close supervision and control a point may be reached where such activities are self-defeating. If the subordinate has to be so elaborately controlled the supervisor might just as well undertake the task. Conformity to rules relies primarily upon compliance, upon a willingness to work within a regulated framework which Etzioni has suggested rests either upon acceptance of a 'utilitarian' financial bargain or upon a 'normative' commitment.[11] A key point about the former is that it also invokes in practice some measure of 'tolerance' on both sides; some concept of 'trust'.[12] This applies limits to the things the supervisor can require the subordinate to do, and involves acceptance by the superior of limited deviations by the subordinate from the activities that are expected.

It is not necessary to elaborate this diversion into industrial sociology unduly. The general point is that the mindless conformist implementation is rare. More common, even in a wide range of situations in which subordinate staff are primarily motivated by 'utilitarian' rather than 'normative' considerations, is some concern about the justification for the policy that is to be implemented. Indeed, as the recent concerns of trade unions in, for example, the health services and in social security suggest, there seems to be a growing 'rank and file' interest in policy. This extends beyond a tendency to influence policy delivery by the characteristic 'insubordinate' responses of evasion, delay and so on, into a desire to feed back views into the policy-making process.

The studies of rule enforcement particularly indicate that in most tasks, and particularly in the more elaborate tasks, there will be a strong elememt of discretion. In the last section three sources of discretion were identified, arising from (a) a deliberate recognition of local autonomy, (b) 'political' difficulties in resolving key policy dilemmas, and (c) 'logical' problems in prescribing 'standards'. This discussion adds a fourth, the inherent limits to the regulation of tasks.[13] In practice, prescriptions for policy implementation convey discretionary powers to field-level staff for reasons that are combinations of these four 'sources' of discretion. An alternative way of looking at this phenomenon is to see the field official as a 'street-level bureaucrat'.[14] His or her job is characterized by inadequate resources for the task, by variable and often low public support for the role, and by ambiguous and often unrealizable expectations of performance. The official's concerns are with the actual impact of specific policies upon the relationships with specific individuals; these may lead to a disregard of or failure to understand the wider policy issues that concern those 'higher up' in the agency. The 'street-level' role is necessarily uncertain. A modicum of semi-professional training defines the role as putting into practice a set of ideals inculcated in that training. Yet the 'street-level' bureaucrat is also the representative of a government agency, one that is itself subject to conflicting pressures. In day-to-day contact with clients and with the community at large, he or she becomes to some degree locked into the support of individuals and groups that may be antipathetic to the employing agency. In such a situation of role confusion and role strain, a person at the end of the line is not disposed to react to new policy initiatives from above as if he or she were a mere functionary. New policies are but factors in a whole web of demands that have to be managed.

It is interesting how many of the social workers who regard themselves as identified with their clients, sharing some sense of oppression by the 'bureaucracy' that weighs upon them both and working therefore to help the clients receive resources from the 'system', have a view of social security field staff that is directly in contrast to their view of their own position. They see social security staff as biased and prejudiced against the poor and only too ready to evade their responsibility to help. They demand, therefore, that the social security bureaucracy should more effectively control and discipline its subordinates. Without taking sides on these views it can be acknowledged that there are 'two faces' to street level bureaucracy. It may be seen as the effective adaptation of policy to the needs of the public, or it may be seen as the manipulation of positions of power to distort policy towards stigmatization, discrimination and petty tyranny. Which it does will vary according to the policy at stake, and the values and commitments of the field workers, but it will also depend upon the scope accorded by the organizational control system, for this phenomenon is not necesarily independent of 'biases' built into the policy delivery system. Social workers can manipulate their 'system' in favour of some clients because their agency grants them licence to deploy such commitments. Social security officers can discriminate negatively because they are encouraged to be vigilant to prevent fraud and abuse.

Consideration of discretion and of the roles of 'street-level bureaucrats' must also involve looking at the implications of professionalism for implementation. For Etzioni the compliance of professionals to their organizations rests upon 'normative' commitments.[15] But policy makers may be said to have to 'pay for' a lessening of day-to-day control problems with concessions in the implementation process; professionalism tends to involve participation in the determination of policy outcomes. In the health service, for example, doctors have been able to secure a very full involvement in policy making within the service as one of the prices for participation. Three interrelated points may be made about professionalism:

1   that it may entail a level of expertise that makes lay scrutiny difficult;
2   that professionals may be, for whatever reason, accorded a legitimate autonomy;
3   that professionals may acquire amounts of power and influence that enable them to determine their own activities.

These sources of professional freedom clearly have a differential impact depending upon (a) the professional involved, (b) the organizational setting in which professionals work, and (c) the policies that they are required to implement. The importance of the level of expertise for professional power has led some writers to make a distinction between professions and semi-professions,[16] with doctors and lawyers in the former category but social workers and teachers in the latter.

Point (b) has been the subject of controversy about the impact upon professional activities of organizational, and particularly public, employment, the conclusion to which would seem to be, in short, that 'it depends on the profession and upon the organization'. On point (c), once again, a good deal depends on the nature of the policy involved.

There are a large number of situations in which it is expected that professional judgement will have a considerable influence upon the implementation process. Clearly explicit in many policies is an expectation of this. This applies to many decisions made in face-to-face relationships between professionals and their clients. Many of the issues involved are increasingly the subject of controversy, involving arguments about 'rights' versus 'discretion'. Within these arguments disputes occur about the significance of expertise and about the scope for effective limitation of discretionary power. The effective resolution would also impose many difficult policy questions – about moral rights to choose (for example, with reference to abortion) and the best way to allocate scarce resources (for example, with regard to kidney machines) – which are at present partly masked by professional discretion. There are also some important questions here, which are very hard to resolve, about the way to link together professional autonomy in dealing with an individual relationship with a client, and a policy-based concern (or 'public concern') about the way in which professionals allocate their services as a whole.

A further important complication for the study of implementation introduced by the involvement of professionals is that some activities depend upon the co-operation of two or more professional groups. Studies of attempts to co-ordinate the efforts of various professions concerned to protect children from injury by their parents have suggested that particular professional practices, activities and terminology may intensify communication problems.[17] There are also, clearly, some key problems about the boundaries between the various professional 'territories'.

It is important to recognize the extent to which professional involvement with policies implies not merely scope to influence implementation but also an impact upon policy itself. Within the health service the very direct influence of the doctors has been subjected to considerable attention by policy analysts.[18] What has perhaps been accorded less attention has been the ways in which policy and implementation have involved a feedback from implementation as policies have been found inadequate to meet the demands of 'good professional practice'.

Packman has examined the way in which social workers in children's departments gradually found that good child care practice required not merely the control and care powers possessed under the 1948 Children's Act but also preventive work to keep children out of 'care'.[19] They innovated as far as possible under the 1948 Act but eventually secured a further Act, in 1963, which legitimated 'preventive' work. A similar concern to extend social work practice, to enable integrated work with whole families, led, as Hall has shown, to further legislation in 1970 bringing all local authority social work within one department.[20]

The discussion in this section has developed the key points about inter-organizational practice by means of consideration of the rules–discretion dichotomy. But to end it three issues must be raised, which have been implicit rather than explicit within the argument so far: the relevance of the lack of clarity within much policy, the significance of value conflict; and the importance of rewards.

The first of these points does not require much further emphasis at this stage. A lack of clarity in policy has already been identified as one explanation for discretion. But equally when the relationship, within a system of rules, between means and ends is far from evident, then implementers may be more disposed to break rules, and their supervisors may be disinclined to enforce them.

A lack of clarity about policy goals and conflict about values, as already suggested, often go hand in hand. Burton Clark has written of 'precarious values'.[21] Policies may have among their goals objectives that lack support in the community. Implementers will be aware of the controversial character of the policies and may not themselves subscribe to the goals entailed. The social security official required to secure the delivery of benefits to one-parent families, but also expected to prevent abuse, may well take the latter consideration more seriously than the former, letting his or her conception of morality and stereotypes about the social behaviour of the claimants influence behaviour.[22]

But the implications of Clark's analysis go further than this, seeing the problem of precarious values as affecting not merely day-to-day behaviour but also the way in which a whole organization may conceive its tasks. In particular, an organization that is given a task that is controversial and unpopular in many quarters, such as an organization charged to promote racial and sexual equality or one providing help to a stigmatized group such as vagrant alcholics, may find that it is given an unclear mandate and is placed in a position in which it finds it hard to acquire 'legitimacy' for its activities. This may lead to the adoption of 'safe' and uncontroversial activities, organizational security being put before any movement towards potentially disruptive goals.

The problem of 'precarious values' may also be related to the problem of rewards. We return here to Etzioni's analysis of the distinction between 'utilitarian' and 'normative' rewards. Clearly the official placed in a position of 'role-strain' between the demands of superiors and the expectations of the public, or of 'value conflict' between his or her own ideals and those embodied in policy, will be influenced by rewards of both kinds. Benefits now and hopes of advancement may curb an inclination to deviate from the requirements of superiors; a feeling that some parts of the job are 'worth doing' may be even more influential. But the substitution of 'unofficial' or 'official' goals may be a product of recognition that more 'worthwhile' activities may thereby be undertaken. The motivation of field-level staff is an important issue even within the most integrated organization. Where, however, 'control' is attenuated by a gap between those concerned with policy and the implementing agency, it may assume crucial significance.

## THE SOCIAL, POLITICAL AND ECONOMIC ENVIRONMENT

Policies are evolved in a wider environment in which problems emerge that are deemed to require political solutions, and pressures occur for new political responses. Implementing agencies continuously interact with their environments. Much has already been said that has a bearing upon the underlying significance of the environment.

Whatever the relationship between state and society, policies may be interpreted as responses to perceived social needs. Government is concerned with 'doing things to', 'taking things from' or 'providing things for' society, or for parts of it. Putting policies into practice involves interactions between the agencies of government and their environment. Those who do that are, of course, themselves a part of the social environment in which they operate.

However, in looking at social policy we must also question whether the distinction between the policy system and its environment can be easily made. In chapter 1 it was established that it is misleading to see any single equation between the activities of the social policy system and the enhancement of social welfare. But just as the policy determinants of welfare are multiple, and sometimes unexpected, so individuals' welfare is influenced by phenomena that have nothing to do with the activity of the state. The determinants of an individuals' welfare can be broadly classified as depending upon their own capacity to care for themselves combined with (a) market activities and relationships, (b) the behaviour of 'significant others' as providers of 'informal care', amongst whom family members are likely to be the most important, and (c) the role played by the state. To study welfare requires attention to all 'determinants', and changes in the way in which welfare is provided are particularly likely to involve shifts in the roles played by these 'determinants' and shifts in the relationships between them. In other words, the process of interaction between policy system and environment is a very active one, and those interactions occur across an ambiguous and shifting boundary. To give a concrete example, personal social services care is only one element in individual care systems in which family, neighbour and purchased care are likely also to play a part. A shift in the availability of, or character of, any one of these care ingredients is likely to have an impact on the others. Day to day policy implementation in the state-provided sector involves the management, or indeed mismanagement, of its relationships to the other elements.

Accordingly studies of social policy have conceived of the system as a 'mixed economy of welfare'.[23] Furthermore, 'social divisions of welfare' have been identified recognizing not merely that there are different sources of welfare for individuals but also that individuals differ in the access they have to different welfare systems. Titmuss,[24] who originated the notion of 'social divisions of welfare', identified alongside mainstream 'public welfare' 'fiscal welfare', the system of relief from taxation (of which the relief for mortgage interest payments and pension contributions are among the most important examples); and 'occupational welfare' (the range of fringe benefits available to some employees). Titmuss, together with others who developed his work such as Sinfield and Townsend,[25,26] argued that these other welfare systems may provide large benefits additional to, or quite separate from, the benefits provided by the more central institutions of the welfare state. They may operate in a direction quite contrary to any egalitarian tendencies in the mainstream policies. The 'social divisions' theme has been taken up in another way by some recent feminist writers who have been concerned to show not merely that many welfare provisions discriminate against women, but also that female services within the family and neighbourhood form crucial separate welfare systems, enhanced in importance when other systems fail or are withdrawn.[27]

These points have been emphasised in this chapter because the implementation of many contemporary policy initiatives – privatization, the limitation of social expenditure, the extension of community care – involve changing the balance between the various ingredients in the 'political economy of welfare'. Where government withdraws or reduces its direct contribution to welfare it may still make an indirect contribution if the social security system subsidizes private provision, or it may have to acquire a new range of regulatory concerns about the quality of private services, or it may face increased problems in the other areas of concern because of the new pressures placed upon individuals and families.

Those who are directly affected by policies, the public, may be crudely divided into unorganized and isolated public – who pay taxes, receive benefits, seek planning permission, visit doctors and so on – and the organized public, the organizations upon whom policies have an impact. These relationships may be studied with a view to ascertaining whether implementation proceeds in terms of the even-handed justice that Max Weber suggested is, or should be, characteristc of bureaucratic administration.[28] Clearly, questions about bias in the behaviour of public officials, the mechanisms by which scarce benefits or services are rationed, the roles played by 'gatekeepers' and the problems of securing effective 'take-up' of some benefits are issues of concern for the implementation of policies. In study of these issues many of the issues about the motivation of implementers – about 'role-strain', 'precarious values' and the exercise of discretion – concern the interaction between the nature of policy, the implementation system and the characteristics of the public. Policy delivery is not easily made an 'even-handed' process; class differences influence access to professional services, some social security applicants are less well informed and more easily deterred than others, and 'street-level bureaucrats' who may be regarded as highly responsive to local needs in a white neighbourhood may be seen very differently in a black one. Here the 'environment' affects the way the policy is received.

The relationships between implementers and organizations may well involve elements of bargaining. Moreover it has been suggested earlier that one important issue for social policy that arises in relationship between public authorities and private agencies is that the latter may be the instruments by which government executes policy. One of the clearest examples of this is provided by the building societies. The government today sees them as important for housing policy as are the local authorities. It has sought to get them to extend loans to borrowers, who hitherto, because of their low incomes or because of the areas in which they want to buy houses, have not been able to get help from the societies. Government seeks to influence the prevailing borrowing and lending rates, and was even, in the 1970s, prepared to lend money to prevent the latter being raised.

Hence, the analysis of implementation is complicated by the extent to which many organizations participate in policy implementation. The blurred boundaries between the public sector and the private sector complicate the study of implementation, particularly when the government engages in private and obscure bargaining processes with private organizations.

Other organizations with an impact upon policy implementation may include the public organizations. There is a difficulty here about drawing the lines between the categories used in the analysis. Reference has been made to the complexity of policy. An extensive discussion has also been provided of the extent to which implementation requires inter-agency co-operation. What has not been emphasized, however, is the extent to which, in addition to the clear and close relationships involved, in a system so cluttered both with policies and with agencies there is a very wide range of interaction involved. Indeed, any new policy may be described as having a ripple effect. Policies may be understood as being interlocked with other policies. Successful policy implementation depends upon resolving problems of incompatibility between policies over often quite a wide range. Even policies with little direct impact on each other will be 'rivals' for scarce resources. Such issues will not be merely inter-policy issues but also inter-agency ones. The resolution of conflict between different policies depends upon mutual adjustment. At most this may require re-definition of one or other policy; more often it probably requires the exercise of discretionary powers associated with one or other to enable special circumstances to be recognized. The flexibility required of the policies implies a flexibility required of different agencies. This means that policy implementation may require bargaining and dealing between agencies, and that therefore considerations may be brought into the inter-policy relationship that are very much wider than the ones that appear to be at stake. Just as every new policy enters an arena already full of other policies, so every time interrelations imply agency interrelations there is a whole history of relationships that must be taken into account.

This chapter has portrayed the implementation process as a complex one, in many respects inextricably bound up with the policy-making process. It has suggested that in the study of social policy it is important to give attention to implementation problems that arise directly from the characteristics of policy, but to recognize also that there is a complicated interrelationship between these and a range of inter- and intra-organizational factors. Finally, all these complications interact with a complex environment.

An approach to the examination of social policy has been introduced here that has not been given much explicit attention in relation to the study of specific policies. One justification for this lengthy examination of policy implementation is that, while we all experience the effects of the implementation process, and many of us participate in various ways in it, very few of us are involved in policy making. Yet it is this policy making, often particularly that which occurs at the highest level, that receives very much more attention. It is hoped that, in considering the detailed discussions of particular areas of policy contained in the next section of this book, readers will bear in mind the importance of the implementation process for the actual impact of social policies upon the public.

SUGGESTIONS FOR FURTHER READING

The author has contributed to further discussions of the issues raised in this chapter in chapters 8 and 9 of his book with Glen Bramley,

*Analysing Social Policy*,[29] and in chapters 6–9 of his book with Chris Ham (see n. 31 in ch. 3). Susan Barrett and Colin Fudge's *Policy and Action* is also an important source.[30] Other key works on implementation are those by Pressman and Wildavsky (see n. 6) and Bardach (see n. 4) and an article by Van Meter and Van Horn.[31]

The theme of discretion has been a particular concern of the author's work cited above. Those who want to follow up this issue should also look at the writings of Jowell (see n. 3) and Davis,[32] and a collection of papers edited by Adler and Asquith.[33]

# Specific Areas of Social Policy

Each of the chapters in this part of the book will contain the following:

1 an account of the policies involved, which deals with their scope and coverage in Britain at the present time, and examines their organization;
2 a consideration of the particular characteristics of the British system, which seeks to give some insight into the reasons why it takes the form it does and the general consequences of that form for the service provided for the public;
3 the more detailed examination of a selection of specific issues of contemporary importance: these will consider particular policy problems and interesting current policy innovations. New directions suggested for policy, and solutions to policy problems, will be related to the factors that will influence their chances of adoption and implementation. Readers should note that some of the sections of specific sub-topics may be relevant to more than one chapter. Thus, issues about the relationship between personal social services and both income maintenence and health services are discussed in the personal social services chapter, and the discussion of the education of ethnic minorities in the education chapter makes many points relevant to other policies.

# CHAPTER 5

# Social Security

## INTRODUCTION

The expression 'social security' is used here to cover all the British state systems of income support. These fall into three categories: contributory benefits, non-contributory benefits which are not means-tested but are contingent upon the individual being in some specific category (a child or disabled), and means-tested benefits. The Beveridge plan for contributory benefits[1] envisaged that they should provide the main source of protection in old age, sickness, unemployment and widowhood. The legislation of the 1940s, picking up the main pieces from earlier contributory social security schemes, attempted to provide this coverage. The major contributory benefits date from that time but the system of contributions, the nature of the benefits and the character of the alternative benefits available to back up the contributory system have all changed a great deal since then.

The Department of Health and Social Security administers the main social security benefits, using a network of local offices. There are centralized computer systems for the contributory benefits. Means-tested benefit administration is more localized. Housing benefit is administered by the lower-tier local authorities, under either housing or finance departments. The DHSS lays down a strong rule structure for the whole system, including housing benefit. The only part of the system for which there now remains extensive local discretion is the Social Fund (see p. 99).

## CONTRIBUTORY BENEFITS

All employees, together with the self-employed, contribute on a weekly basis towards the national insurance scheme for sickness and unemployment benefits, and pensions. They do so on an earnings-related basis, subject to a maximum contribution level. Normally these contributions are deducted by employers, who also have to pay additional contributions for their employees. These should not be confused with income tax deductions.

Since 1977 there has also been in operation a State Earnings Related Pensions Scheme that will provide earnings-related pensions; these will begin to reach a satisfactory level for those retiring in the 1990s. Individual employees must contribute either to this scheme or to officially approved private schemes. Those who 'contract out' in the latter way will secure only the basic retirement pension from the state, which is the main present form of income support for the retired. (There has been a limited 'supplementary' earnings-related pensions scheme in operation since 1959, but this is an unimportant source of retirement income.)

The employee who is unable to work on account of sickness is initially dependent, since the enactment of the Social Security and Housing Benefits Act of 1982, upon his or her employer for support. The latter is, with some exceptions, required to provide sick pay at least up to minimum levels prescribed by Parliament for twenty-eight weeks. After that anyone still unfit for work moves on to invalidity benefit, set at a flat rate level. There is also a state sickness benefit scheme, providing benefits lower than invalidity benefits for people in the first twenty-eight weeks of sickness who have recent insurance contribution records but were not in employment immediately before they became sick. Also those whose incapacity for work arises out of an industrial accident or a prescribed industrial disease may get special, higher, benefits after fifteen weeks of incapacity for work.

There are similar systems of statutory maternity pay, payable for eighteen weeks, backed up by a reduced state maternity allowance for women with recent work records who do not qualify for pay from their employers.

Unemployment benefit is available after three days out of work, subject to complex previous contributions conditions, to the formerly employed. After a year on this benefit, entitlement is 'exhausted', and recipients cannot requalify until they complete a period of thirteen weeks in work. There are, for both sickness and unemployment benefit, rules designed to prevent abuse of the scheme. The rules with regard to unemployment benefits are, however, much more obtrusive. There are provisions for disqualification from receiving benefit for up to thirteen weeks if individuals are judged to have left work voluntarily, lost their jobs through their own fault or refused a suitable vacancy. Under legislation before Parliament at the time of writing, this disqualification will last for up to twenty-six weeks. There are also rules to prevent persons involved in industrial disputes and seasonal workers from benefiting from the unemployment scheme.

Widows have an entitlement, based upon their husband's contributions, to widowed mother's allowance if they have children to support and to widow's pension if they are over forty-five. For the widow's benefits and for retirement pensions during the first five years after reaching pensionable age (sixty for women, sixty-five for men), there are 'earnings rules' which reduce the income received, on the basis of sliding scales which allow some but not large amounts of earnings. These rules only apply to earned income; in this sense they differ from the fuller forms of means tests. Widows lose their benefits on remarriage; there is also a 'cohabitation rule' which may be operated to treat widows living 'as wives' the same as 'married wives'.

## NON-CONTRIBUTORY, NON-MEANS-TESTED, CONTINGENT BENEFITS

Child benefit is paid to the parents or guardians of all children under sixteen, and children between sixteen and eighteen who are still at school. The only qualifying condition is a residence one. 'One parent benefit' can be claimed as a modest addition to child benefit for single parents. There are some non-contributory benefits available to the long-term disabled, which must not be confused with the industrial injury disablement provision or with invalidity benefit. Amongst these are the attendance allowance, for those who need very high levels of attention from another person; the mobility allowance, available to those virtually unable to walk; and the non-contributory invalidity pension, available to those among the long-term sick who have not been able to contribute to secure invalidity benefit. There is a range of detailed rules concerning these benefits which cannot be discussed in the space available here.

## MEANS-TESTED BENEFITS

The 1986 Social Services Act, which was implemented by April 1988, radically altered the structure of means-tested benefits. The attention given in the Act to the rationalization of means-tested benefits, although it did also make changes to the pensions scheme and to some of the contributory benefits of lesser importance, is indicative of the extent to which the government recognizes that means tests are now very central to our social security system. People dependent upon contributory benefits often need means-tested support as well, at least in respect of their housing costs. At a time of high unemployment a contributory scheme for those out of work, which has initial qualifying rules and the exhaustion of entitlement after a year, leaves many in need of means tested benefits. In particular, young new entrants to the labour force are unprotected by the unemployment benefit scheme. In addition many people in work earn insufficient for their needs, and have to apply for means tested family and housing benefits to supplement their incomes. The figures in table 5.1 give some idea of the extent of coverage of contributory and means-tested benefits respectively; they relate, of course, to the period before the introduction of the 1986 Act. Bear in mind that many people can qualify for more than one benefit, and that, in particular, means-tested benefits may supplement contributory ones.

TABLE 5.1   The main social security benefits in Great Britain 1986–1987

| Benefit | Recipients (thousands) | Expenditure (£ millions) |
|---|---|---|
| *Contributory* | | |
| Retirement pensions | 9,525 | 17,776 |
| Invalidity benefit | 910 | 2,617 |
| Unemployment benefit | 935 | 1,618 |
| Widows benefit and industrial death benefit | 435 | 902 |
| *Non-contributory, non-means-tested* | | |
| Child benefit | 12,035[a] | 4,425 |
| Attendance allowance and invalid care allowance | 595 | 66 |
| Mobility allowance | 450 | 507 |
| *Means-tested* | | |
| Supplementary pensions | 1,805 | 997 |
| Supplementary allowances | 3,030 | 6,267 |
| Housing benefit | 5,010 | 3,154 |
| Family income supplement | 215 | 158 |

[a] Numbers of qualifying children

*Source*: Central Statistical Office, *Social Trends 17*, London, HMSO, 1987, p. 89

In setting out their objectives for reform, in the White Paper which preceded the 1986 Act, the government said:

We believe that resources must be directed more effectively to areas of greater need, notably low-income families with children. We want a system that is simpler to understand and better managed. We want sensible co-operation between the social security and tax systems. And we want a system which is consistent with the Government's overall objectives for the economy.[2]

As far as the means-tested benefits were concerned, the Act provided new schemes to take the place of supplementary benefit and family income supplement, and changed the housing benefit scheme. It also swept into the means-tested system two contributory benefits of previously near to universal availability, maternity grant and death grant.

The scheme which has replaced supplementary benefit is known as 'income support'. It operates a means test based upon a simple personal allowance structure, enhanced in some cases with 'premiums'. The specific personal allowance rates are for a couple, a single person over twenty-five, a person between eighteen and twenty-four and three age-related rates for children. Then there are premiums for families, lone parents, pensioners under eighty, pensioners over eighty, disabled people, and seriously disabled people. The idea running throughout is that the determination of the appropriate overall entitlement for a household should be a simple and predictable process. Additions for special needs have been abolished. Then rules, not so dissimilar to those operating under the former supplementary benefit scheme, determine how any income should be taken into account. People in full-time work are disqualified from receiving 'income support', but part-time workers may obtain it. To deal with this an earnings rule is used, based on net income, which involves disregarding a small amount and then deducting the rest from any entitlement. Similar 'disregards' are used for some other kinds of income, but state benefits are taken into account in full. Savings under £3,000 are not taken into account. People with savings over £6,000 do not qualify at all. There is a sliding scale of 'notional income' taken into account which applies to savings between £3,000 and £6,000. These are the only figures quoted in this brief description of the scheme, since most of the calculation parameters will change annually to allow benefits to be adjusted to take inflation into account.

Alongside the 'income support' scheme is a means-tested benefit available to low-paid full-time workers. This is 'family credit', and it has replaced 'family income supplement'. The calculation rules for this benefit are based upon those for 'income suppport'. The maximum credit is payable where net earned income is approximately equal to, or below, the personal allowance available to a family on 'income support'. Hence the government aims to ensure that most families where there is a full-time breadwinner are better off than comparable families on 'income support'. Above 'income support' level the credit is withdrawn at the rate of 70 per cent, that is, for each £1 of income above that level 70p of credit is lost.

The housing benefit scheme has been designed to be compatible with these two other means-tested benefits. The 'income support' rules are used in the calculation of benefit so that anyone at or below income support income level gets the full housing benefit entitlement. Thus, an anomaly which occurred before, under which people on housing benefit but not supplementary benefit could be worse off than people on both benefits, has been eliminated. Housing benefit provides support for rent and rates; it does not provide support for house buying. But people on 'income support' may get help under that scheme to enable them to keep up mortgage interest payments. One controversial feature of the revised housing benefit scheme is that all ratepayers, regardless of income, have to pay 20 per cent of their rates. It is expected that when the government introduces the 'community charge' scheme (see p. 53) housing benefit together with the 20 per cent rule will apply to that.

Under the former supplementary benefit scheme there were provisions enabling single payments to be made to help people with exceptional expenditures – removal costs, furnishing, house repairs etc. An elaborate body of rules dealt with these entitlements. The 1986 Act has swept away single payments. But it set up a Social Fund, to be administered by a specially trained group of DHSS officers. Under the Fund there are two kinds of grants available as of right to people on 'income support' or 'family credit': a lump sum maternity needs payment, and a funeral needs payment (the amount of which depends upon funeral costs). There is also provision for grants to be made from the Social Fund to assist with the promotion of 'community care'. These may be available when someone needs help in establishing themselves in the community after a period of institutional care, to assist with some travelling expenses to visit relatives in hospitals and other institutions, and to improve the living conditions of defined 'vulnerable groups' in the community. Elaborate guidance is provided to Social Fund officers to help them determine needs of this kind. They are expected to liaise closely about such matters with social services and health services staff, and to take into account powers these other departments may have to provide assistance in cash or kind. Apart from the grants, outlined in the points above, all other help from the Social Fund is by way of loans, normally repayable by weekly deductions from benefits. Again officers have been given elaborate instructions on the circumstances in which they may provide loans. The Social Fund, excluding the two items of benefit as of right, is 'cash limited'. This means that local officers will have annual budgets, and will be expected to relate a set of rules about priorities to the total sum available. Claimants for help from the Social Fund, other than claimants for maternity and funeral payments, have no formal right of appeal against decisions, though there is provision for internal 'review'.

This description of the new structure for the main means tested benefits does not exhaust the list of benefits. One quite important means tested benefit administered by local authorities, entitlement to free school meals, had its availability restricted under the 1986 social security changes. Free school meals are now available only to children whose parents are on 'income support'.

Other means-tested benefits include grants to students in higher education, relief from payment of National Health Service charges, and legal aid. Local authority social services departments also use means tests to determine charges for residential care and domiciliary services.

## THE DISTINCTIVE CHARACTERISTICS OF THE BRITISH SYSTEM OF SOCIAL SECURITY

The British national insurance scheme today bears little resemblance to commercial insurance. There is no 'funding' and investing of contributions. Invalidity benefit continues for as long as the claimant is sick, assuming an initial fulfilment of the contribution conditions. It is impossible to relate flat rate pensions to contributions; the rate of inflation of recent years has destroyed any correspondence between contributions and payments in terms of the face value of the money involved, and no inflation-proofing assumptions were built into the original scheme. When the State Earnings Related Pension Scheme (SERPS) was set up in 1977 some consideration was given to the future relationship between amounts to be paid out to qualifiers and amounts to be contributed by participants in the scheme still in work. Concern about the relationship between these groups in the early years of the next century, when SERPS beneficiaries will increase rapidly but SERPS contributors seem likely to be comparatively low, was seen by the Thatcher government as a justification for reducing the benefits offered. This change, together with measures to increase the extent of contracting out of SERPS into private schemes, was included in the 1986 Social Security Act.

The unemployment benefit scheme maintains an insurance principle of sorts. Despite the fact that, as early as the 1920s, the scheme was rendered insolvent by the extension of protection to 'bad risks' and the lengthening of the period for which benefit was payable, the exhaustion of benefit after a year, and the special re-qualification rules, provide some limits to expenditure upon this benefit. It is these restrictions that have, at a time of high unemployment, substantially limited the extent to which unemployed people can avoid applying for 'income support'. In 1986–7 26 per cent of the unemployed receiving benefits were getting unemployment benefit alone, 8 per cent were getting unemployment benefit *and* supplementary benefit, and 66 per cent were getting only supplementary benefit.[3]

The presence in the British system of a 'safety-net' group of means-tested benefits to back up the contributory scheme is by no means peculiar to Britain. Such assistance schemes are very widespread, and in many countries they remain under local control and more closely resemble the British scheme's predecessor, the poor law. What is perhaps rather anomalous about the relationship between contributory benefits and means-tested benefits in Britain is that, despite the fact the former are so widely available that the insurance principle is comparatively meangingless, the means-tested schemes remain of considerable importance. We may contrast Britain with the United States, where contributory income support is less widespread and more strictly based upon insurance principles, and where it is therefore not surprising that means-tested forms of relief assume considerable importance. In Britain, on the other hand, the contributory scheme appears to provide close to universal coverage but in fact has to be supplemented in a large number of ways.

The abandonment of the 'insurance' relationship for unemployment benefit, and some relatively slight increases in contributory benefit rates, would markedly reduce dependence on means-tested benefits. Yet these changes are open to objections. The main effect of increasing the availability of unemployment benefit would be to shift the support of a large group of people from 'income support' to contributory benefit with little change to their income, whilst a relatively small number of people with other sources of income (the early retired with private pensions) made actual income gains. Similarly, an increase in contributory benefits relative to 'income support' would produce income gains for a group not among the most poor (not on 'income support'), while merely altering the source of help for the very poor (who would then accuse governments of giving with one hand and taking away with the other).

On balance the shift in the British system in the early 1980s has been in the opposite direction. The ending of earnings related supplement to short-term benefits, the introduction of the employer-based sick pay scheme, and measures which have diminished the value of benefits have reduced the contribution of contributory benefits to income support and increased that of means-tested benefits.

LEVELS OF BENEFITS

Clearly it is important in assessing a system of social security not merely to look at the structure of the system but also to look at the level of benefits provided by it. There are examples, for instance, within the

British system that look most impressive until one scrutinizes the levels of benefit available. This is particularly true of the various benefits for the disabled. For example, attendance allowance does not compensate for the substantial income losses likely to occur for someone who gives up full time work to care for a disabled person. Similarly, the mobility allowance provides only a very limited contribution towards the cost of obtaining and running a vehicle suitable for a disabled person.

It would be pointless, in discussing the main social security benefits, to provide specific figures, which would be dated by the time many read this section. Instead, some of the general issues about the setting of benefit levels will be outlined. Reference has already been made to the relationship between contributory benefit levels and 'income support' levels. Any government setting these relative levels not merely has to look at its stance on means-tested benefits but also has to take into account that the costs of any shift away from the selective approach entails a cost made up of the extra benefit paid to those *not* already on 'income support'. If these include large numbers of people who have failed to claim the means-tested benefit, this will be a contribution to the reduction of poverty; but what if the new arrangement mainly provides a bonus to those already above the poverty line? This is a cruel irony for the commitment of egalitarians to universalism. The pragmatism of everyday politics leads away from a commitment to a more ideal system of social security.

Hence a great deal of debate about poverty in Britain is concerned not about the contributory benefits as such but about the means-tested benefit levels, and about the people and families whose incomes fall below those levels. There are three ways to try to assess the adequacy of this 'poverty level': in relation to absolute concepts of need; in relation to other incomes; and over time in relation to the movement of prices and other incomes. In the early years of national assistance studies which attempted to relate poverty to an absolute standard, based upon the cost of providing a basic minimum of necessities, were still regarded as providing a sound basis for the fixing of benefit levels.[4] More recently this approach has been discredited. It has been pointed out, notably by Townsend,[5] that poverty is a relative concept. The British bare minimum would be quite a good standard of living for people in the more deprived countries of the world. At the same time, British views about what is necessary for an adequate way of life change over time. These changes are related to developments in living standards within the nation as a whole. When the national assistance scales – which today, much updated for inflation, form the basis for the 'income support' scales – were first set in 1948 television was not even available; in the next few years it was regarded first as a luxury then as a necessity, and now colour television has moved in the same way out of the luxury category. If poverty is regarded as a relative concept, the key questions are, for example: to what extent should those on the official poverty line have incomes that make it difficult for them to share a way of life of the majority of the people? Or how large should be the gap between the incomes of those on the poverty line and average incomes? Or even, what should the relationship be between the lowest incomes in our society, most of which are provided by the social security system, and the highest incomes. In other words, the crucial questions are about relationships between the official poverty level and other income levels.

This has been effectively examined by Peter Townsend in his large study of poverty. He persuasively makes a case for regarding large numbers of British people, including both people dependent upon social security and many on low wages, as in poverty.[6] A more recent study by Mack and Lansley lends support to Townsend's argument.[7] This demonstrates the extent to which low income people lack things which according to a public opinion survey, are regarded as necessities.

A variant on this theme of considerable importance in contemporary political debate concerns the relationship between social security incomes and average earned incomes over time. After all, the real political questions are not so much about the setting of levels in the abstract as about the need for, or the amount of, benefit increases. The pressure groups regularly draw politicians' attention to the ways in which, over a period of time, those whom they represent are losing ground. Two important alternative kinds of yardsticks are used for these judgements: indices of earnings and indices of prices. The plural form is used in both these cases since there have been extensive arguments about the best ways of calculating these. In particular it has been argued that a price index for the poor should be rather different from a more general one, since the poor spend their incomes in rather different ways. However, the general problem of choice between earnings and prices as bases for judgements on benefit levels over time is that, while attention to earnings presumes relative positions, it may be important to protect the living standards of the poor at a time when prices are rising faster than earnings.

Before 1973 there was no statutory requirement for government to take specific notice of wages or price movements in determining benefit levels. *Ad hoc* political judgements governed uprating decisions. However, there was a tendency, over time, for the relationship between short-term benefit rates and wage rates to remain roughly the same.[8]

In the Social Security Act of 1973 the Conservatives provided a statutory link between benefits and prices. In 1975 an amendment to the Social Security Act committed the Labour government to uprating long-term benefits in line with prices or earnings, whichever was greater, and short-term benefits in line with prices. Heavy price inflation in the late seventies did produce some relative gains to social security recipients. In 1979 the Conservatives amended the statutory requirement so that long-term benefits were only to be linked to prices. Also, short-term benefits might be increased by up to 5 per cent less than the inflation rate. These rules relate only to the contributory benefits but, in most cases, means-tested benefit rates have been uprated on a similar basis.

The relationship between social security incomes and low wages is clearly important. Several studies of poverty have related incomes to the level provided by the main means-tested scheme. Apart from drawing attention to numbers falling below it because of a failure to claim benefits, they have shown that there is a significant group which fall below that standard because of low wages. Developments in the family benefits, and in housing benefit, have been designed to tackle this problem. However, there is an alternative way of responding to it. This is to argue not that something must be done to augment the earnings of the low wage-earner, but that means-tested benefit levels must be kept below the lowest wage levels. There was at one time a provision within the supplementary benefits rules – the wage stop – to enable individual benefits to be kept down. This was abolished soon after the introduction of family income supplement, which reduced the numbers of cases involved considerably. It has been argued that few of the unemployed are in fact deterred from obtaining work by benefit payments being above the levels they can obtain as earners. However, there is undoubtedly a relatively small gap between the benefits paid to some families, particularly large families, and the wages paid for low-skilled work. The deterrent effect of this will depend first upon the actual costs of going to work, second upon individual views of the psychological costs and benefits of work, and third upon the benefits still obtainable when in work. It is difficult to estimate the actual extent of deterrence at a time when jobs are scarce. However, there is a widespread public belief that this deterrent effect actually contributes to our high unemployment rates. Politicians share, or are sensitive to, this belief. It accordingly influences their attitudes to increases in the short-term benefits. However, the government sees the introduction of the 'family credit' scheme, which provides benefit to anyone in work whose net income is at or below the 'income support' level as dealing with this 'unemployment trap' problem. That, however, depends upon 'take up', an issue to which we will return.

As well as a concern about the relationship between benefits and other incomes there is also a concern about relativities within the benefit system. The 'income support' scheme rules make assumptions about the extent to which a couple may live more cheaply than a single person, about the extra needs of the elderly and the disabled, about the different costs of children at various ages, and about the lower needs of single adults under twenty-five. Some of these judgements are clearly controversial. In particular the low 'income support' rate for the single under twenty-five seems to be related to an assumption that such people can live with their parents, and not form separate households. The assumptions about the costs of children made by the rules have also been challenged as unrealistic about the costs of teenage children. It seems fair to suggest that considerations about the evidence on actual costs have been mixed with views about who are the most deserving amongst the poor in the determination of some of these rules.

## SOCIAL SECURITY ASSUMPTIONS ABOUT FAMILY LIFE AND WOMEN'S ROLES

The assumptions about family life operated under the poor law involved a household means test under which all a household's needs were taken into account and also its resources, so that adult children of a needy couple were expected to contribute to their maintenance. The contributory benefits developed in 1911 treated the insured claimant as the sole beneficiary, providing flat rate payments at the same level regardless of his or her family commitments. However, in the 1920s the principle of additions to benefits, taking into account theneeds of wives and children, was introduced. The improved contributory scheme developed in the 1940s carried forward this principle, while means-tested assistance shifted from a household means test to a family one. Broadly, then, British social security policies have been developed on the assumption that the typical claimant is a married man with a non-working wife and dependent children. That is not, of course, to say that the system cannot cope with claims from single people, but that it has had difficulty in coming to terms with both female employment and with multi-person families constituted other than on the basis of legal marriage.

Until recently, married women have been required to pay lower contributions and have received lower benefits than men. There has additionally been an arrangement, now slowly being phased out, under which they could contract out of all the contributory scheme except the industrial injuries part. While this anomaly is being eliminated there are still others. Married women cannot claim contributory benefit increases in respect of dependent husbands and children. The continuation of provisions for non-employed wives to be treated as 'dependants' for whom husbands can claim additions to benefits implies that the return an employed woman receives on her contributions may in some cases be worth only the difference between the full pension or benefit and the addition for a non-working wife. In other words there are difficulties in securing a fair balance in a scheme that tries, on the one hand, to make provision for 'dependent' wives and children and, on the other, to enable the married woman to be a contributor and claimant in her own right.

The position with regard to means-tested benefits is naturally even more complicated when men and women live together, and perhaps have children, but are not married. A family means test requires judgements to be made about whether family situations exist. Generally this is straightforward; claimants agree with official interpretations of their situations. Indeed, it is to the advantage of a male claimant, living with a non-employed 'wife' and children (even if they are not his) to claim them as his family. However, difficulties arise where claimants, normally female, wish to be treated as independent but find that the DHSS regards them as the 'wives' of male friends. DHSS have tried to develop a definition of 'living together as man and wife', which distingushes stable relationships from more casual ones, but difficulties and disagreements still occur. It is of course only heterosexual relationships that are treated in this way – in all other cases claimants' needs are assessed separately. The issue here, which as was pointed out above also applies to widow's benefits, arises from the family-based approach to benefits. While it would be possible to treat unmarried 'couples' differently from married ones, the only fair way to avoid problems of this kind is to cease to make assumptions about family patterns of support, but instead to have a structure of *individual* entitlements.[9]

PROBLEMS OF MEANS TESTING

There is an extensive literature on the problems of means testing. Much that has been written on this subject comes from those who advocate, as an alternative, the strengthening of the contributory benefits system so that it becomes more universal in its coverage and provides better benefits. We have seen already some of the political objections to this approach. Not surprisingly the political climate of the 1980s is not sympathetic to it. Alternative approaches to this issue are also found. One of these suggests that we could have a structure of 'basic income' in which all would be guaranteed a minimum income, and some of us would secure earned incomes (necessarily more heavily taxed) to supplement this state minimum. This would be a radical departure from our current system. It finds little support close to the corridors of power. Another alternative which has awakened a wider interest is 'negative income tax'. The British 'pay-as-you-earn' system for the deduction of tax would seem to be the ideal vehicle for the development of a system whereby additions rather than deductions could be provided in some cases. However, the basis for the assessment of tax would have to be shifted from an annual to a weekly one, arrangements would have to be made for the system to operate when people were both in and out of work, and some more precise information on need would have to be available to the tax authorities.

When the Conservative government announced its radical review of social security in 1983 it seemed possible that the negative income tax idea would be adopted. In practice the 1986 changes have been influenced by this approach, in the adoption of a common set of rules to determine benefit rates and in the use of 'net' rather than gross income (that is, income after tax). But the income tax system itself remains 'untainted' by social security considerations. Hence the standard problems about means testing remain, albeit in a form much affected by the 1986 Act.

The general case against means tests is that they confuse, deter and stigmatize those who need help. People prefer benefits to which they have clear-cut rights, and about which they can obtain unambiguous information. Those who have to claim help are often already in trouble, about which they are ashamed or for which their neighbours criticize them; to have to reveal intimate details to an offical in order to obtain benefits deepens the sense of 'stigma'. The low take-up of some benefits is attributed both to this 'stigma' and to the complexities surrounding the administration of means tests.[10]

It is undoubtedly the case that take-up levels for the means-tested benefits are lower than other benefits. But there are marked variations between the various means-tested ones. The National Consumer Council produced in the 1970s the estimates shown in table 5.2.[11]

TABLE 5.2   Take-up of means-tested benefits

| Benefits | Estimated Take-up (%) |
|---|---|
| Student grants | 100 |
| Free school meals | 80 |
| Family income supplement | 75 |
| Supplemetary benefit | 75 |
| Rent rebates | 70–5 |
| Rate rebates | 62 |
| Rent allowances (unfurnished) | 30–5 |
| Rent allowances (furnished) | 10 |

These estimates have, of course, been rendered out of date by the social security changes. It is however useful to start from them, since this chapter is being written just before the full implementation of the 1986 Act and studies of the new system are not available. The position with regard to free school meals may be improved simply because the new scheme excludes so many low income people. However children will have to establish to the education authorities' satisfaction that their parents are on 'income support'! The government considers that the rules for 'family credit' are more comprehensible than those for family income supplement, and that this will increase take-up. Pressure groups are sceptical. The figures for supplementary benefit given in table 5.2 are probably already rather out-of-date, but 'income support' will not be obviously easier to obtain than its predecessor. One thing which must be said here, in fairness to the DHSS, is that much supplementary benefit non-take-up involved quite small amounts, where contributory benefits were in payment. However, some of the punitive measures applied to young people, limiting their accommodation opportunities and pressurizing them into low income jobs or training may depress take-up. The other benefits in the table are all now collectively called housing benefits. Those who qualify for rate rebates alone are still likely to be unsure about entitlement. The take up of housing benefits paid to private tenants is likely to have increased significantly between 1982 and 1987 because of the way supplementary benefit was a 'passport' for housing benefit. The new scheme partly breaks that link. There is good reason to believe that many low earners in private accommodation, particularly the geographically mobile young, have a low take-up of housing benefit.

Not only is it the case that some means-tested schemes are much easier to understand than others; the big disparity between rent rebate and rent allowances take-up occurs because local authorities, as the administrators of those means tests, could much more easily publicize the former among their own tenants. Another factor that facilitates take-up of benefits is that 'income support' is regarded as an automatic 'passport' to others. This is most evidently the case with relief from NHS charges. However, this implies a cause for concern about the needs of those just above 'income support' levels, together with those who, in not claiming small amounts of income support, may also be shutting themselves out from ready access to other benefits.

One particular problem about the multiplicity of means tests is that, operating together, they may create a 'poverty trap'. This is a kind of income tax effect under which an individual whose earned income rises may find that tax and insurance contributions increase while benefit income decreases and together they diminish any gain to a very low level, or even exceptionally produce a loss. The goverment stated that one of the main benefits of the 1986 Act was to be that, by using earned income after tax and national insurance deductions and having the main means tests operate with a common framework, they would eliminate the 'poverty trap' problem for most people. Housing benefit entitlement is calculated *after* taking into account income tax and any 'family credit' entitlement; if the latter two change they affect the net income used to determine housing benefit so that poverty trap losses over 100 per cent cannot occur. However the housing benefit taper is 85 per cent (65 per cent on rent and 20 per cent on rates), so an individual gaining £1 of net income will in fact lose all but 20p of it. This is much higher than the highest level of income tax! What the government can say is that the poverty trap has become more 'predictable' and uniform in its impact, not that it has been eliminated.

This 'poverty trap' problem must afflict any unified means-testing system, including negative income tax. If the tapering off effect is to be reduced benefit receipt will logically spread further up the income distribution, adding to the cost of the scheme. In the last resort this can only be compensated for by increasing tax rates, either across the board or through alterations to the higher rate bands. Moreover, in many households where there are adjustments to both family credit and housing benefits the ultimate 'actual' loss will be 98p.

CONCLUSIONS

The British system of social security has been built up by the development of a contributory system together with a limited system of family benefits, which were conceived to minimize dependence upon means tested benefits. However, the latter have not been reduced to the 'safety net' role envisaged for them by Beveridge and others. Indeed in recent years an alternative strategy has been suggested, to confine expenditure on social security by placing an emphasis upon means-tested benefits. While the main issue for debate about the system seems to be the conflict between the case for a comprehensive system of non-means-tested benefits, probably founded upon contributory principles, and the alternative means-testing approach, this conveys an oversimplified notion of its character. In fact, the two approaches are mixed together in the system, and the overall picture is further confused by a range of *ad hoc* responses to special issues and problems – the needs of the disabled, the compensation of industrial injury victims, the requirements of support for students and schoolchildren, and so on.

The 1986 Social Security Act has simplified the means tested part of the system. This eases administration, and limits the opportunities for errors, differential rule interpretation and outright discretion within the main means tests. It is an approach to reform around which a broad consensus might have formed were it not for the fact that the government was determined that the new scheme should be no more costly than its predecessors, and that it should make it easier for government to contain the future growth of social security costs. Therefore simplification inevitably implies rough justice, gainers being counterbalanced by losers. In addition the very controversial Social Fund has been introduced, with loans as its main form of aid, and with cash limits, to take up the strain on the system previously imposed by the complex single payments rules.

The growth of means-tested relative to contributory benefits since the 1960s, caused by political reluctance to increase the expensive contributory benefits, and the use of *ad hoc* measures to cope with problems of low wages and high housing costs, had produced a great deal of turbulence in social security policy. Will the 1986 Act bring in a period of stability? Or will it lead to further attacks on the contributory system on the grounds of its irrelevance for the determination of most non-pensioners' incomes? Or will we see a future government attempting to turn back the tide and revert to a modernized version of the Beveridge approach?

### SUGGESTIONS FOR FURTHER READING

There is not at present a textbook on the social security system or on social security law which has caught up with the recent rapid succession of changes to the system. The Child Poverty Action Group (CPAG) handbooks on means-tested and contributory benefits are the best sources. These are produced annually and keep up with benefit rate changes.

The White Paper outlining the proposals for the 1986 Act provides a good guide to the government's thinking. All but a few details of its proposals were enacted. A summary of the Act and a critique is provided in the Social Security Consortium's *Of Little Benefit*.[12] Doubtless a variety of other critiques will soon appear.

CPAG pamphlets are useful critical sources of information on the system. Deacon and Bradshaw's *Reserved for the Poor* (see n. 10) is an excellent review of the issues about means testing and the various alternatives to it, but was completed before the government proposed its changes.

The best discussions of poverty and social security are Townsend's important poverty survey, and Mack and Lansley's more recent book (see nn. 5 and 7).

# CHAPTER 6

# The Personal Social Services

## INTRODUCTION

This chapter will deal with those services which are the responsibility of the local authority social services departments in England and Wales. The decision to treat the personal social services sector as equivalent to that of the local social services departments is an arbitrary one, justifiable only in terms of existing departmental boundaries in England and Wales. In Scotland, for example, the relevant departments are the 'social work departments' and their responsibilites include duties carried out by the probation service in England and Wales. The justification for refraining from giving attention to the probation service is that a proper consideration of its role raises issues about relationship to the courts and to other aspects of penal policy, which it is not intended to cover in this book. In England and Wales, before the creation of social services departments in 1971 a chapter like this would have had to deal with activities carried out within several public departments. There are still now some variations between authorities in the services that are the concern of the social services departments – a few departments have taken over the education welfare service, and child guidance remains an interdepartmental 'hybrid' service – but broadly the activities of these departments can be made the focus of attention.

One way of classifying the personal social services is in terms of their contributions to the needs of specific groups in the population: the elderly, the physically handicapped, the mentally ill, the mentally handicapped and children. This 'client' group classification is encouraged by the DHSS's concern to relate social services planning to health planning with reference to such categories.[1] An alternative classification is in terms of kinds of services: residential care, day care, domiciliary services and fieldwork. These two modes of classification can, of course, be related to each other. A two-dimensional table could be drawn up, relating kinds of clients to kinds of services. This is difficult only where client groups fall into two or more categories – where the elderly are also physically handicapped, for example – unless the service is seen as being provided for families rather than for specific individual clients. It is the new integrated service's commitment to families that is seen as fitting unsatisfactorily with the various client group classifications. However, in most cases the focal beneficiary of the service will be identifiable. It is field social work, rather than the provision of concrete benefits like residential care, that is most difficult to classify in these terms. However, even in this case the problem is not so much frequent doubt about the focal clients, as a lack of clear information to enable social workers' activities to be clearly classified for the purposes of budget documents and planning activities.

In this section personal social services' activities will be discussed in terms of the kinds of services involved, treating their relevance for specific client groups as the basis for consideration under each service heading.

RESIDENTIAL CARE

There are two main groups of residential accommodation supplied by local authority social services departments: accommodation for the elderly, provided under Part III of the 1948 National Assistance Act, and accommodation for children who have been removed from parental care. The old people's homes have faced the problem, since 1948, of living down their heritage as 'workhouses'. While authorities have steadily replaced those institutions that were established under the poor law, putting in their places smaller and generally more homely institutions, they have faced difficulties in eliminating the public view that these are places to which people go only 'as a last resort'. The limited number of places available has emphasized the 'last resort' character of these homes, in more senses than one. It has been difficult to establish within them a mixed population of elderly people with varying degrees of frailty. Instead there is very often a problem of maintaining a distinction between the population of these homes and the patients of the overburdened geriatric wards of the hospitals. The group the local authorities cannot readily refuse to help are those so frail that they cannot any longer manage in their own homes, whatever the level of domiciliary service provided. Many of these people require extensive nursing care but cannot secure hospital places.

About 120,500 elderly people were accommodated in these local authority homes in the United Kingdom in 1985.[2] There is a widespread concern about the best way to use the supply of residential places for the elderly, and about the implications, for the future supply of these places, of an ageing population and of a diminishing capacity to provide family support. The distinction between the local authority's responsibility and the health service's responsibility is a difficult one, producing planning problems and 'boundary' conflicts over individual cases that are seldom in the old people's best interests. Local authorities would like to maintain a distinction between those for whom they supply domiciliary care and those for whom they supply residential care that is based upon individual preferences and needs and not upon a desperate attempt to spread scarce resources in the most economical way. A typical problem here is the desire to make temporary residential accommodation available to support family care within the community on an occasional 'holiday' basis. This comes into conflict with the pressing demand for all units of accommodation to be used for long-term accommodation.

However, an added complication for the determination of the local authority's responsibility for the residential care of the elderly is that there is a large, and growing, number of privately run homes available. About 102,200 people were accommodated in registered voluntary private homes in the United Kingdom in 1985.[3] The number of places in this sector had doubled since the mid 1970s. By contrast the number of public sector places has gone down. Local authorities are responsible for the registration of voluntary and private homes, and have therefore to monitor their standards. They are thus placed in the anomalous position that they are the ultimate judges of the quality of services which relieve them of their own statutory responsibilities to provide care.

This rapid growth in private care has been stimulated by the availability of social security benefits to enable old people to pay charges. It has been an uneven growth. In some areas it has dramatically reduced the demand for local authority care. In others its impact has been quite slight. The greatest growth has been in the south and west of England, particularly in the seaside areas. An Audit Commission report on this issue has described this growth as a 'perverse effect of social security policies', distorting efforts to get the balance right between residential and community care and increasing regional inequalities. They point out that, for example, 'there are now nearly ten times as many places per 1,000 people aged 75 and over in private and voluntary residential homes for elderly people in Devon and East Sussex than there are in Cleveland'.[4]

We thus have an odd situation. Local authorities have been seeking to extend forms of care within the community. The local authority burden has been reduced in the 1980s, but not particularly through the evolution of community care. Rather a private sector has grown, unconstrained by public authorities' concerns about the importance of maintaining people in the community and using residential places for the most needy. As the situation stands at the time of writing responsibility seems to be moving to the DHSS, to use its controls over the social security system to determine who should be supported in private residential care.

Despite the slight decline in the public sector contribution to the residential care of the elderly, nearly a quarter of local authority personal social services expenditure is devoted to this item.[5] That figure would be larger were it not that some of the cost of care is recovered by means of charges to residents. Charges are determined by means tests, with a minimum charge set by the secretary of state and recoverable from 'income support' where necessary. Local authorities cannot recoup all, or large parts of, their costs from social security as the private homes can!

The cost of residential services for the elderly, together with a concern about institutionalization, has stimulated the search for ways of enhancing community care. One important experiment in Kent,[6] on providing localized budgets to enable service managers to construct 'packages' of care for people in order to keep them out of institutions has attracted wide interest, and a number of attempts to replicate it are proceeding.

The position with regard to residential care for childen is complicated, and rather confusing. A large proportion of the children who are in legal terms 'in the care of the local authorities' are not in fact in any kind of institution, indeed a significant proportion of them are living in their parents' homes. There were about 72,800 children 'in care' in England and Wales in 1985. Of these fifty per cent were boarded out, in foster care, and 17 per cent were under the 'charge and control' of a parent, friend or relative. The remainder, 33 per cent, were in some sort of institutionalized care, about two-thirds of them being in local authority run 'community homes'.[7]

Children may be taken into the 'legal' care of a local authority where parents are unable to care for them, or are deemed to be unfit to care for them. In the first category there is also a group of children, generally older, who are considered to be out of parental control. Care decisions are the responsibility of the courts, but most action to take children into care will have been initiated by social workers in the social services departments. Once a child has been taken into care the local authority will seek to ensure a settled future for him or her. In many cases this will mean return to parental care. Where this is not possible foster care is widely used. Hence, institutional care is likely to be regarded as a temporary expedient in many cases, while the situation is assessed and longer-term plans are made.

Under the 1969 Children and Young Persons Act local authorities acquired increased responsibilities for the care of children brought before the courts for delinquent acts. The object of this legislation was to move further from the labelling of young offenders as criminals, and to make the issue for decision by the juvenile courts one about responsibility for care rather than punishment for crime. Social services departments may now have to undertake the 'supervision' of such children, or they may be given legal custody of them under a 'care order'. They may fulfil the parental responsibilities entailed in a care order in a variety of ways, including the supervision of a child within a residential institution. The former remand homes and approved schools became specially staffed 'community homes' under this legislation. Since many local authorities do not possess the residential resources to fulfil responsibilities of this kind on their own, and in particular lack the necessary range of resources that must include (exceptionally) a 'secure' institution, there are regional planning committees to facilitate the use of homes by authorities other than the ones responsible for their management.

Where the care responsibilities of local authorities are discharged through the use of foster parents, payment will be made and the arrangements will be supervised by social workers. The cost of residential care for children, including fostering, remains a significant element in social service department budgets, consuming over 10 per cent of the total.

This discussion of residential care has involved only two client groups: the elderly and children. The mentally ill and mentally handicapped receive institutional care within the public sector, primarily from the health services, though there is a gradually growing local authority involvement in the provision of hostels and 'half-way' houses. The physically handicapped may exceptionally be accommodated in the old people's homes when they are under pension age, not in need of hospital attention, but unable to care for themselves, or be cared for, within the community. There is some public disquiet about this, and generally the special facilities provided by some of the charities for the younger physically handicapped offer a much preferred alternative.


DAY CARE AND DOMICILIARY SERVICES

Social services departments organize a variety of day care services. For the elderly most provide day centres where people can go for company, social activities, occupational therapy, perhaps cheap midday meals, and maybe some aid or advice. Similar facilities are often provided for handicapped people. For the younger handicapped, and particularly for the mentally handicapped, local authorities provide centres where company and therapy may be accompanied by productive activities. In many cases these are more or less sheltered workshops, doing commercially sponsored work and paying pocket money to handicapped people. There are some difficult distinctions to be drawn here between sheltered work, therapy and provision for some daytime life outside the home.

Social services departments also provide day care for preschool children. These day nurseries were largely developed during the Second World War, but this service has not since grown to a really effective level. Places are few, and are generally only given to children from very deprived backgrounds. In recent years there has been a considerable growth of private provision for day care for young children – daily minding, day nurseries and playgroups – for which the social services departments have supervisory responsibilities. In 1985 there were 679,000 maintained or registered day care places for children under five (not to be confused with nursery school places) in the United Kingdom. Only 33,000 (5 per cent) of these were in local authority maintained day nurseries. 470,000 (69 per cent) were in registered playgroups and 144,000 (21 per cent) were with registered child-minders.[8] There are undoubtedly large numbers of unregistered child-minders.

The primary form of domiciliary care provided by social services departments is the home help service. This has developed remarkably from a service primarily conceived to help in maternity cases to a large enterprise serving predominantly the elderly, and thus playing an important part in helping old people to manage in their own homes. Local authorities in England and Wales provide around the equivalent of 57,000 full-time home helps.[9] The development of the services is, however, uneven. According to the Audit Commission

home help provision varies by a factor of six or more among authorities – from under seven full-time home helps for every 1,000 people aged over 75 (equivalent to less than eight minutes of actual help every week for each person aged over 75) to 44 full-time home helps.[10]

This is another area of care where the public sector is accompanied by a large private sector. People may purchase their own help, and of course, where services are inadequate, the gap is likely to be filled by large amounts of unpaid work by relatives and neighbours. Local authorities may charge for home help services, and may use means tests to determine the level of the charge.

Local authorities may also provide meals, taken to people in their own homes. This 'meals on wheels' service is often provided through a voluntary organization. Again, the extent of coverage by the service varies widely from area to area, from, at one extreme, a 'token' meal a week to, at the other, the provision of a comprehensive, seven days a week service. Local authorities may set charges for this service; the extent to which they subsidize it is also variable.

Local authorities provide a range of other 'benefits in kind' to assist with the care of people within the community. The Chronically Sick and Disabled Persons Act of 1970 suggests a wide range of services that local authorities may offer to the handicapped. Despite the emphasis in that Act upon local authority duties, the word 'may' in the last sentence is appropriate. There are wide variations in the adequacy of the help provided. Authorities may provide, and pay the rental costs of, telephones; they may adapt houses to meet the needs of the disabled; and they are able to provide a variety of aids to daily living. They tend, however, to impose budgetary limits that ration quite severely the money available for such benefits. However, a further piece of legislation, the Disabled Persons (Services, Consultation and Representation) Act of 1986, increases the rights of the disabled to be informed about provisions and consulted about their needs. This should have the effect of increasing the flow of services to the disabled.

## FIELDWORK

The services provided by local authorities that were described above as 'fieldwork' include visiting by social workers, social work assistants, occupational therapists and volunteers recruited and organized by social services departments. The social work aspect of this is often emphasized; in Scotland the departments are called 'social work departments', and in England and Wales social workers are the dominant professional group and occupy many senior management roles. But it is important to recognize that the support of people in their own homes is carried out by a variety of workers, not all of whom are, or should be regarded as, social workers. The distinction here between the social work task and other tasks is a difficult one to make. The public often makes no distinction between social work and many other 'caring activities', yet social workers are increasingly preoccupied by a concern to define their task. This has implications not only for social workers' 'professional' aspirations, but also for the costs of various services, since trained social workers are relatively expensive.

The activities of fieldworkers arise from a range of duties of social services departments: the responsibility for the care of children, under various Childrens Acts, which requires visiting where child abuse or neglect is suspected; the supervision of children both under directions from courts and under a duty to prevent harm and keep them wherever possible with their families; the investigation and supervision of adoption and fostering arrangements; and a general readiness to respond to cries for help from families under all kinds of pressure. Fieldworkers are required to help in various ways with the care of the mentally ill and handicapped within the community, and social workers have statutory duties under the 1983 Mental Health Act to assess and take appropriate action when the mentally ill appear to require compulsory hospitalization. The care of the elderly and handicapped in the community involves a need both for visiting to give support and advice, and for the assessment of special needs for services or aids. Where authorities employ occupational therapists they play an important part in assessing the needs of, and helping, the disabled. Authorities often also employ specialist social workers for the blind, and sometimes for the deaf. Occupational therapists have a range of responsibilities, often including the teaching of mobility skills, in addition to their social work tasks.

On the reorganization of the National Health Service in 1974 the local authority social services departments were given responsibility for hospital social work. This service evolved from two very different traditions. In connection with the more advanced mental hospitals a quite sophisticated psychiatric social work profession had developed, often leading the way in the provision of case work both within hospitals and among their out-patients. In the general hospitals, on the other hand, social work had its origins in the activities of the almoners required, before the coming of the National Health Service, to assess patients' capacities to pay fees. Once hospital treatment was free this group of social workers took on a variety of different jobs. In many cases they were regarded primarily as important for links between hospitals and the community, and in particular therefore for arrangements with regard to the discharge of patients. Yet others, particularly in the more sophisticated hospitals, developed forms of case work and counselling, to help patients deal with the psychological and social problems that often accompany medical ones. Hospital social work therefore has very mixed traditions, and is very patchily developed today. Now an important issue for hospital social workers is how to integrate with community-based social work while remaining one of the professional groups involved in the hospital service.[11] They share this last problem with the social workers employed in the child guidance service, who are social services employees working alongside psychiatrists from the health service and psychologists from the education service, within administrative arrangements that are a product of local compromises between the three services involved.

## FORWARD PLANNING, NEEDS AND PRIORITIES

The integration of the local authority social services occurred at a time
when local government was becoming increasingly conscious of the need
for forward planning, and for co-ordination between services by means
of corporate planning. The new social services departments brought
together services that had hitherto been poorly co-ordinated, and that
had made relatively low demands on local authority resources. Clearly
the departments had to plan much more coherently for the future.
Indeed, central government gave these new departments specific duties
to carry out research and undertake forward planning. A similar
increased emphasis upon planning was affecting the organization of
central government. The DHSS, which acquired responsibility for all
the personal social services after their local reorganization, was required
to assess the needs both of these services and of the health services, and
to integrate the two.

The DHSS initially required local authorities to prepare ten-year
forward plans. Subsequently it was decided that such long-term plans
could not be co-ordinated successfully at a national level. Moreover, the
reorganization of local government, which followed only three years
after the creation of social services departments, and the fairly dramatic
change in public expenditure plans as a consequence of inflation and
efforts to control it by curbing public spending, rendered these long-
term plans comparatively irrelevant. They also had inevitable weaknesses as documents prepared hurriedly, often with inadequate data and
in advance of necessary research. In 1976 the DHSS adopted a more
limited but more systematic approach to forward planning. It required
local authorities to provide figures on levels of provision and expenditure in the current year, estimates for the next year and forecasts for
two further years. This involved filling in a relatively straightforward
form (which related well to the kind of information authorities were
already assembling for their own budgeting needs) and supporting it by
narrative comment. This exercise was sufficiently limited and precise to
enable the DHSS to assemble national data, make comparisons between
authorities and feed its observations back to local authorities. The new
Conservative government abandoned this exercise in 1980, probably
largely because planned expenditure reductions would so limit growth
as to make forward planning statements irrelevant.

An interesting feature of the abandoned exercise, and therefore of
possible future ones, was the way in which the DHSS tried to secure a
more rational basis for loan sanctions based upon a balance between
national and local priorities. The DHSS expected local authorities to
bear in mind its statements on national priorities,[12] but to relate them to

local ones. When it made decisions about the acceptability of new local initiatives, therefore, it endeavoured to relate its views about their compatibility with national policies to the evidence local authorities had provided about different local needs. Cynics within local government saw the planning system as a further DHSS invasion of local autonomy. The DHSS rejoinder was that, on the contrary, the system enabled it to be more sensitive to local needs. There was a conflict, of course, if local and national policies clashed, and there was no special evidence that local needs differed.

There were two important sources of complications for the planning processs, both of which remain important despite the abandonment of a formal national system. One of these is the way in which the personal social services system under local authority control is inextricably bound up with the National Health Service. This issue will be explored further in a later section. The other is, as was seen when the relationship between public and private residential care was discussed, that the assessment of needs for social services is bedevilled by the fact that in many areas of this work the statutory services provide only a small part of the total care and support within the community. The total need for statutory residential or domiciliary services depends upon the other ways in which these needs, or their equivalents, are met. This means in fact that there is a confusing relationship between needs and the availability of services. The scarcity of social care produces not only heavy demands on the local authorities but also extensive efforts to meet the need for it in other ways.

The increased recognition in the 1980s of the limited funds available for public services, and the relationship between this and the growing needs for social care (as a result, for example, of the growth in numbers of the very old) has sharpened concern to find ways of balancing the respective contributions to the 'mixed economy of welfare'. While this is sometimes presented as a new issue, social care has always involved some combination of care within the family and community, care which is bought, care which is provided by voluntary and charitable agencies, and care which is provided by public agencies. What is perhaps new is acceptance that the contribution from the last source is inherently limited. Hence the development of a lively debate about the roles of the other forms of care.

An important part of that debate concerns the search for ways of defining need, and identifying how public agencies should respond to it. Economists have an approach to this issue. They tend to relate need to demand, and stress the virtue of the price mechanism as a means of adjusting services to demands. If there is a high demand for a particular thing then this will be reflected in a willingness to pay higher prices. Higher rewards will attract more suppliers, and may ultimately bring down the price. Always however an equilibrium is maintained in which supply and demand are balanced by the price mechanism. To what extent does this offer a solution to the problem of needs in the social services? Clearly it does not if the local authority is the only supplier of a particular service. Then conditions of monopoly exist in which prices are determined by the supply available, and those who are unwilling or unable to pay them must go without. The attempt to identify real needs regardless of ability to pay is the hallmark of the public service here. Rationing according to the capacity to pay is quite widely regarded as a bad way to distribute many services. The price mechanism solution is also inappropriate where is it arguable that people who need particular services are unlikely to recognize the need and translate it into an effective, money-backed, demand. Social work services designed primarily to protect children from their parents will fall into this category. There remain services, however, like the home help service, that are provided both by the statutory authorities and by the private market. In some senses the need for these services can be regarded as fairly limitless – most of us would like our domestic chores to be done by someone else. The price mechanism seems to offer a basis for distinguishing this absolute need from effective demand, and of allowing for the existence, side by side, of a public and private sector.

This is all fair enough in theory, but what about those with high needs, in some absolute sense, but a low capacity to pay? There are two possible answers to this objection to the use of the price mechanism. One is that social affairs should be arranged in such a way that what are really income maintenance problems do not have to be solved by the provision of subsidized services. This is an attractive argument, but one that poorly matches the real world. The other is that means tests should be devised to enable cheaper services to be given in some cases. The trouble with this solution is that it can cope with situations in which only a minority have to be helped outside the market place, but it quite destroys the market concept when it has to be very widespread. The reality is, for many of the personal social services (including the home help service), that some more fundamental way of defining need is required: a minority can buy the services on the open market; there remains a large group who appear to need them free or at a reduced price, only some of whom receive them. The problem remains of determining how much the service should expand to meet the unmet needs.[13]

This digression into the market approach to need was necessary, first because it has significant advocates and second because it offers an approach to the definition of need. The alternative is the ascertainment of some more absolute way of determining need. In some cases this does not seem so problematical; in relation to some diseases, for example, there may be a finite group whom it is generally agreed are in need of treatment. But in other cases the problem is one of making a distinction between 'absolute need' and some more limited concept. While I may contend that I need my house cleaned in order to free me to write books, you may argue that I am still physically capable of doing this work while others are not. They, you will say, are the ones really in need. But would this be a disagreement about needs or about priorities?

For the personal social services, then, the determination of needs is complicated, first, by the fact that the departments do not have the sole responsibility to meet certain kinds of needs, and second because their views of needs must be determined by their views of priorities. Both of these problems are not ones that can be solved by more and better research. Research may be required once they have begun to answer the more fundamental questions, but first they have to resolve difficult questions about the limits of the statutory social services' contribution to the solution of the social problems, and about the importance of any specific service relative to others.

These are dilemmas for all public policy, and particularly for all social policy. Finite resources require choices, in the last resort, between more education and more health services, for example. Within specific departments, and particularly within personal social services with their very mixed collection of services to various client groups, the weighing of priorities is a particularly difficult political exercise.

These, then, are the fundamental problems for forward planning. But it would be misleading to suggest that departments, and committees, necessarily spend a great deal of time worrying about these issues. They are perhaps more likely to give attention to what are, in effect, second-order problems. How many people are there who are not getting help despite the fact that they are at least as disadvantaged as those who obtain services? To what extent does the authority's level of provision fail to meet the needs of people who are helped in other areas? Is it possible to identify specfic consequences of help, or failure to help, in terms of family breakdown, hospitalization, etc.? What alternative sources of help are there in the area and can these be supported as well as supplemented? Is the composition of the population who are helped changing in ways that will make the present package of services inappropriate in the future? The importance of questions like these should not be minimized, but they must be placed against a background of extreme uncertainty about needs, about the roles of social services departments in relation to those needs, and about the difficulty of what seem to be invidious judgements about the relative priorities to be accorded to various groups of needy people. These fundamental questions seem to call for political solutions. But politicians are reluctant to try to answer them; they often respond by providing roughly the mixture as before. In chapter 3 it was suggested, moreover, that the British form of democratic politics does not provide very satisfactory mechanisms for settling issues of this kind. Often the key issues are pushed back to the administrators and professionals, and believed to be matters for expert judgement. This is an issue that will be raised again in chapter 7 on the health service.

## THE PLACE OF SOCIAL WORK IN THE SOCIAL SERVICES DEPARTMENTS

One of the most difficult elements for forward planning and priority determination within social services departments is that part of the service that is provided by social workers and related staff. It has already been suggested that many of the needs for social work help are seldom expressed, at least not in any straightforward sense. The pressures that lead to calls for more social work come from the anxieties of the public and politicians about child abuse, the deterioration of old people who live alone, or the disturbance caused by aggressive mentally ill people, for example. These are issues of social control as much as of service. Pressure also comes from the many requests that come to social services departments that are not so much for specific services as for help with a wide range of problems of poverty and deprivation. Social work is seen as having a contribution to make to the problems of underprivileged communities in many different ways; indeed, often these expectations go far beyond the profession's capacities, particularly when political and economic problems are perceived as social or individual ones.

There is a wide but essentially diffuse demand, therefore, for the social services workers. Forward planning exercises in social services departments find it difficult to categorize the actual contribution made by social workers. Social workers, inasmuch as they seek to protect their day-to-day activities from hierarchical scrutiny and control, contribute to this imprecision. It is also fostered by their own uncertainty about their work, and by controversy within the profession about the essential ingredients of the social work task.

There has been in recent years an extensive debate about what social work is, and a related one about whether it can be practised within local authority social services departments. This seems to have various interlocking dimensions. There is a concern about the relationship between social work and a variety of, perhaps more mundane, supporting tasks that may be performed. Thus Butrym distinguishes between:[14]

1  'provision for the quality of inner life', which she regards as the social work task above all;

2   providing 'support and containment', which is partly a social work task but may also be performed by others, including volunteers;

3   dealing with 'matters of right and entitlement', where social workers need to know of the services available but should not be concerned with the day-to-day administration;

4   dealing with other agencies, where the social worker's task is to transmit relevant needs 'to appropriate institutions and to press for necessary changes to policies'.

A British Association of Social Workers working party has similarly published an elaborate attempt to distinguish some of the more complex tasks which require special skills, including in particular skills in dealing with interpersonal relationships, from more mundane activities.[15] A quasi-official investigatory committee looked at this issue in response to growing criticism of social work, and in a report published in 1982 broadly endorsed these attempts to distinguish a core of tasks requiring social work expertise from the wider activities surrounding them.[16]

But critics of social work have condemned the quasi-psychiatric emphasis in some of this theorizing, suggesting that above all social workers should give relatively straightforward and practical help to people trying to cope with problems of deprivation.[17] The significance of this debate is, first, its implications for the balance to be achieved by departments between the use of trained social work staff and the use of less trained personnel (including perhaps volunteers). Second, if at the core of the social work task lies intensive work with individuals with special problems, to what extent can such work be done in public authorities and, if it can be done there, what arrangements need to be made to protect this case work from the other pressures upon social work time? Third, and alternatively, if a wide range of work with problems of deprivation is to be performed by social workers, how are the boundaries to this work to be determined, and what are its implications for relationships between social services departments and other agencies?

The traditional model of social work, with its concern with individual problem-solving, sees as its key method 'case work', requiring intensive relationships with individuals and families. But two other approaches to social work given increasing attention these days are 'group work' and 'community work'. To these should be added a fourth, an 'integrated' approach embracing all of the other three approaches according to the demands of the situations.[18] Group work clearly has a place within the statutory framework for local authority social work. This is emphasized by the inclusion within the 1969 Children and Young Persons Act of provision for 'intermediate treatment', involving help to delinquent children through shared activities with others. The position of community work is more controversial. This kind of work involves working with the communities to help them solve their own problems. There is, however, a radical school of community work which stresses the importance of the mobilization of groups against the power structure in the community. There is scope for argument, first, as to whether this work really is social work and, second, whether it has a place within the framework of the local authority social services department. Schools of social work offer community work training, or a community work option, to their students. But community workers are also trained in other ways. Local authorities employ community workers to some extent, and some authorities tolerate relatively radical activities. They vary in the extent to which they see a need to integrate this work with social work. This argument for a more radical approach to social work is particularly pertinent where traditional case work methods come up against cultural differences, as in ethnic minority communities.

There is one further dimension to the debate about the social work task which must be mentioned here. Before the integration of local authority social services departments, many social workers specialized by client group; indeed, this specialization was determined largely by the department in which they worked. Part of the case for integration of the personal social services was the argument that social work involved skills usable with, or transferable to, varying client groups. The new generic departments matched a generic concept of social work. The initial problem for most departments was to get social workers from different backgrounds to work together. To this end the generic approach was emphasized. Once the achievement of integration was no longer an issue, social workers began to explore the scope for specialization within the generic department. This specialization might be in terms of methods of work, or in terms of kinds of problems tackled; but it might also be a return to client group specialization.

At the same time, however, an informal, *de facto* kind of specialization is developing within departments. Child care work is particularly seen as deserving of expert attention. This may be attributed to a variety of things: the clear statutory requirement about visiting and reporting where the courts are involved with child care problems, the very high anxieties raised within social work and the public at large by child abuse and neglect, and the importance within the departments of staff with children's department backgrounds. Mental health work is also seen as important in some areas, and its underlying significance is emphasized by the emergency powers possessed by social workers and by the recognition, in the 1983 Mental Health Act, of the need for special additional training for this work. Work with the mentally handicapped, physically handicapped and elderly, on the other hand, is seen as less pressing and more routine. The consequence is that child care work and mental health work is regarded as requiring the attention of the most experienced qualified staff, while the other activities are more readily delegated to others. Social work teams are likely to contain both qualified staff and some social work assistants (or social service officers). Matching this division of 'skill' there tends to be a division of work on the lines suggested above. Often social work assistants are the only 'specialists' in work with the elderly.[19]

Recently, attempts have been made to ensure that real specialization occurs in social services departments as opposed to this *de facto* specialization with its unfortunate assumptions about kinds of clients and levels of work. However, the argument for and against specialization continues to be a live one. One movement back against specialization has emphasized the need for social workers to relate to small areas or 'patches'.[20] This derives its strength from the concerns with community work or with 'integrated' work discussed above.

### THE RELATIONSHIP BETWEEN THE PERSONAL SOCIAL SERVICES AND INCOME MAINTENANCE

Some of the functions that today are within the social services departments have at earlier times been within local authority health, education or even housing departments. However, further back in time, before 1948, there was a strong association between the personal social services and income maintenance within the poor law. It is worthwhile to look a little more at the separation of these two services that exists today, and at some of the factors that partially undermine that separation, particularly because they have important implications for some of the dilemmas about the social work role.

The political commitment, in the 1940s, to separating income maintenance from the personal social services was influenced by a hatred of the poor law. It was seen as possible to develop services for all freed from the stigma of the means test and the workhouse if the National Assistance Act of 1948 gave all income maintenance responsibilities to a national body and the duty to provide residential and domiciliary care to the local authorities. The services for children were given a quite distinct identity by the Children Act of 1948, and developed their own special approach to community care within the children's departments of the local authorities. A concept of social work was able to develop, very different from that within the United States welfare departments, where income maintenance and social work are closely linked. Social workers, regardless of their political persuasion, have come to see it as very important that they are able to give aid, advice and support to their clients without at the same time having responsibility for their incomes. What this implies is that, whereas personal social services under the poor law were essentially for the poor, and were very involved in the control of the lives of the poor, today in the British system it is possible to conceive of the benefits of the services as available to all without discrimination.

That, then, is the ideal; the reality is a little different.[21] It is clearly the case that a very high proportion of the users of the personal social services are low income people. It is quite hard to envisage a situation in which it could be otherwise. The peculiarity of the personal social services is that they are concerned with a range of benefits that is also provided in other very different ways, by both commercial enterprises and voluntary activities. The very existence of a statutory group of services of this kind poses some delicate questions about the nature of the balance between this and individual, family and community, provisions. The assumption is that the statutory provisions are necessary when the others fail. Politicians get worried about the possibility that private responsibilities will be abandoned in favour of public ones. This is possible; it is in the nature of statutory intervention into areas generally the realm of private action that it may alter behaviour. However, the evidence is that typically those who seek help from the personal social services do so when other possibilities no longer exist. An absence of other ways of meeting such needs is particularly associated with poverty.

Several connections between income maintenance and the personal social services therefore exist. Many of the services are rationed by means of charges, motivated at least partially by that political concern to keep down the expected volume of demands upon the service. If charges are not to deter the poor, however, they must be abated through means tests. These need to be related to the other means tests within the social security system. That is one connection; the other is more complicated and more clearly explains the social workers' concern about separation of their services from income maintenance. There is a correlation between the forms of pathology that come to the attention of social workers – delinquency, child abuse, even publicly threatening mental illness – and poverty.[22] It is difficult to summarize here a very complex, and deeply value-laden, debate. Strands within it include arguments about the extent to which the rich can hide their pathology, or seek help from sources other than social services departments; about the extent to which poverty *causes* social pathology and vice versa; and about the extent to which this 'deviancy' simply involves a labelling of the non-conformity of the poor. The fact is, however, that it is primarily low income people who become the clients of publicly employed social workers.

It is this fact that leads many who have written about social work to stress the importance of a relationship with the poor that does not include responsilbilty for their incomes.[23] Yet at the same time many social workers recognize a need to help clients with their income maintenance problems. There is a power under Section One of the 1980 Child Care Act and under a related but rather more all-embracing provision in Scotland, enabling money payments to be made to help social services clients where these might assist in keeping children out of care. Here, then, is a statutory recognition of a connection between lack of money and social pathology. Yet this power is comparatively little used, and several writers have drawn attention to the danger that it might be used to reward good behaviour and become a social control device within social work.[24] In general, an alternative approach is preferred in which social workers assist clients to claim benefits from other agencies. Such work is generally described as 'welfare rights work'. To some degree, in many authorities, specialist workers, who are often not social workers, have been taken on to do this sort of work. There has also been a considerable growth of aid and advice work on welfare benefit problems in voluntary agencies and advice bureaux. However, social workers are bound to have to take on some of this work; some do it with great commitment while others feel it will distort their activities and pull them away from 'real' social work.

The character of welfare rights workers has changed as the social security system has changed. Before 1980 the concern was to get supplementary benefits officers to exercise their extensive discretionary powers. After 1980 the complex structure of apparent 'rights' required that poor people secured help in finding their way through the regulations, identifying things to which they were entitled and getting the increasingly hard-pressed social security administration to grind into action. The social security changes brought in by the 1986 Act have thrown the social workers and welfare rights specialists into turmoil. Rights to single payments have more or less disappeared. The new Social Fund scheme seems to require social services personnel to replace the conflictual pattern of behaviour required to secure rights by collaboration with social security officers to determine need for 'community care' grants. The loans provisions for other forms of help, administered by officers with high levels of discretion, similarly suggest a need for a very different approach to getting resources for clients. The position is further complicated by the fact that social services departments retain a power to make grants, under the 1980 Child Care Act. This is a power that has been little used, and most departmental budgets for this item are limited. If this were to change, or if social workers are co-opted into helping determine needs for Social Fund grants and loans, social workers could be back to money-rationing responsibilities in a big way.

## THE ROLE OF THE VOLUNTARY SECTOR

Reference has already been made to the 'mixed economy of welfare'; voluntary agencies are, alongside family, community and private enterprise, an element of considerable importance. Voluntary organizations carry out many functions on behalf of social services departments. These entail large grants, and in some cases the voluntary component of the work is small. Thus some departments use a voluntary agency to provide a range of services to the blind. A service widely provided in this way, but involving a large component of voluntary work, is the 'meals-on-wheels' service. The Women's Royal Voluntary Service is often responsible for this.

Social service departments also help to support the activities of voluntary organizations. These range from large organizations offering special forms of residential and domiciliary care to quite small local community ventures. While some of this work may be meeting needs that would otherwise be met by the departments, in many cases the voluntary ventures that are subsidized undertake tasks that are quite distinct, and perhaps innovatory.

There is a variety of ways in which individul volunteers are used in the personal social services. They may be deployed under the auspices of voluntary agencies; they may be organized under schemes requiring community services of convicted offenders, or schemes to provide work for the unemployed in return for special allowances (should those in these two categories properly be called volunteers?); or they may be individuals who undertake, by direct arrangements with the departments, to help with particular tasks. A wide range of tasks may be involved: supportive visiting of clients, taking people from residential homes out in cars, helping social services clients withdecorating or gardening, helping to run clubs and day centres, and so on.

All this voluntary input into the personal social services may be seen as helping to multiply the amount and range of services available for a given amount of public expenditure. It may also be seen as adding a community dimension to a service that is in danger of becoming too bureaucratized and professionalized. Some of it is a logical extension of the way in which the personal social services are called in to replace or buttress independent caring in the community. It may be seen in this way as helping to put back a community support system that, in the best of all worlds, should have been there.

However, there are problems about this balance between statutory effort and voluntary effort. It may be seen as a way of achieving personal social services 'on the cheap', with departments helping to provide partial and inadequate voluntary services instead of meeting their obligations to provide more comprehensive direct ones.

While above it was suggested that volunteer services may be better than bureaucratic or professional ones, they may alternatively be worse. Social workers who are reluctant to make use of volunteers suggest that they may be unreliable, they may be indiscreet, they may give gratuitous advice where none is desired, and they may give bad advice and interfere in problems they do not understand.[25] Voluntary help typically comes from people who are very unlike the people who need help – groups such as middle-class, middle-aged, married women are prominent among the ranks of volunteers.

It may be argued that what is needed in many situations is the development of community-based self-help activities, not the importation of volunteers from outside. On the other hand it would be rash to suggest that this form of voluntary activity is without its problems. Some of the points about reliability and discretion certainly apply with this form of voluntary activity. Equally, encouraging situations in which communities help themselves may also be seen as providing social services on the cheap. If it is not to be seen like this then another problem must be confronted, that community self-help may also entail the making of demands for new services from the departments. This form of voluntary activity may therefore imply situations in which departments subsidize their own pressure groups. Some social services departments have been able to accept relationships with the voluntary sector that involve this. However, many others have been unwilling to see volunteers in other than traditional, supplementary, service-giving roles.

## THE RELATIONSHIP BETWEEN PERSONAL SOCIAL SERVICES AND THE HEALTH SERVICE

In many respects the concerns of the health service and those of the social services departments overlap. The following are a few key examples. In the planning of services for the elderly, the mentally ill, the mentally handicapped and the physically handicapped attention has been given to the way in which people are likely to require mixtures of health care and social care. In this example what is particularly relevant is the modern concern to maximize care within the community rather than inside institutions. What this implies is a combination of medical care from general practitioners and community-based nursing staff, on the one hand, and social care, from home helps, social workers and so on, on the other. Deficiencies on either side may have to be made up by extra services on the other.

The discharge of patients from hospital in itself has substantial implications for personal social services provision. It is important that social support services are readily available at this stage. Hence day-to-day co-ordination between the two services is crucial. Reference has already been made to the extent to which discharge of people from geriatric wards will have implications for residential homes. Conversely, when old people's homes can no longer cope with their sickest inhabitants hospital services need to be readily accessible. Indeed this two-way exchange encourages forms of 'trading' between the two departments.

A very different example for the need for inter-service co-ordination and co-operation is supplied by the problem of child abuse. Non-accidental injury to children is frequently discovered by doctors and health visitors, yet it is the social services departments that have the responsibility for preventive and legal action in these circumstances. On the other hand, where social workers suspect child abuse they may need medical confirmation of their suspicions. Once child abuse is suspected continued vigilance is necessary. Sometimes it is a health service worker who is best placed to maintain a watching brief, sometimes it is a social worker. In many cases both departments accumulate evidence on this problem; it is important that they share that evidence both formally through case conferences and informally.[26]

These are just a few examples of situations in which the relationship between the two services is significant. Many others could be given, both where joint planning of services is important and where joint action and cross-referral is required. Their importance has led the DHSS to encourage, and the local agencies to adopt, a variety of means of developing links.

At the service planning level the DHSS has led the way by emphasizing the need to look at National Health Service and personal social services together.[29] Within individual localities it has encouraged the development of formal joint planning activities. A particular stimulus to this has been provided by 'joint financing'. Money from within the health service budget is made available to help to finance projects within the social services departments that can be considered to meet needs that might otherwise have to be met by the health service. In the long run social services departments are expected to take over the full cost of these ventures. However, where positive progress can be made in the shift of people from institutional to community care a more direct transfer of resources from health to personal social services may occur.

There is nevertheless still concern about the extent to which the boundaries between the NHS and local government hinder the development of integrated community care. This was one of the main concerns of the Audit Commission report on Community Care.[28] It pointed out the extent to which the local government grant system continues to inhibit developments and felt that much more could be done to shift resources from the health service. It argued that the management arrangements for individual services are still too fragmented and the joint planning systems are ponderous and time-consuming. It therefore suggested that the organizational framework for community care could be radically altered, to provide for integration of services in respect of specific client groups. Specifically it suggested that local authorities could be made responsible for the long-term care of all but the most severely disabled amongst physically and mentally handicapped people, a single budget from both local authority and NHS under the control of a single manager could be provided for the care of the elderly, and services for the mentally ill could be largely brought under the control of the NHS. The government has asked Sir Roy Griffiths to report to them on these issues. His report is expected by the end of 1987.

CONCLUSIONS

The responsibilities of the social services departments, in England and Wales, involve a wide collection of activities. These range from the provision of relatively precise benefits, through a variety of residential and day care facilities, to a number of very personal and individualized services. They include a high proportion of the social work practised in this country.

The mixture of activities has grown rapidly. This growth is perceived with quite considerable anxiety by the public, since most of the activities were hitherto undertaken outside the statutory sector, within the family and the community. One interpretation of this growth is that public services can now be provided to help to strengthen family and community life. If this view is taken then residential care replaces the neglect of the isolated old, and social work helps families to cope with crises that would hitherto have destroyed them, and so on. But there is an alternative view that the growth in these services is in itself an index of social pathology, that people are not coping so well with aspects of life that in the past were of little concern to public services. This ambivalence is compounded by widespread uncertainty about what social services departments do (indeed, they are often confused with social security departments), a very vague conception of the social worker's role (shared, it seems, by many social workers), and a deep uncertainty about the circumstances in which help may be sought from the various specific services.

## SUGGESTIONS FOR FURTHER READING

Two general books on the personal social services which are recommended are Christine Hallett's *The Personal Social Services in Local Government*,[29] and Adrian Webb and Gerald Wistow's *Social Work, Social Care and Social Planning: The Personal Social Services since Seebohm*.[30] Books by Judge (see n. 13) and Booth also deal with many of the financial and planning issues in this area of policy.[31] The book on the social work task cited in n. 16 gives a portrait of the activities of fieldwork teams, as does Goldberg and Warburton's *Ends and Means in Social Work*.[32] A variety of different perspectives on what the social work task should comprise are provided in the books by Butrym (see n. 14), Specht and Vickery (see n. 18), and Jordan (see n. 21).

A good account of community work in social services departments is provided by Thomas and Warburton.[33] The author and Peter Laing have explored the issue of the relationship between social work and income maintenance in their *Social Work and Money* (see n. 21), though, as has been pointed out in this chapter, this is at the moment a rapidly changing scene.

The issue of the 'mixed economy of welfare' is explored in an article by Judge.[34] Issues about community care and public expenditure in ‚the social services have been explored in Webb and Wistow's *Planning Need and Scarcity*,[35] and in Glennerster's *Paying for Welfare*.[36] The Audit Commission's report (see n.4) quoted in the chapter offers an incisive critique of community care in practice.

# CHAPTER 7

# The Health Service

## THE ORGANIZATION OF THE SERVICE

By contrast with the beginning of chapter 6 on the personal social services, the first part of this chapter needs to be less concerned with what the service does – people are relatively clearer about this – but more concerned with how it does it, and particularly how it is organized. Clearly, the ingredients of the health service are hospitals, the primary care practitioners (doctors, dentists, pharmacists and opticians operating outside the hospitals), and other community-based services (community nursing and health visiting, and preventive medicine). One of the most confusing aspects of the health service is the structure that has been designed to contain, and if possible integrate, these various activities.

The basic structure of the system within England can be represented diagrammatically, as in figure 7.1. England is divided into fourteen regions. In addition to planning and advisory responsibilities, the regions have a range of responsibilites for the hospital sector: the appointment of specialist medical staff (except in areas containing medical schools) and the planning and management of capital expenditure in particular. The districts, of which there are 192 in England, have overall responsibility for the planning and provision of comprehensive services in the territories they cover. It will be seen from the diagram that at that level there are also separate family practitioner committees responsible for primary care. The districts are concerned with day-to-day running of the hospital and community services (but not general practitioner services). Within the districts there are subdivisions for administrative purposes, known as units.

In Scotland and Wales responsibility for the service is that of separate ministers (the secretaries of state for Scotland and Wales) and separate departments. This devolved structure enables the omission of the regional tier in the system. In Scotland the next tier authorities are called health boards, and most of them have another tier of districts

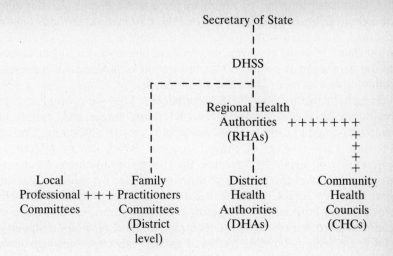

FIGURE 7.1　Basic structure of the health service in England (only those links indicated --- can be called 'hierarchical', see text, where all the links are described)

under them. In Northern Ireland there are four health and social services boards with 'area' responsibilities, each responsible for a number of units.

The structure described here was set up in 1982. Soon after it was set up the government commissioned Sir Roy Griffiths, Managing Director of Sainsbury's, to lead a team to examine the management structure for the NHS in England. Griffiths reported in 1983, recommending a structure which was a radical departure from the collegial approach, involving management teams of administrators and professionals (doctors, nurses etc.), then prevailing in the service. His recommendations were adopted, and extended to the other parts of the United Kingdom.

As a consequence of the Griffiths recommendations there is now in England a Health Service Supervisory Board chaired by the Secretary of State for Social Services; included on it are the Minister of State (Health), the Senior Permanent Secretary in DHSS, the Chief Medical Officer (another DHSS official) and the Chairman of the NHS Management Board. The last named is a special appointee, from the private sector, who heads a board set up to control the service as a whole. Then each region, district and unit has also had to appoint a general manager, each on a fixed-term contract. Many of these general managers were already health service administrators, but there have been appointments from outside and in some cases senior professionals, particularly doctors but occasionally nurses, have received these posts. A centralized system of accountability has partly superseded the system of decentralization to regional and district authorities. What this implies in practice is still far from clear. What is, however, very evident about the Griffiths changes to the management system is that the system of professional representation in management has been undermined.

Hospital doctors are NHS appointees. They are organized in consultant-led teams. Consultants are RHA appointees, and continue to exercise, despite Griffiths, a considerable degree of autonomy. Crucial for this is the concept of clinical freedom, which can be effectively extended from a right to determine the treatment of individual patients to a right to plan the pattern of care as a whole. Consultants may be part-time appointees, enabled to combine private practice with NHS work. Junior hospital doctors, below consultant status, are organized in consultant-led teams. Many of them are in short-term appointments, which are seen as building blocks of trainee experience leading up to consultant status. There are problems of relatively low pay, heavy duties and insecurity for junior doctors, enhanced by difficulties in advancing to consultancies.

The access of patients to the hospital system is normally by way of a general practitioner referral, though direct self-referral is acceptable in the event of accidents and emergencies. Once under hospital care individuals may be treated as in-patients or out-patients. The general notion here is of a hospital-based service for problems that are beyond either the expertise or the resources of general practitioners and the 'primary care' teams. However, the lines are sometimes blurred. Modern health centres can often provide services that are elsewhere provided by hospitals. Similarly community hospitals provide, in some areas, limited service of a kind traditionally provided by 'cottage hospitals', and they will involve general practitioners in their work.

The general medical practitioners operate, under contracts granted by the Family Practitioner Committees, a system in which, broadly speaking, they are free to decide how they will organize their practice and free to accept or reject patients. They are paid primarily on a 'capitation' basis, so much for each patient on their list together with an allowance for practice expenses and special payments for various exceptional tasks undertaken. The system of payments has been the subject of extensive negotiations and conflict between the doctors and the secretary of state, in the course of which the scheme has been elaborated in a variety of ways to include such things as additional fees for elderly people on doctors' lists, and payments for night and weekend work. While the doctors have clearly been eager to secure maximum rewards but to remain within a system that preserves their freedom, the government's objectives in these negotiations have included the encouragement of forms of group practice, the development of health centres and an increase in the number of doctors practising in some areas. In the last few years the general practitioner service has grown much more sophisticated. Isolated independent practice has declined, and health centres, providing a wide range of medical services, have multiplied.

Dentists, opticians and pharmacists are paid on a fee-for-service basis. The complications over maintenance of lists do not apply in their cases. However, there are problems, particularly as far as dentists are concerned, about the setting of a system of remuneration that rewards most adequately the best practice, is administratively straightforward and can be supervised without detailed surveillance of day-to-day activities.

The dental, optical and pharmaceutical services are, like general medical practice, administered by the family practitioner committees. These are set up by the secretary of state and include DHA appointees, local authority nominees and representatives of the local medical, dental, pharmaceutical and optical committees, which are entirely in the control of the relevant professional groups. The family practitioner committees have responsibilities to see that the various services are available in their district, to help patients obtain practitioners and to deal with complaints.

Prior to reorganization in 1974 the local authorities provided some of the community health services, under the direction of the medical officers of health. They were responsible for community nursing services, the running of maternity clinics, measures to prevent the spread of infectious diseases, and a range of public health responsibilities (controls against impure foods, insanitary living conditions etc.). There was also a separate school health service, although usually the medical officer of health was also in charge of this. Reorganization left the district councils with the public health responsibilities, but shifted all other services under the wings of the health authorities.

The service reorganization of 1982 and the introduction of the Griffiths system of management has rather dispersed this 'community health' group of activities. In 1974 one possibility was that community medicine would assume a key role in the planning of the service, extending concerns about preventive medicine. Now such specialists are rarely found in key management roles. The community nursing services remain in some areas within district management units, but in others have been dispersed into units also containing hospital staff. At local levels there has been some scope for the development of 'primary care teams', groups of health service workers based upon a health centre and sharing a common clientele. But at that level community teamwork is made more difficult bý the independence of the general medical practitioners. It is ironic that the use of the medical practice as the basic building block of a community-based organization requires the members of the team who are not in the employment of the DHA, the doctors, to be the linchpins of the system.

The NHS is financed out of national taxation. In 1985–6,[1] in Great Britain, it cost about 17,500 million. Of this 72 per cent was spent on hospital and community services, 24 per cent on family practitioner services and the remaining 4 per cent on a miscellaneous group of centrally run services. Throughout its history the growing cost of the health service to the Exchequer has been a matter of political concern. Demographic changes affecting need, technological changes affecting the quality of treatment, and rising staff costs mean that the cost of the NHS increases without the public necessarily being aware of any improvement in the service it provides. Attempts have been made to estimate how much expenditure has to grow each year merely to maintain a consistent level of services to the public. A conservative estimate puts it at 2 per cent, but many suggest it is nearer 4 or 5 per cent.[2] This is important in explaining how, in recent years, we have found both the public and NHS practitioners complaining of falling standards, supported by concrete evidence from increasing waiting lists for operations, whilst governments claim they are spending more, in real terms, than ever before on the health service. This is a theme to which we will return when we look at trends in public expenditure in the final chapter.

Charges to recipients of services bring a small amount of money back to the health service. These only account for about 3 per cent of the health service's budget.[3] Charges cover part of the cost of the supply of drugs, medical appliances, spectacles and dental treatment. They are not applied to hospital in-patients or to children and the elderly. There are means tests that enable low income people to secure the remission of charges.

NEED AND THE RATIONING OF THE HEALTH SERVICE

The British health service is thus, broadly speaking, free and universally available. The general issues raised by the absence of a price mechanism to convert needs into effective demands was discussed in chapter 6 on the personal social services. One of the political preoccupations ever since the founding of the National Health Service has been the apparently limitless character of need.

There seem to be two crucial problems that were given insufficient attention by those who forecast a decline in need for health services. One is that, to put it crudely, everyone whose life is saved lives on to become ill again. More precisely, increases in life expectancy bring with them the likelihood of increased work for the service in dealing with the chronic illnesses that particularly affect the elderly. Even without the benefits of the health service the elderly would be a growing proportion of the population during the last decades of this century. The other is, again, the difficulty about defining need. There is a growing understanding that the relationship between having a medical need and seeking medical attention is complex and obscure. Individuals may experience considerable suffering from a condition that manifests no pathological abnormality. Conversely, they may have serious medical problems and yet experience little suffering. Perhaps more significantly, in quantitative terms, minor deviations from 'good health' are tolerated by many people for long periods without medical attention being sought. This applies, for example, to problems like indigestion, recurrent headaches and skin complaints. The evidence is therefore that, according to Tuckett:

> As a result of several epidemiological enquiries, using many different methods and many different definitions, we have become aware (surprising as this may seem) that the medical services deal with only a rather small proportion of the symptoms of disease experienced by members of the community.[4]

There is a choice between the policy conclusions to be drawn from these findings. One is that a great deal more should be spent on the health service, and in particular many more efforts should be made to screen for unidentified illness in the population. The quite opposite view is that the fact that many people manage without medical treatment for many complaints suggests that those who do 'bother' doctors about similar problems should be encouraged to become more self-reliant and to make more use of self-medication. A less extreme version of this view suggests that, since medical resources are clearly limited, it is important to control access to the services in such a way that the more serious complaints are treated while doctors are not overburdened with the trivial. At the moment the system depends primarily on general practitioners' judgements for this necessary filtering process. Are there ways of pushing the responsibility for it back to the patients? This provides one argument for the exploration of the case for a charging system to control demands upon the service.

A case for health service charges is also argued in terms of the desirability of choice and competition. This has been made most cogently in the United States by Eliot Friedson,[5] who sees the power of the consumer as enhanced by a relationship with the doctor in which he can 'hire and fire' him. For Friedson the British model of health service organization places individuals in a very weak position in dealing with doctors, and provides the community at large with an absence of weapons for bargaining with a medical profession that would not be so united were doctors in competition with each other.

The fundamental point in favour of a free service is that charges may deter people from seeking necessary help.[6] This is, as suggested in the last chapter, particularly likely to be the case when incomes are low. Moreover, one of the effects of ill health is naturally to reduce income and to increase other costs. The issue at stake is not simply therefore one of inequality in general, but specifically of inequality between the sick and the well (regardless of other determinants of their income and expenditure). Clearly also, while in other areas of life people may be expected to make choices between different ways of spending money, serious illness leaves little choice. Individuals will bankrupt themselves to save their lives, and those of their loved ones.

Where much of the health service is still 'in the market place', as for example in the United States, the issues are rarely actually as stark as these. There are two reasons why they are not. One is that many people insure themselves against sickness. The other is that a 'safety net' means-tested medical system exists for the poor. Arguments in favour of a free service must therefore deal with the weaknesses of these two alternative forms of provision.

The key problems with insurance schemes are that they will not insure the 'bad risks', they often exclude some conditions (especially preventable ones, for example pregnancy), and they may collapse. While it is true that these schemes may reduce the powers of doctors, who are dependent upon the patronage of the insurance agencies, they do not necessarily curb trivial demands since subscribers may be determined to obtain their money's worth. It is, however, the exclusion of certain groups from insurance cover that is the main problem. In the 1980s the case for an insurance-based approach to health care has re-emerged on the political agenda. Private insurance schemes have grown rapidly. Debate has developed, therefore, about the extension of such schemes nationwide. The case for such a new approach involves suggesting that individuals might be required to insure themselves privately, and that the state might underwrite such schemes and make special means-tested provision for those for whom they cannot cater.

The problems with a means-tested health service are the requirement of a test of means before treatment, the likelihood of situations in which individuals will have to abandon resources – or wait to 'hit the bottom' – before they can get treatment, and the probability that (as was the case in Britain when such a system operated) two classes of health service will exist. In the last resort, as implied above, the case for a free service is not that it helps to distribute resources from the rich to the poor, but that it enables the healthy to support the sick. If it is believed, on the other hand, that it is in the interests of the evolution of society that the 'weak should go to the wall' it will of course be comparatively easy to take an alternative view.

These issues about ways of funding health care have been brought to a head by the evidence that, despite increases in expenditure, the capacity of the health service to meet all the demands upon it is falling. While largely attributable to an ageing population, escalating health costs also add to this problem. Demands for more resources for the service, and better pay for the lower paid workers within it (particularly nurses) have been met by government willingness reopen the issue of insurance, despite the complications it involves,[7] and to explore other ways to use privatization to try to reduce health costs. Whether this will result in a radical shift away from the principles of a free health service remains to be seen.

## EQUALITY OF TREATMENT WITHIN THE HEALTH SERVICE

While the current Conservative government has not come up with any proposals to undermine the general principle of a free health service, there is a great deal of discussion in Britain today on two related issues: the most appropriate relationship between the health service and the residual private medical sector, and the extent to which the health service provides equality of treatment to all the population.

These two issues are related, since the diversion of medical resources into a private sector, largely accessible only to the better off, reduces the resources available to other sectors of the population. However, the defenders of private medicine argue that the resources involved are, in a sense, extra ones, which would not necessarily be diverted into public medicine in an entirely nationalized sector. Particular bones of contention, however, have been not so much the right of the private sector to exist, as the support that sector receives from a variety of special links with the health service.

Both general practitioners and consultants are able to take on private patients as well as health service ones. This enables health service resources to be used in various ways in support of private medicine. Moreover, situations arise in which it is possible for doctors to say to people that, while health service treatment will be inadequate, or long delayed, they may secure a better deal by becoming private patients. Perhaps the most widespread examples of this come from the dental service, where a range of more sophisticated treatments are available only on a private basis.

Within the hospitals, consultants are able to engage in private practice by taking part-time health service contracts. A particularly contentious issue in this sector has been the presence within NHS hospitals of 'pay-beds', which facilitate the undertaking of public and private work side-by-side, the use of public resources (such as expensive equipment) for private patients, and 'queue-jumping' when public beds are scarce. Early in 1974 ancillary workers in a London hospital forced the newly elected Labour government to act on its commitment to eliminate pay-beds by threatening to withdraw services to private patients.[8] This brought it into fierce conflict with the hospital doctors, and it was this, together with conflict over doctors' pay, that led the government to set up a Royal Commission on the National Health Service. Without waiting for the Commission to report the government initiated a procedure to phase out pay-beds. However, the Conservatives quickly reversed the policy on coming to power.

The development of private insurance schemes has also helped to prop up a system of private medicine in Britain. The use of NHS hospitals has been crucial here, but now private resources are increasingly going into separate hospital developments. It is unclear to what extent these will be available to sustain on their own the more expensive kinds of treatment. However, at the time of writing situations are arising in which the NHS buys the use of private hospital equipment.

The growth of private insurance raises the question of the overall impact on the state service of alternative ones. Is there scope here for desirable competition? Is it a valuable addition to consumer choice, enabling people who are so inclined to pay a little extra for a superior service? Or does it threaten the basic service, and reduce its capacity to meet the needs of all?

The health service's capacity to meet need has been subjected to extensive scrutiny. Epidemiological studies of the differential impact of mortality and morbidity have been of importance here. These show considerable differences in the experience of ill health between different regions of the country, between different social classes,[9] and between different ethnic groups. The statistics on infant deaths have been given particular attention. Twice as many children of unskilled workers die in the first month of life as children of professional workers. The infant mortality rate (deaths in the first year of life by 1,000 live births) varies widely from region to region. The Royal Commission on the NHS quoted figures on this for 1977. The highest rates were 17.2 in Northern Ireland, 16.1 in Scotland, and 15.5 in the Yorkshire region. The lowest were 11.2 in East Anglia and 11.6 in South West Thames region.[10] Statistics for districts would have shown even greater disparities. Similar evidence can be adduced from studies of illness experience in other age groups.

The policy questions this evidence raises obviously concern, first, the extent to which these differentials are attributable to differences in the availability of health services; and second, inasmuch as they are attributable to other factors (low income, poor housing and so on), to what extent better health services can and should offset these disadvantages. On a narrow interpretation of the first of these questions there is evidence of differences between different parts of the country in terms of the availability of health care. The Royal Commission showed variations in health spending per capita between regions in 1976–7 from £122.38 in North West Thames, to £91.52 in the West Midlands and £93.80 in Trent region.[11] Similar disparities may be noted in numbers of doctors and other health service practitioners per head. It should, however, be stressed that these figures do not clearly correlate with the data on mortality. Indeed Northern Ireland and Scotland had expenditure per head considerably above those for North Thames. Expenditure on health care and numbers of doctors needs to be related to the differential incidence of needs, taking into account such factors as the age structure of the population.

The government, after the first reorganization of the health service, set up a Resource Allocation Working Party (RAWP) required to develop a formula to facilitate comparisons between the resource needs of different regions. This has used population estimates weighted to take into account differential mortality and different utilization rates based upon differences in the age and the structure of the population.[12] Allocation of new money to the regions has been based upon the RAWP formula, and allocations by regions to districts are based upon similar principles.

This is proving a difficult and controversial exercise in the light of the inadequacy of the statistics available, the difficulties in relating such data to needs and the uncertainty about the relationship between costs and effectiveness. Furthermore, an attempt to relate resources to needs within geographically defined territories must take into account the fact that patients cross boundaries for some services, and particularly for some of the most expensive specialized hospital services.

While this start on tackling some of the problems of 'territorial injustice' that have beset the National Health Service since its foundation has been widely welcomed, there are some other issues about the availability of services that require attention. Social class differentials in the use of health services suggest that efforts need to be made not only to ensure that adequate resources are available in underprivileged areas but also to facilitate access to the use of those resources by all in need. This raises policy questions about the siting of surgeries and hospitals, the arrangements made by doctors to enable patients to secure appointments, the extent of the use of health service personnel – such as health visitors – who actively seek out those in need of health care, the extent of health education, and the significance of screening services (such as in industry).

Finally, these questions lead on to the other question raised: the extent to which there might be an expectation that health services should be better in some areas, or for some people, to help to compensate for other social disadvantages. The opposite is generally the case in Britain; there is a correlation between poor health services and other social, economic and environmental deficiencies. To what extent should the concept of a state health service embrace a responsibility to point out how other social factors contribute to ill health?

These last questions have led some critics of the National Health Service to say that it is really a 'national illness service'.[11] Academic studies of the health progress of the nation have suggested that changes in the environment and in behaviour have been more important than medical advances.

There are a number of interrelated approaches to the prevention of ill health. Healthy lifestyles may be regarded as a matter of personal choice. It is evident that many people have become aware of the need for exercise and the need for a healthy diet. At the time of writing a forceful junior minister at DHSS, Edwina Currie, has been outspoken on these issues. Yet lifestyle options may be influenced by income and environment, constraining choices. They may also be influenced by the practices of the food and drink industries, the additives they use and the things their advertisements promote. Other aspects of our living and working environments may be quite outside our control. It may be argued that governments have important regulatory responsibilities to help protect our health. Recently the government abolished a body, with a modest budget from DHSS, which had been quite outspoken on the need for regulatory policies. That was the Health Education Council. It was replaced by the Health Education Authority. It remains to be seen whether this new body will have any impact. The limited list above of points about this vast subject indicates that the health of the nation depends upon much more than the efforts of the NHS.

THE REPRESENTATION AND PROTECTION OF THE PUBLIC

When the formation of the National Health Service was debated in the years before 1948 many doctors made clear their opposition to local government control. While some community services were kept within local government between 1948 and 1974, the main forms chosen for the local control of the health service were hybrid organizations in which ministerial appointees served alongside local authority nominees. Another feature of these organizations was the presence of members of the professions (mainly doctors) working in the health service. In the executive councils, and their successors the family practitioner committees, direct representation of the professions was secured. In other bodies the official nominees included professionals. These general principles have continued to govern the membership of the various management bodies in the service, the main difference between the old system and the new being merely that local authority membership has been reduced and the government has made it clear that it does not expect such members to see themselves as indirect public representatives. The system therefore provides for a minimum of public participation but a substantial professional involvement. Public representation is, in a sense, only at the national government level, and even at that level there are professional advisers with a similar status to the top administrators and an elaborate structure to allow for professional representation.

An interesting innovation in 1974 was the setting up of community health councils (CHCs) to enable the public viewpoint to be expressed. But the status of these bodies is as officially recognized and subsidized pressure groups, with rights to make representations and to seek information. Such power as they have primarily rests upon their capacity to embarrass health authorities. Even in relation to this weapon, they have an awkward choice to make between seeking a close day-to-day working relationship which may inhibit its use, and remaining more aloof but loosing opportunities to secure information and to make informal representations. One other point not to be forgotten about CHCs is that they are not themselves representative bodies in any of the senses in which that term is used in democratic theory. Half of their members are appointed by local authorities and one sixth by the RHAs; the remainder are elected by relevant voluntary organizations (by means of rather haphazard election processes which do nothing to ensure that they are representative of the patients in their areas).

This, then, is the pattern of public representation within the health service. Those who advocate the bringing of the service under local authority control are unlikely to secure a shift now, both against professional opposition and against a structure of organization that fits ill with the pattern of local government in many parts of Great Britain.

However, for many members of the public what matters more than representation is protection from abuse and malpractice, and the chance to be heard when dissatisfied with the service provided. Apart from the general opportunities to make representations, which apply to all the public services, there are, for the health service, a number of special procedures available. Practitioners and hospitals may be sued for tort damages, and professional malpractice may result in debarment from practice by the relevant professional organization. Patients may complain, through a procedure involving primarily the family practitioner committee, that practitioners have acted in breach of their terms of service, and penalties may be imposed including, at worst, 'sacking' from health service employment. Complaints against hospitals may be formally investigated by the DHA, and exceptionally the secretary of state may order an inquiry. Examples of the latter have thrown important light upon weaknesses in the services for the mentally handicapped. Finally, a patient may complain to the health service commissioner, though the powers of this official broadly preclude investigations in areas where other forms of investigation or litigation are available.

There is thus no absence of avenues for further action by individuals with grievances. However, the multiplicity of procedures is confusing to patients; and all involve very formal approaches which deter action. This formality is regarded as important for the protection of vulnerable professionals from frivolous complaints. But the general problem here is that evidence that things are going wrong in particular parts of the service, particularly the family practitioner parts, does not come to light easily, and thus attract corrective action, when complaints involved are insufficiently serious to activate the formal machinery. Community health councils may contribute to the correction of problems of this kind, through the accumulation of evidence on grievances brought to their attention or through surveys of patients' experiences. Their lack of formal powers, however, implies that they must then seek to influence the behaviour and practices of staff who see themselves as accountable to no one. This is a challenge to CHC subtlety and tactical skill.

There is one other source of influence upon day-to-day practice within some parts of the health service. This is the Health Advisory Service, accountable to the secretary of state and manned by seconded professionals. It is required to conduct a limited audit of the operation of particular services. This body is concerned with the overall performance in specific areas, particularly where institutional care is involved, and not with the scrutiny of individual professional decision making. It clearly could be developed into a more all-embracing, and perhaps more public, medical audit system.[13]

## CONCLUSIONS

An American student of the British National Health Service described it as 'something magnificent in scope and breathtaking in its implications'. He went on to say:

In the light of past accomplishments and future goals, the Health Service cannot very well be excluded from any list of notable achievements of the twentieth century. So much has it become a part of the British way of life, it is difficult for the average Englishman to imagine what it would be like without those services that have contributed so much to his physical and mental well-being.[14]

That expresses rather well the peculiar mixture of utopian expectations and of taking the service for granted that gives a slightly exaggerated quality to British discussions of policy issues in the health service.

We have expectations of the service that often go quite beyond any capacity to deliver results. We oscillate wildly therefore between pride in our system and disquiet about its waiting lists and overcrowded wards. We put doctors on a pedestal as the magnificent experts who dominate the system, and we get angry about their arrogant presumptions. We demand more and more from the service, and we get worried that we are perhaps becoming a nation of hypochondriacs who can too easily make demands upon it. These mixed emotions colour the reactions of both politicians and the public to the main policy dilemmas that inevitably confront the service.

Undoubtedly a public approach to medicine, which is by no means exclusively a characteristic of the British, involving disproportionate expectations about its capacity to solve the problems of suffering and death, lies at the root of some of our difficulties in putting health policies in context, and coming to terms with the strengths and weaknesses of our health service. There are signs, however, that the 'demystification of medicine' is beginning to occur. This is helping us to assess much more realistically decisions about the allocation of resources between the hospital service and the community services, and between the health service and other public policies. Some of these issues have been considered in this chapter. Others were given attention in the discussion on 'forward planning, needs and priorites' and on 'the relationship between the personal services and the health service' in chapter 6.

We are beginning to ask whether we have not so far been too ready to delegate decisions involving moral questions as well as medical questions to professional practitioners. We are beginning to achieve a better understanding of the extent to which many of the determinants of the health of the nation have little to do with the quality and nature of its clinical medical services.

## SUGGESTIONS FOR FURTHER READING

Two good textbooks, both at the time of writing in editions that take into account the 1982 health service reorganization but only just comment on the emergence of the Griffiths proposals are Christopher Ham's *Health Policy in Britain*,[15] and Ruth Levitt and Andrew Wall's *The Reorganized National Health Service*.[16] An account of the work of family practitioner committees is found in Allsop and May's *The Emperor's New Clothes*.[17] The Royal Commission report (see n. 7) and *Inequalities and Health: The Black Report* (see n. 9) are vital sources on the activities and performance of the health service. Glennerster's book, recommended at the end of the last chapter (n. 36 in ch. 6) deals with many of the finance and public expenditure issues.

# CHAPTER 8

# Education

## EDUCATION POLICIES AND THE ORGANIZATION OF THE SYSTEM

The state's role in education is a dual one; it is the major provider of education, and has also assumed a responsibility to supervise it in the sector for which it is not directly responsible. This chapter will confine its attention largely to the publicly maintained education system, but some consideration will be given to the private sector inasmuch as some key policy issues concern the relationship between the two sectors. About 6 per cent of the United Kingdom's schoolchildren are in private schools.

As in the health service chapter it can be taken for granted that readers will be aware of the basic services provided by the system. Furthermore, the organizational structure of the education system is relatively simple and relatively well known.

The provision of state schools is the responsibility of the counties and the metropolitan districts in England and Wales except in inner London, where an *ad hoc* authority (the Inner London Education Authority) exists. In Scotland it is the concern of the regions, while in Northern Ireland it comes under appointed education and libraries boards. These authorities are also concerned with the provision of many forms of higher and further education, often combining for this purpose.

The universities are outside local authority control, the government-appointed University Grants Committee (shortly to be replaced by the Universities Funding Council) deals with their affairs. At the time of writing the government is starting to engage in an attack on local government control over most of education. They are proposing to bring polytechnics under central control, using an intermediary body rather like the University Grants Committee. They are setting up City Technology Colleges, on an experimental basis, to provide some centrally funded secondary education; and they are enacting legislation to 'enable the governors of county and voluntary maintained schools, with the support of parents, to apply to the Secretary of State for maintenance by grant from Central Government instead of maintenance by local education authorities and to enable inner London Boroughs to take over education from the Inner London Education Authority.'[1]

In Scotland, Wales and Northern Ireland education other than in universities is the responsibility of the Scottish, Welsh and Northern Ireland offices respectively. In England the relevant central government department is the Department of Education and Science, and this is the department to which the University Grants Committee is accountable for all the United Kingdom universities.

The school system can be identified as involving three sectors: a very small pre-primary sector, primary education and secondary education. In most cases these sectors can be identified respectively with the education of children under five, between five and eleven, and between eleven and the school leaving-age of sixteen (with many pupils continuing at school until eighteen). However, some authorities have developed systems that deviate from the strict break between primary and secondary education at eleven-plus. These have generally introduced an intermediate, middle-school system, for children in two or three of the year bands between nine and thirteen. A few have developed separate schools to split the secondary age group.

One innovation of the latter kind has been the introduction of 'sixth form colleges' for the over-sixteens. The educational arrangements for those over the minimal school-leaving age is further complicated by the fact that some further education colleges offer both practical and academic courses for children in the sixteen-to-eighteen age brackets.

The arrangement for the starting of compulsory education at the age of five differentiates Britain from many other countries, which do not make it compulsory until six or seven. However, the concomitant is that public preschool education is ill-developed. Despite considerable public pressure, and considerable emphasis by educational experts on the importance of the preparation for education that may be provided in nursery schools, and may thus particularly assist those children who receive but limited help from parents, the preschool system has remained small.

The main point of note about policies for primary education has been the extent to which, very often on the basis of local initiatives, innovatory approaches to education have been developed. Many primary schools have been transformed over the last twenty to thirty years from formal institutions in which uniformed children sat in straight rows in classes streamed on the basis of tests of educational ability, to very informal places where pupils move about freely to work together in little clusters drawn from mixed ability classes. The gradual elimination of selection at eleven-plus has clearly contributed to this 'liberation' of primary schools. It is an interesting example of a change that developed from the bottom and has never required any formal recognition in legislation, which may nevertheless be regarded as a major policy development. Its implications are now beginning to receive attention. Politicians are starting to ask whether this largely professionally motivated innovation has gone too far. There is a growing concern about levels of literacy and numeracy, and responsibility for their alleged inadequacy is sometimes attributed to this educational revolution.

In chapter 2 it was shown how the idea of the comprehensive secondary school gradually replaced the bipartite or tripartite system envisaged at the time of the passing of the 1944 Education Act. In 1986 about 86 per cent of secondary school children in the public sector in England were in comprehensive schools. The percentage was 98 per cent for Wales and 96 per cent for Scotland.[2] The growth of the idea of the comprehensive school may be identified with that same development in professional educational thinking that created the 'progressive' primary school. But this change in policy required much more positive decision making by local politicians. The internal organization of a school may be changed gradually and subtly over a period of time by its head teacher and staff. Change in the organization of the local education system requires more centralized and publicly apparent decisions. Comprehensivization received an impetus not only from new ideas on education but also from an increasing Labour Party opposition to the divisive character of the old system. Popular support was forthcoming largely, it may be suspected, because of discontent about the inaccurate and necessarily arbitrary distinctions that had to be made between children by tests conducted at the age of eleven.

By 1979 the development of comprehensive education was nearing completion. The Labour government had, in the 1976 Education Act, required local authorities to develop plans for comprehensivization. A minority of authorities were holding out on this. But on coming to power the Conervatives repealed this law. This had the effect of stemming the tide, but not reversing it.

One aspect of the resistance to comprehensive education has involved the argument that the abandonment of selective schools leads to a lowering of educational standards, and to the neglect of the needs of the most able children. This view seems to have been taken increasingly seriously in recent years by the advocates of comprehensive education, so it has not merely been an aspect of the 'backlash' against comprehensivization. It has also inhibited the extension of the educational changes going on in the primary schools into the secondary schools. In particular it has contributed to the maintenance of ability-based 'streaming' in many comprehensive schools. This phenomenon, which can have the effect of creating a divided education system within an apparently integrated school, is further reinforced by the imminence, in the teenage years, of the public examinations. These involve a sixteen-plus examination the General Certificate of Secondary Education, just introduced to integrate the two previous examination schemes, the General Certificate of Education (GCE) 'Ordinary Level' and the less academic Certificate of Secondary Education, and the Advanced ('A') Level examinations normally sat at eighteen-plus.

Two further current government initiatives are likely to strengthen the hands of those who stress the need for formal, and probably 'streamed' education. These are the proposals for a national common 'core' curriculum, and the testing of children at seven, eleven and fourteen.

Studies of comprehensive schools have suggested that as children approach the school-leaving age there are many factors, often out of the control of the schools, that contribute to the divisions between the school-oriented 'academic' pupils and the anti-school group, who increasingly see their education as irrelevant and who drop out of participation in all school activities.[3] An increasing concern therefore in secondary education is not so much the fate of the brighter pupils – the comprehensive schools have been eager to 'prove themselves' by doing justice to the needs of this group – as the difficulties entailed in developing a relevant syllabus for those at the other end of the ability range. There are related problems here, of course, of absenteeism and delinquency. Overall the issue concerns the relationship of the education system to the needs of underpriveleged groups in society – for example, low-skilled workers and racial minorities. Since, moreover, such groups are located in specific areas, there is a geographical dimension to this problem. One of the arguments advanced in favour of the comprehensive school is that it is able to take all the children of a limited geographical community. But suppose such a 'community' is manifestly not truely 'comprehensive', and worse still, suppose atypical residents in that community take steps to get their children educated elsewhere; then new distinctions arise between schools in which their catchment areas rather than their selection policies influence, or are believed to influence, their characters. This is a growing problem for comprehensive secondary education in Britain.

The education of handicapped children requires the system to develop certain special resources. However, the trend is to try to integrate the education of the handicapped as far as possible into the ordinary system. There is a range of special voluntary schools for groups such as the blind and the severely physically handicapped, at which local authorities may pay for places. No local authority has sufficient children in these groups to justify provision on its own. On the other hand there is a large group of children in each authority who are classified as sufficiently below normal intelligence levels to require special provision. Until 1970 these were divided into two groups: the 'educationally sub-normal', for whom most education authorities supplied special schools, and the 'severely sub-normal', who were deemed unsuitable for education and sent instead to junior training centres run by local health authorities. The latter group are now the responsibility of the education system, but are still generally sent to the schools that are merely the old training centres under other names. There is scope for the integration of education for these two groups. An official committee which reported in 1978, the Warnock Committee,[4] made a number of detailed suggestions for increasing the integration of this part of the education system with the rest of the service, while not neglecting the special attention required for handicapped children. These are slowly being put into operation.

The concept of further education embraces a number of different activities: vocational education, further academic education (both of a kind provided generally in schools and at higher levels) and non-vocational adult education. Education for degrees and for post-graduate qualifications is provided in universities, in polytechnics, and in colleges of higher education. In 1984–5 there were about 541,000 full-time students (not counting students from abroad) in higher education. About 270,000 of these, roughly 50 per cent, were in universities.[5]

There are a number of non-teaching activities that make contributions to the overall performance of the education system. Schools may provide meals and milk to children. The former may be available free to the pupils whose parents are on 'income support'. The extent to which these should be subsidized for others has been something of a political football, and extensive cuts have been made recently to these services. Means-tested grants are also available towards the cost of school clothing, and towards support of children in the sixteen-to-eighteen group who are still at school. These are among the benefits that complicate the social security system.

The welfare of schoolchildren is also given attention through the school health service and the education welfare service. Exceptionally the latter is a social services department responsibility (in Cheshire and Somerset for example); more typically it comes under education departments. Historically the main concern of this service has been truancy. Today its objectives have been widened to embrace the whole range of problems that may affect educational performance. In this it has the support of the child guidance service, which was described earlier, in relation to the personal social services, as an inter-departmental hybrid. The relationship between social workers and educational welfare officers is a delicate one, since the latter are a relatively untrained group who are anxious to upgrade their skills and abandon the 'attendance officer' image.[6] An established ethos and working style is, however, hard to change, and truancy does remain a central problem for the service.

## PAYING FOR THE EDUCATION SYSTEM

Public education in Britain is, broadly speaking, free. There is a system of fees for higher education but nearly all British students, regardless of parental income, are able to obtain grants for undergraduate courses that cover at least these. Some further and non-vocational education has to be paid for by students, but generally these fees are subsidized. Hence the provision of education in Britain makes heavy demands on public funds. Most of this money has to be provided by the local authorities, but of course a high proportion of local expenditure is actually covered by central government grants. In 1984–5 education in the United Kingdom cost £16,008 million. £14,390 million of this was spent on the local authority sector.[7]

The gradually falling numbers in the school age groups has, since the mid-seventies, encouraged government and local authorities to see education as a target area for expenditure cuts. Places in teacher education have also been dramatically cut. In 1981, in advance of the fall in the numbers in the eighteen to twenty-two age group, the government also identified higher education as an area in which it might apply disproportionate expenditure cuts.

The selection of education as a target for cuts, using falling numbers as a justification, involves a refusal to accept, on the one hand, the relevance of the argument that rationalization of a system in which units are lumpy is hard to achieve, and on the other, the case for raising standards in the face of lessening pressure. A class that halves its numbers still requires a teacher, and that teaching will be better if the numbers demanding attention are less. In addition, as far as higher education is concerned, where scarce places are rationed by a selection system, falling numbers could offer the chance to extend educational opportunities.

Whilst the government has made the quest for greater efficiency in the use of diminishing resources the central thrust of its education policy, right-wing ideologues have also called into question the case for free education. The only practical inroad into this principle has been a tendency for schools to be forced to charge for extra benefits not seen as strictly part of the core curriculum – music lessons, educational trips etc. There has been some dispute about the legality of some of these charges under the law as laid down in the 1944 Education Act. At the time of writing the government has promised legislation which will legitimate such charges. Will it be opening a door a little, which will subsequently be pushed much wider open? It should also be pointed out that expenditure restraints have increased the extent to which parents, individually or collectively, have needed to purchase textbooks and equipment for their children's education.

Another idea for change to the education system which has come from the political Right is that an education voucher system could be developed which would enable parents to place their children within either the private or public sector, paying supplementary fees to private schools where necessary. The Conservative government has encouraged a local experiment to explore the feasibility of vouchers. It has also enabled local authorities to provide 'assisted places' in the private sector for selected children. Expenditure constraints have kept this development to fairly modest levels. In 1985–6 there were 24,500 children in such schemes in Great Britain (out of a total secondary school population of about 4.5 million). Of these children 40 per cent received full remission of fees, the rest part remission.[8]

The other major area in which there is a serious controversy about the use of public funds is in relation to grants to university students. In this case it is not the basic tuition fees that are at issue but the grants provided to pay students' living expenses. The present system involves means-tested grants for which, unless the student has been self-supporting for three years before restarting full-time study, parental income and other commitments are taken into account. (There are also special and rather anomalous arrangements for the means-testing of married students, which cannot be explored properly here.) This system is criticized from 'both sides'. The National Union of Students would like to see the means test abolished. It draws attention to the many anomalies involved, and to the problems faced by the many students whose parents do not pay their contributions towards the grants.

But there is an alternative line of criticism of the British system which has involved the advocacy of a loan system, as operated in many countries, as a preferable approach to the maintenance of students.[9] It is argued that students receive public funds whilst delaying starting to make a contribution to national income. Nevertheless by studying they enhance their future earning potential. It is therefore suggested that it may be reasonable to expect students to repay all or some of the benefit bestowed upon them in this way. A number of schemes have been suggested. The more sophisticated attempt to avoid heavy demands on resources in early career, and to allow for the possibility that individuals may go into low-paying but socially useful work. There are various special problems, such as for example the appropriate treatment for a woman whose career and earning power is affected by marriage and child-rearing. Administratively sophisticated schemes might become complex and costly. Critics of loan schemes point to the benefit the nation gains from its educated people, and warn that loan schemes might deter some people, particularly people from low income families, from entering higher education.

The existence of a comprehensive and relatively generous means-tested grants system for entrants to universities must be compared with the rather unsatisfactory situation with regard to some other students and particularly with regard to schoolchildren between sixteen and eighteen years of age. It is mandatory upon local authorities to pay grants to university students. Other higher education grants are discretionary; this clearly has unfair consequences from time to time. Local authorities may pay limited means-tested maintenance awards to the parents of schoolchildren who are over the school-leaving age. These again are discretionary and are not very extensive in coverage. Children who have left school but are unemployed may claim social security benefits. Moreover, under the new measures to combat youth unemployment, many of these youngsters may now be put on training or further education courses and paid allowances. Not surprisingly, the case for a more universal grant system for this group of scholars has been argued.

CONTROL OVER THE EDUCATION SYSTEM

The control of education in Britain involves what has been described as a 'partnership' between central and local government. Yet clearly that partnership is under threat. At a time when central government is trying to curb local government expenditure it must focus attention upon education in that it accounts for around half of this expenditure. Furthermore, politicians at national level take a great interest in the way education is organized and conducted.[10] The development of comprehensive education and the elimination of direct grant schools were issues that fundamentally divided the parties. Governments have also felt it important to take stands, on such matters as literacy, the core content of the curriculum, the role of nursery education and the future of higher education. Strong commitments in national politics have been met by equally strong ones in local politics. Hence battle-lines have been drawn, particularly on the comprehensive issue. Local authorities have even had recourse to the courts to resist what they see as central government interference. The main example of this was the battle in Tameside in 1976 when, after a local election victory, the Conservatives reversed a Labour plan to 'go comprehensive'. The secretary of state sought to intervene, arguing that the change was too far advanced to be reversed. The court upheld the local authority's position. The change of government ended this particular battle.

The uneasy balance between central and local government is not the only delicate balance of power in the British educational system. At the local level the running of the system involves a number of different groups which are contending for influence or protecting their prerogatives. Each local authority appoints an education committee, consisting primarily of councillors but including some other representatives of groups interested in education, such as teachers, churches and local universities. It is a generally accepted convention that on contentious political matters the non-councillor members should restrain their intervention. The committee is served by a chief education officer who leads a team of officials who generally have teaching qualifications. There is thus a strong professionally oriented administrative group at the centre of the system. In the schools themselves head teachers expect a considerable measure of freedom in the determination of the way the school is run and the content of the curriculum. They operate, of course, in consultation with their teachers, but vary extensively in the extent to which they allow staff participation in decision making. In the last resort, however, the class teacher clearly has some autonomy in determining his or her input and relationship to pupils.

Schools are required to have governing bodies. As a result of the implementation of the recommendations of the Taylor Committee in 1980,[11] there was some extension of the powers of these bodies. Further legislation in 1986 extended this process. They are required to consist of an equal mix of local education authority nominees and parents. The Taylor Report urged that they should participate much more fully than had hitherto been the case in the running of schools, and this should include (although the wording of the report was deliberately rather general and guarded) participation in the determination of the curriculum. These proposals were, therefore, important in recommending much clearer parent participation and a much more positive approach to involvement in key decision making within schools. They were not popular with the teachers' unions, another important element in the 'partnership' at both national and local levels. However the Conservative government has been keen to further governor control over schools; at the time of writing it is enacting a measure to require local authorities to delegate budgetary responsibilities to schools. Thus the government seems to be squeezing local authority powers both by increasing central controls and by extending governors' powers.

A related issue which has received considerable attention has been parental choice of schools for their children. Whilst there were high pupil–teacher ratios, and pressure upon school numbers in many parts of the country, the scope for parental choice was fairly limited. But as school rolls have fallen the situation has changed. In urban areas, in particular, variations in the popularity of schools have often become very clear. In the Education Act of 1980 the government has tried to provide parents with some measure of choice over schools. It requires local authorities to give information which will help with choice, and it lays down an appeal procedure for those whose wishes are not granted. Parental choice seems to be operating as a curb on innovation by teachers. It may also be helping to determine where cuts will fall. Inasmuch as it is more likely to be exercised by middle-class parents, it may be enhancing the tendency for there to be a hierarchy of schools, under the influence of geographical location.

## EDUCATION AND THE DISADVANTAGED

Education plays a significant role in relation to the distribution of occupational opportunities in British society. On the Left there is considerable concern about the extent to which education contributes to upward mobility. There are two versions of this preoccupation. One of these involves a commitment to equality of opportunity, and therefore a demand that the able children of 'lower-class' parents should have access to educational openings. The other is a concern about equality in a more absolute sense. A naive version of this places faith in the possibility of an education system that can help to create a more equal society. A more sophisticated approach recognizes that education cannot be, by itself, an engine of social change but stresses that it must play a part by ensuring that children are not socially segregated and that schools attempt to compensate for other sources of inequality.

'Equality of opportunity' is a slogan that finds political support beyond the ranks of the Left. A rather mixed commitment to both forms of equality has informed the evaluation of education policy. Differential educational opportunity and achievement has been extensively studied by sociologists and psychologists. The evidence accumulated by research in the 1950s and early 1960s was used in making the case for comprehensive education and for the abandonment of streaming.[12] More recently attention has shifted to those problems of underachievement in the education system that cannot be directly attributed to the way that system is structured. Two particular themes have been emphasized: the significance of home background for educational success, and the extent to which the 'culture' of the school system is alien to some children.

It has been shown that poverty and poor housing conditions militate against educational success.[13] There is little the education system can do about these problems, but it can try to compensate for them with extra efforts to help deprived children. Home backgrounds are relevant in another sense, too. There are wide variations in the extent to which parents help with the education of their children. Such help takes many forms, involving not only the more obvious forms of encouragement and the provision of books and study facilities, but also a great deal of implicit 'teaching' through interaction with children. The latter starts when babies are very tiny, and one of its most significant ingredients is the learning of language. The children who are most deprived in these respects are often those also most deprived in a material sense. But parental educational levels and abilities are also relevant. There is a variety of practical ways in which the education system may help to compensate for these less straightforwardly material disadvantages, both before and after children reach compulsory school age.[14]

The issue with regard to the 'culture' of the schools is a more difficult one. Partly the problem is one of identification of the needs and special interests of children whose backgrounds differ from the white educated middle class who dominate the system. There is a variety of ways in which stories, educational situations and examples can be devised that seem relevant to these children. Hence there is ample scope for change here. However, there must be limits to the extent to which this issue can be fully met, if only because of the extent to which it implies a conflict with the objective of facilitating social mobility through education. If a key concern of education is to prepare children to operate in a middle-class world, even perhaps to join that world, then it may not be particularly functional for it to be too obsessed with relating to working-class culture. There is a terrible dilemma here, very relevant to the alienation of some children from an education system in which they are becoming the 'failures'. You cannot eliminate the concept of failure so long as you still have the objective of enabling some to 'succeed' through the education system. It may be desirable to eliminate the more invidious aspects of competition within the system – to recognize for example, that progress *relative* to ability may be as important as the easy success of the advantaged and talented – but notions of achievement, and consequently non-achievement, are fundamental to the role of education in our kind of society.

There are some special, and slightly different, issues about the 'culture' of education and the needs of racial minorities. These will be examined in the next section in relation to the whole range of problems, and therefore policy dilemmas, about the education of immigrant children and children of immigrants.

The idea of attempting to compensate for disadvantage by providing special resources for the schools in some areas was suggested in a report of a government advisory committee (the Plowden Committee) in

1967.[15] Many of the measures adopted did no more than attempt to redress the imbalance of educational resources between run-down inner-city areas where the schools were old and facilities were limited, and newer suburban areas. Additional money was made available for capital projects and current expenditure in areas where there were high levels of deprivation. But in addition the government provided for extra teachers, above the normal quotas, and special additional allowances for teachers in those areas. Areas were designated on the basis of statistics on the socio-economic status of parents, the extent of absence of housing amenities, proportions of children receiving free school meals, and proportion of schoolchildren with serious linguistic difficulties.

Some action research projects were initiated to monitor special compensatory education ventures in some of these 'educational priority areas'. These gave particular attention to the value of preschool education, along the lines of the American 'Headstart' programme. In 1968 the government developed a special 'urban programme' of social policies for deprived urban areas. Under this programme local authorities could receive grants to expand nursery education and to support preschool playgroups. The emphasis upon this stage of education led eventually in 1973 to the easing of limitations upon the development of nursery education.

The issues with which this section has been concerned have received rather less attention in the political climate of the 1980s. With diminishing work opportunities for school-leavers there has perhaps been less room for a generous concern about educational underachievers. The author contemplated leaving this section out of the revised edition of this book, but in the end decided that there was not a case for ignoring such an important issue just because of its contemporary low political salience. In any case, urban riots in the early 1980s have helped to keep the issue to be considered in the next section on the political agenda, and the two issues are closely related to each other.


## THE EDUCATION OF THE ETHNIC MINORITIES

Britain has a non-white population of around two and a half million. About 40 per cent of these are British-born. The remainder are predominantly migrants from the West Indies and the Indian Subcontinent. There is thus a substantial non-white school population, concentrated in urban areas. Most of these youngsters are the British-born children of migrants, as immigration has been tightly controlled since the 1960s.

When many non-white children were themselves immigrants the system saw their language problem and cultural difference as the main issue. Some of these are still evident. Many Asian children are encouraged by parents to make the most of educational opportunities, and many have made remarkable progress within the British system. They face problems, however, in coming to terms with strong contrasts between patterns of home life and school life. This is particularly an issue for girls coming from homes that cherish traditional ideals of feminine behaviour, expecting daughters to remain close to the family, to have no career ambitions and perhaps to accept an early arranged marriage.

Some Asian groups have begun either to make demands for new developments in the education system in tune with their cultural needs (appropriate religious education; courses in Asian languages) or to call for separate state-subsidized schools for their children on the lines of Catholic schools. A look across to Northern Ireland, where a division in education on religious lines has many of the characteristics of a division on cultural lines, and contributes to the division of that community, gives pause for thought on this model of education for a culturally diverse society. Yet there is an important question here about the extent to which education is to help to effect the assimilation of minorities, or whether it can accommodate cultural diversity.

West Indian children come from a society where European cultural models have a strong influence, and are reinforced through the education process. It is precisely this bias in West Indian society, and in American Negro society, that has been attacked by those concerned about the development of black consciousness. It is argued that this dominance of a white cultural model contributes to the maintenance of a subordinate self-image. Black leaders in Britain have become deeply concerned about the underachievement of children of West Indian origin. They attribute this to a variety of factors, but see the white racial and cultural bias in the education system as reinforcing other aspects of disadvantage.

Hence whilst the education system continues to see the issues about non-white children as ones about *their* characteristics it may alternatively be suggested that the central issue is *its* racial and cultural assumptions, the phenomenon which is described as 'institutional racism'. An official committee, chaired by Lord Swann, reported on its 'Inquiry into the Education of Children from Ethnic Minority Groups' in 1985. In a brief guide to the report Lord Swann, whilst not using the expression 'institutional racism', made it very clear that the issue of society and the education system's response was of central importance in explaining the problem of underachievement by non-whites. He argued:

On the evidence so far there is at least a dual problem. On the one hand, society must not, through prejudice and discrimination, increase the social and economic deprivation of ethnic minority families. On the other, schools must respond with greater sensitivity, and without any trace of prejudice, to the needs of ethnic minority children.[16]

Lord Swann saw the latter to be achieved through the concept of 'Education for All':

The fundamental change needed is a recognition that the problem facing the educational system is not just how to educate the children of ethnic minorities, but how to educate *all* children. Britain has long been an ethnically diverse society, and is now, mainly because of her imperial past, much more obviously one. All pupils must be brought to an understanding of what is entailed if such a society is to become a fair and harmonious entity.[17]

Some Afro-Caribbean groups have set up weekend supplementary schools. In these, children receive a mixture of teaching that emphasizes the black cultural heritage, correcting the European biases of history teaching, for example, and helps with the learning of basic skills. The fact that such a development seems necessary poses a different sort of challenge to the education system from that posed by Asian 'separatism': it suggests a need to tackle the biases in the system through the encouragement of culturally relevant studies, and the acceptance that there is a problem about the white view of society. It calls for a sophisticated understanding of the issues by all teachers, and special efforts to recruit black teachers.

This last problem about the education of black children links up very closely with the issue of the place lower-class white children find themselves occupying within the system, and with the quite concrete disadvantages of children from lower-income homes. Inasmuch as black entrants to Britain have generally been forced to accept many of the poorest jobs and worst houses, children find that the 'inferior' stereotype of the black person seems to be reinforced by their, and their parents', experience. Moreover, the fact that many black parents have had relatively little education themselves, and use a dialect form of English very different from that used in the schools, means that, like comparable lower-class white parents, they are ill-equipped to help their children tackle the education system. There is a web of reinforcing disadvantages here which makes the development of compensatory education particularly important for this group of children.

Readers may observe that this is the first time a section in this book has explored the issue of the impact of an area of social policy on ethnic minorities at any length. Many of the points made here are relevant to other policy areas. In particular the chapter on the personal social services might have discussed some of the issues about the inadequacies of service for minorities; and explored, in terms not unlike those used about educational separation, the issue of trans-racial adoption. Similarly the chapter on the health service could have dealt more with the extent to which there is an ethnic dimension to inequalities in health, and explored some of the communication difficulties which arise when white health professionals pay insufficient regard to cultural and language problems. Lack of space prevented those discussions, but readers are urged to think about the relevance of the points made here for those other policy areas.

## CONCLUSIONS

The state system of education had roots in a mid-nineteenth-century concern with the training of an effective workforce able to operate in an increasingly complex industrial system and society. Its growth has been inextricably bound up with the development of a democratic society. The original view that the newly enfranchised should be literate has been answered by a belief among the electorate that education holds the key to social advance. This may be in part an illusion. The opportunity structure is determined by the economy and by the political system. Increased education does not in itself increase the supply of 'top jobs'; it merely increases the competition for them. The fact that educational qualifications are widely used as a basis for discrimination between applicants for jobs emphasizes the link between education and social and economic advancement, regardless of whether or not those jobs require education at the level, or of the kind, possessed by those deemed best suited to fill them. Hence the nature of the education system and the opportunities it provides is of central political importance in Britain.

In this sense demands that 'politics should be taken out of education' are based upon a total failure to comprehend what either politics or education are all about. A study of education policy controversies in the past thirty years demonstrates a great deal about politics and administration in British society. A most complicated balance of power will be found between central and local government, and between politicians and professionals. Perhaps some of the demands that politics should be taken out of education come from a sense of individual frustration, among parents and pupils, about conflicts in which they feel fairly impotent. Education is perhaps the sector of social policy that people feel they understand best; they try hard to influence it but find that many of the key problems elude their grasp. The educational system's elusive quality should not however be explained simply in terms of the reluctance of political and professional elites to accept participation. Its very sensitive relationship to the economy and society makes controlling its interaction with social change very difficult.

## Suggestions for Further Reading

For a discussion of education policy with a particularly sociological slant readers should look at Finch's *Education as Social Policy*.[18] Regan has provided a very sound factual introduction to the organization of the education system,[19] while a book by Kogan provides a lively discussion of the key political issues.[20] The EPA report edited by Halsey (see n. 14) contains a good review of compensatory education in Britain. While it is now very dated, the literature on education and social class (see n. 12) and particularly the book by Jackson and Marsden, provides excellent insight into underlying issues that are still with us despite the near demise of the grammar schools.

Stone provides a useful examination of the issues surrounding the education of racial minorities,[21] as does chapter 6 of Rex and Tomlinson's study of race relations in Birmingham.[22] To them should be added the Swann Report, discussed in this chapter (see n. 16).

# CHAPTER 9

# Employment Services

## INTRODUCTION

Britain's manpower policies are the responsibility of the Department of Employment, but the running of the main employment and training services is delegated to the Manpower Services Commission (MSC) set up in 1974. The MSC has ten members drawn from both sides of industry, from local authorities and from education, and, of course, a large staff of civil servants. In the financial year 1985–6 about £3 thousand million was spent on employment and training services.[1]

At the centre of the work of the employment services are the Jobcentres, which seek to link potential employees with employers. At the time of writing the government has just announced that Jobcentres are to be brought back under the control of the Department of Employment in order to link them better with the administration of benefit.

This is the first of the two chapters in which, as was pointed out in the introductory chapter, a considerable amount of attention has to be given to economic issues. In the next chapter, on housing, it is a fact that a great deal of the provision is through a private housing market which requires attention. In this chapter, while it is true that employment services are provided by both public and private agencies, what forces particular attention to be given to the interaction between social and economic policies is that employment services represent a form of public intervention in the economy and that job opportunities are determined primarily by the working of that economy rather than by the specific interventions of the employment services. Effective employment services may contribute to the creation of a healthy economy, but they cannot in themselves 'cure' an unhealthy one.

Many discussions of employment services give little attention to their social role. They are seen as concerned with the effective working of the labour market, and not as services which provide social benefits. There are two reasons for disagreement with this approach to the study of employment services. The first of these is simply a dissatisfaction with the conventional distinction between social and economic policies, as suggested in chapter 1. Economic policies have social effects, and clearly the social effects of a service designed to help people secure satisfactory jobs as quickly as possible are most important. The second is that considerations other than concern to make the labour market operate efficiently enter into the employment services. The alleviation of unemployment is as much a social issue as an economic one. Indeed economic 'realism' may involve unconcern about unemployment and even a desire to maintain a 'reserve army of labour'.

A government may manage the economy without making any use of employment services, and the case for employment services as necessary for either economic or social ends is less easy to make than the case for, for example, health services or education. The employment services date from the early years of this century, and have played a fairly low key role until recentlly. Even today employment services expenditure, at about 2 per cent of public expenditure, is dwarfed by that on the other services discussed in this book.

The objectives of the employment services can be classified in terms of four functions. These have varied in importance over the history of the services in Britain with only the first two of them assuming much importance until fairly recently. The third was stressed as the great new goal for the services in the 1970s but has now fallen right away in importance to be replaced by the fourth. These four functions are:

1   the provision of basic help and training for the unemployed;
2   the policing of the unemployment benefit system;
3   'active manpower policy', in which the employment service is seen as playing a crucial role in preserving full employment without high inflation;
4   the mobilization of special initiatives to mop up unemployment, other than general economic measures to stimulate the economy.

Of course, these four functions are not entirely separable. Any specific measures may perform more than one function. Function 1 appears in most activities; in this chapter traditional, longstanding measures for the unemployed which have operated regardless of labour market conditions will be considered in the discussion of this function, while more recent innovatory measures are discussed in the relation to others. It should also be recognized that 'functions' may be determined by the perspective of the observer, or proclaimed by the government in order to justify itself. Hence the discussion of policies which is to follow, set out in terms of these four functions may be rather less detached than much of the rest of this book. For example, the British government still justifies many of its employment policies in 'active manpower' terms despite high unemployment and a much weakened trade union movement. To many observers, therefore, including the present author, much that it does seems more explicable in terms of functions 2 and 4 than in terms of a continuing commitment to function 3.


## THE PROVISION OF BASIC HELP, ADVICE AND TRAINING FOR THE UNEMPLOYED

The Jobcentres are the modern successors of the employment exchanges, set up in 1908 to do just what their name suggests, to link employers seeking workers with employees. In the 1970s the Jobcentres were seen as replacing the large institutional employment exchanges with modern shop front offices in commercial and shopping centres. In them there is an emphasis on self-service, individuals can select jobs from open display advertisements, only turning to staff when they think additional advice is necessary. The hopes for this approach have, however, been somewhat dashed by the rise of unemployment.

The Jobcentres have been seen as needing to work very like private employment agencies. One area of employment work where that principle has been taken to its logical conclusion is in the operation of the Professional and Executive Recruitment service. This charges employers for its services, and is required to 'break even' financially every year.

There is also a specific employment service for disabled employees, set up in the 1940s with assistance to injured ex-servicemen very much in mind. This service employs specially trained staff who give advice and help with job placement. Individuals may register as disabled workers, and employers have a statutory obligation to ensure that disabled people form at least 3 per cent of their workforces. This quota has been poorly enforced throughout its history. In the contemporary context of high unemployment the disabled have fared badly, and the quota has become so irrelevant that there has been some debate about repealing the legislation.

Before 1974 the provision of unemployment services to those under eighteen years of age was the responsibility of a separate youth employment service. The split between the youth service and the adult service was widely criticized. The government considered the option of abolishing the former, but in the end decided that the youth service, renamed the careers service, should continue to operate as a source of vocational and employment assistance for school-leavers and should be available to continue to help them for a time if they preferred to keep in touch with it. At about the same time the limitation of the service to help for the under-eighteens was abandoned. The new system requires close liaison between the local staff of the MSC and the careers service, run by the local education authorities.

Until the late 1970s the training activities of the MSC concentrated upon the re-training of adult workers to enable them to move to new employment. Since that time the training side of the employment services work has been increasingly concerned with the provision of training for young people who are unable to move directly into the labour market on account of the lack of jobs. In 1985–6 364,000 people were involved in the main youth initiative, the Youth Training Scheme.[2] Roughly half that number of adults were catered for by the job training programme. The Youth Training Scheme will be discussed separately below, under the measures considered to belong in function 4. What is stressed here is that special training measures for young people have come to dominate the system. It should be added also that since the traditional adult training emphasis was on training people for *real* labour market opportunities the decline in job openings has inevitably considerably altered its role.

## THE POLICING OF THE UNEMPLOYMENT BENEFIT SYSTEM

In chapter 5 it was shown that the unemployed are supported by the state, according to their previous work records and length of unemployment, on either flat rate unemployment benefit or means-tested 'income support' or some combination of the two. It was pointed out there that unemployment benefit could be stopped for up to thirteen weeks where individuals were found to have lost employment unnecessarily or to have failed to take employment opportunities. It might have been added that there are also powers to make deductions from 'income support' when these things occur.

There has been extensive controversy in recent years about the impact of the social security system upon the behaviour of the unemployed. High benefit levels are alleged to deter efforts to find work. Arguments centre upon two issues, the levels of income acquired by the newly unemployed, and the phenomenon of long-term unemployment.

It has been suggested that the introduction, in the mid–1960s, of earnings-related benefits and redundancy pay contributed to an increase in unemployment at that time. Economists have sought, by comparing other evidence on the state of the economy with data on unemployment, to test this hypothesis. It seems possible that these new benefits did have a slight effect upon employment durations among the short-term unemployed. They were, in a sense, designed to do this. They reduced the impact of redundancy and helped workers to avoid hasty relocation into inappropriate jobs. However, the difference they made was marginal, and in the long run the only effect of the particular cushioning of the newly unemployed may be slightly to increase the job prospects of rather longer unemployed people. Since they have their maximum effect near the beginning of a spell of unemployment they have no effect upon the phenomenon of long-term unemployment, which is of great significance at the present time.

However, it has also been suggested that unemployed people on means-tested benefits have been deterred from seeking work by the high levels of benefit relative to the lowest earnings levels. This has been used as an argument for ensuring that the unemployed gain less than any other group from the benefit system. The introduction of the 'family credit' scheme has been seen by the government as ensuring that people with family responsibilities will be better off in work than on benefit. The particularly harsh treatment of those under twenty-five under the 'income support' scheme helps to ensure that young people without family responsibilities cannot achieve benefit levels comparable with even exceptionally low wages.

In 1986 the government introduced the Restart Programme. This was designed for unemployed people who, the government said, 'need special help to return to work'.[3] It involves the interviewing of people who have been unemployed some time. They may then be offered a variety of things. This may include a job, of course, and in this case if it is a low-paid job then there may also be a temporary Jobstart Allowance of £20 per week. It may include reference to some other special scheme (see later discussion). Initially all that was offered to most people was attendance at a Restart course 'which remotivates and re-equips people to get back into employment' or at a Jobclub, 'which helps people in their own job searches with expert advice and free facilities'.[4] However in 1986, on an experimental basis, the government started up the Job Training Scheme. This involves provision by 'managing agents', who are paid for their services, of work experience and training for a period of six months. Trainees must be given a minimum of 300 hours training, in skills needed to equip them for the normal labour market. Allowances are paid consisting of the equivalent of social security benefit rates plus travelling expenses. At the time of writing, in 1987 the scheme is being extended from its pilot origins. There are 350 managing agents and about 15,000 places.

In many ways Restart is an extension of the helping services outlined in the last section. Why then include it under a section on the policing of the benefit system? There are two answers to this. One is simply to ask why government should be so concerned to develop a specific technique for reviewing the circumstances of the long-term unemployed at a time of very high unemployment. The other is to observe that at the time the government introduced Restart it also tightened the provision enabling the stopping of, or reduction of, benefits to those seen as failing to take employment opportunities so that the rejection of a specific job no longer has to be proved. In fact failure to attend a Restart interview can lead to the stopping of benefit. This is the verdict on Restart expressed by the civil service union which represents many staff in management and supervisory roles in Restart:

> To devote Jobcentre resources to this work is a diversion away from the primary jobfilling role. More important however is the damage to the relationships between the jobseekers and Jobcentre staff. If the unemployed are summoned to the local Jobcentre to have their continued eligibiliy for benefit scrutinized and challenged then it is difficult to see how an employment counselling service can succeed. Such a session must be based on free and frank discussions based on trust and a simple commitment to the Jobfinding task.[5]

The government's decision to bring Jobcentres back into the Department of Employment, to integrate them better into benefit administration, must be seen as a development of the same policy. It reverses the commitment made by an earlier Conservative government, when the MSC was created, to try to get away from the 'dole queue image'.[6] What is more there has been a persistent rejection of the other more logical move to integrate the administration of benefits for the unemployed with the rest of benefit work in the DHSS, to get away from the inefficient arrangement under which 'income support' for the unemployed is calculated by the DHSS but paid on its behalf by the Department of Employment.

ACTIVE MANPOWER POLICY

When it was setting up the Manpower Services Commission in 1974 the government stated in *People and Jobs*:

> the service is regarded by many workers and employers as a service for the unemployed – and mainly for manual workers at that. As a result, employers do not inform the Service of all their vacancies and some hardly use it at all. During the past five years, for example, workers registering for jobs have normally outnumbered notified vacancies by more than two to one. Thus, whereas the Service fills more than two in three vacancies, it places only about one in three of those who register. The task facing the Service is to break out

of a situation where employers do not use it because they doubt – sometimes rightly – whether it has suitable people on its books and where workers seeking jobs do not visit the local unemployment office because vacancies they want are not notified by the employers.[7]

In modernizing the service the government was clearly influenced by the Swedish concept of 'active manpower policy', in which the employment service was seen as playing a crucial role in preserving full employment without high inflation. Britain's own problem in swinging rapidly from situations of economic stagnation when unemployment began to rise into problems of an 'overheated' economy bringing inflation and balance of payments difficulties were seen as at least partly attributable to problems of labour supply. 'Overheating' was associated with difficulties in securing adequately trained skilled labour. It was felt that a more sophisticated employment service, dealing with a much higher share of the job placings and able to give more expert attention to training problems, would much more effectively match supply and demand in the labour market and thus contribute much better to the maintenance of a balanced economy.

In fact, the modernized employment services have so far had to operate in an economy in which the problems of both unemployment and inflation have been far worse than they were in the period between the Second World War and the end of the 1960s, and in which many economists have abandoned the orthodox 'Keynsian' belief that there is a direct and simple relationship between unemployment and inflation. While it is easy to sneer that Britain's conversion to active labour market policy came too late, it is indeed hard to discern whether or not the new service contributes to the mitigation of problems in a now very troubled labour market. Certainly the system has succeeded in ensuring that it is notified of a better proportion of vacancies than was the case in the past. About a third of all vacancies are notified and about a quarter of all engagements are made through it.

However, while *People and Jobs* saw the future of the service in terms of a lesser concern with the unemployed, and therefore a greater degree of assistance to those who sought to move between jobs, in fact the stagnation that has occurred in the labour market has forced the system to give a great deal of attention to the issue of unemployment. It is interesting to speculate, therefore, whether the creation of the Manpower Services Commission has been instrumental in creating the diverse and imaginative response to unemployment that has occurred (see next section).

Certainly some of the measures adopted – in particular job creation and the use of subsidies – seem to have been influenced by the more active manpower policies of countries like Sweden. Ironically. in

Sweden in the 1950s and 1960s such measures were seen as ways of helping the very small minority of the population unable to secure work on the open market when employment was as full as possible. They take on a rather different character in an economy characterized by a seriously deficient demand for labour. They have been criticized as inadequate alternatives to the effective management of the economy. One distinguished economist, the late Lord Vaisey, argued:

> The sum total of these schemes seems to me to be cosmetic rather than genuine in its economic consequences. What they do in effect is to push employment around a bit without much net effect. They are in no sense a substitute for the substantial regeneration of British industry.[8]

In economic terms the official answer to Vaisey's argument is that these schemes provide or protect jobs with minimal inflationary effects, by comparison with the more direct ways in which the economy might be stimulated. But there is also an interesting social issue here. This is that such policies may be used to influence the impact of the recession on particular groups of people. While they may do little or nothing to affect the overall level of employment, they may help to ensure that particular people – the young, the previously long-term unemployed, the residents in certain areas – experience the ill effects of worklessness rather less than other people.

Politicians, when they justify special measures to provide employment, deliberately obfuscate these issues. They want to be able to claim jobs saved, or created by government intervention, as contributions to the alleviation of unemployment as a whole. The actual macroeconomic effect of these interventions is, happily for them, profoundly obscure.

## The Mobilization of Special Initiatives

This, then, is how the special initiatives that have become of great importance in British employment policy since the late 1970s need to be seen: as measures designed to take the maximum number of people off the unemployment register (and thus to show that the government is doing something about worklessness) with the minimum economic effects. Minimizing economic effects is important since general efforts to re-stimulate the economy have come to be seen by many, and particularly by the Conservative government, as inflationary and damaging to Britain's economic position.

The two main special initiatives are the Youth Training Scheme (YTS) for young people and the Community Programme (CP) for adults. To these is being added, at the time of writing, the Job Training Scheme discussed above.

It has already been pointed out that about 364,000 young people were on YTS in 1985–6. They can remain in the scheme for up to two years; they are paid an allowance a little higher than they could get on benefits. There is a variety of schemes. Some are sponsored by private sector employers, providing work experience and training; whilst these are open to the objection that they provide free labour for profit-making organizations, they are, from the young people's point of view, close to the real world of work and may lead on to engagement in regular jobs. Others are provided by public and voluntary organizations. They may offer a better deal in respect of training, particularly for people who have got very little out of the education system, but may be less effective as bridges to work. As unemployment has tightened its grip upon Britain this scheme has evolved from an earlier group of experiments and has been extended in length. Today it is coming close to being part of the normal post-school experience of those who leave school on reaching sixteen. In 1984–5 28 per cent of sixteen year-olds who had left school were in employment, 23 per cent were unemployed, and 48 per cent were on YTS schemes.[9]

Two further points about the way in which YTS is coming to dominate the experience of sixteen to eighteen year-olds who have left school is the way in which the need for the scheme is coming to be seen as a mark of failure on the part of both the young people involved and the education system. Individuals who would, when the demand for labour was higher, have got work easily are now seen as in need of further 'training' before they can get work. At the same time the education system is seen as having let them down by not preparing them properly for the world of work. Of course, a simpler but more costly way to have removed this group from the unemployment statistics would have been to have raised the school-leaving age. However, there is perhaps something in the view that early school-leavers have had enough of the education system, and it enough of them, and that new and different agencies with a very clear vocational orientation can serve them better. That is a fair comment as far as the best of the YTS schemes are concerned, but many have been devised hurriedly and accepted with a minimum of vetting by the MSC, eager to meet the political demand for a vast increase in youth training.

It is worth commenting that YTS and its predecessors have grown in Britain at a time when the apprentice system, always weak by comparison with systems elsewhere in Europe, has been in decline. Opportunities for youngsters to learn skilled manual trades in this way are now very scarce. But YTS may be accelerating that decline by offering a limited, government-subsidized, version of traditional apprenticeship.

Similarly, whilst YTS was created because of the collapse of the youth labour market, it may be itself contributing to that collapse by allowing employers to get youngsters to work for no more than supervision costs whilst on the scheme.

The Community Programme (CP) provides temporary work, and limited training opportunities, for long-term unemployed adults. There are around 240,000 places at any one time.[10] Individuals cannot hold CP places for more than a year. Wages are paid, but are limited to an average to be achieved by any scheme. In practice this limits many places to less than full-time. The work is supposed to be of community benefit, but rules prevent it from being competitive with regular work. The consequence is that CP sponsors are generally local authorities and voluntary organizations, who have been able to identify activities which supplement their main tasks. We see, here, therefore the way in which CP has been designed to provide work with the minimum of direct impact on the economy. CP sponsors are typically organizations which have been hard hit by public expenditure restrictions. They are not allowed to use CP places to counteract these, but may find them sustaining less important activities than others that they have been forced to cut.

Alongside these measures are a number of smaller initiatives. There is a job-release scheme which helps to promote early retirement, providing subsidies which then create about 50,000 new jobs a year, and a job-splitting scheme to encourage work sharing, which provides under 1,000 new jobs a year. About 8,000 places are provided in the Community Industry scheme of temporary employment for very disadvantaged young people. One scheme which might perhaps have been mentioned in the last section, because it has a more obviously longer-run employment stimulation intent, is the Enterprise Allowance Scheme, which helps unemployed people to set up in self-employment, through initial subsidies. This had about 60,000 entrants in 1985–6.[11]

It could be that the attention in this chapter to the special employment measures will be rendered out of date by a recovery in the economy. Unfortunately this seems unlikely. Such pessimism is primarily based upon (a) the British economy's diminishing capacity to absorb labour as high-technology industry grows in importance, and (b) the present structure of the British population. The size of the group that will want to participate in the labour market is expected, in the absence of new measures, to grow rapidly during the next ten years. At one end of the system there are large numbers of young people leaving school; at the other end a relatively small number of people due to retire (the products of the low birth rate around the time of the First World War). In addition female participation in the labour force is growing rapidly, with increasing female work aspirations and a low birth rate. Hence if we look to the economy's recovery to solve the problem on its own it will require a growth rate higher than any Britain has enjoyed over a sustained period this century, simply to absorb the increasing numbers who want to work.

Clearly this situation has important implications for the contemporary emphasis upon what are essentially temporary palliatives. There is a case for the adoption of measures which reduce the workforce participation of those who form the main body in employment, through shorter hours and longer holidays, or firmer steps to exclude particular groups from the labour market. Since the exclusion of women is unlikely to be on the agenda, the choice seems to be between coming much more effectively to terms with youth unemployment, by accepting that entry to the labour market some years beyond sixteen should be the norm, and providing for earlier retirement. Both options are being taken up to some degree. Early retirement is encouraged, both by measures discussed above and by separately negotiated schemes for specific groups of employees (university teachers, for example). The new measures for the young unemployed are increasingly based on the assumption that 'training' is the most appropriate thing to offer, though it may well be asked 'training for what?'. Both options pose problems inasmuch as a lack of worthwhile alternative activities and a poverty-level income is the likely outcome for many people. But either may be preferable to leaving the ordinary working of the labour market to exclude people involuntarily from participation, particularly since the experience of unemployment is concentrated amongst those with the lowest skills, least education, least income and wealth, and poorest health.

However, many people prefer the shorter working hours alternative. The viability of this depends on how seriously it is pursued by the trade unions, and particularly upon the extent to which it is regarded as something other than a device to raise incomes through overtime. Its viability may also depend, however, upon the extent to which individuals refrain from using the extra time to take on second jobs. Political intervention in the labour market is notoriously beset by unintended consequences. The steps individuals may take to protect or enhance their incomes may sabotage attempts at 'work sharing'. Moreover the present government has shown little interest in working *with* unions in this way; it has been rather more concerned with ensuring that unions are unable to obstruct its efforts to restructure the economy. Work sharing does not generally figure in that restructuring.

CONCLUSIONS

For many years policies for the relief of unemployment, apart from macroeconomic ones, were confined to the provision of benefits and the availability of a relatively passive employment exchange system. The rise of unemployment in the 1970s was met by revitalized public agencies committed to 'active' manpower policy. This has led not only to extensive consideration of the case for intervening in the labour market on behalf of specific groups within the unemployed, but also to the development of job creation measures. These measures have proved difficult to operate because of strong inhibitions upon competition with the 'regular' labour market. In Britain today policies have been designed to maximize removals from the employment register while minimizing their inflationary effects. These policies have been conceived as temporary expedients. They are beginning to look rather permanent.

## SUGGESTIONS FOR FURTHER READING

This is another topic on which recent policy change has rendered many books rather dated. There has been a large number of recent books on unemployment, but few have dealt with the measures for the unemployed in any depth. Moon and Richardson's *Unemployment in the U.K.* is good on the politics of unemployment, and gives a reasonable amount of attention to the special measures.[12] A rather older book which still sets out the issues about unemployment and policies for the unemployed very well in Sinfield's *What Unemployment Means*.[13] Up-to-date analyses of policies are contained in the Unemployment Unit's regular *Unemployment Bulletin*;[14] and Dan Finn, one of the staff of that unit, has recently examined policies for the young in his *Training without Jobs*.[15]

# CHAPTER 10

# Housing

## INTRODUCTION

In 1985 the housing stock of the United Kingdom comprised nearly 22.5 million dwellings. Six million of them (27 per cent of the stock) were rented from local authorities, new towns and the Northern Ireland Housing Executive. About 2.5 million (11 per cent) were privately rented, about half a million of them from housing associations. Nearly 14 million (62 per cent) were owner-occupied.[1] We will see, in this chapter, that public policies influenced all these sectors, if not directly through public provision then indirectly through tax subsidies (in the case of the owner-occupied sector) or rent regulation (in the privately rented sector).

From the end of the First World War until 1979 the owner-occupiers and publicly provided sectors grew dramatically at the expense of the privately rented sector. Since 1979 the former has continued to grow but the latter has begun to decline, as a result of the sale of council houses to their occupiers.

These developments have been enormously influenced by government interventions. There have also, inevitably, been complex interactions between the sectors as the system has changed. For example, increased opportunities for owner-occupation have both diminished the demand for private renting and been partly created by landlords' desires to sell houses that seem no longer to offer a satisfactory return if they are let. We will return later to give more attention to some of the interactions of this kind that have policy implications. However, it is clearly simplest to introduce this discussion of policies by examining each sector separately.

## THE LOCAL AUTHORITY SECTOR

While there had been a small amount of public housing built earlier, the effective growth of this sector dates from the enactment of legislation after the First World War to enable local authorities to receive central government subsidies towards the provision of housing 'for the working classes'. A long succession of subsequent Acts of Parliament have elaborated this initiative, encouraging both the building of large estates designed to meet basic housing needs and the adoption of substantial slum clearance schemes. While the housing no longer has to be specifically 'for the working classes', this sector has become the main provider of houses for those unable to buy their own.

The history of the subsidy system developed in this sector is complicated. For many years the government used, but regularly changed, a system under which local authorities secured a fixed sum per dwelling annually over a fixed period of years. In the 1960s the Labour government adopted a new approach, without terminating the older subsidies, under which percentage subsidies were paid, effectively to subsidize the rate at which authorities borrowed money. However, in the 1972 Housing Finance Act the Conservatives sought to sweep away all the continuing older systems of subsidy. The objective was to move to a system in which general-purpose subsidies were eventually eliminated. They recognized the need to continue to subsidize certain particularly expensive forms of development, and in particular slum clearance. They also acknowledged a case for subsidizing low income tenants by requiring authorities to operate rent rebate schemes which received an element of national subsidy. Otherwise they expected local authorities to move towards balanced housing budgets by raising rents. A national system of 'fair rents', at higher levels than existing rents, was to be developed that might leave some authorities, whose housing commitments were particularly costly, with deficits that would be partly met out of central government grants. But most authorities should reach a position at which general-purpose subsidies would be unnecessary, and some would achieve surpluses which they would have to hand over to central government.

Naturally this new scheme was designed to be phased in gradually. Rents were to be increased in stages, and a 'transitional subsidy' was paid. Before the transition could be completed the Conservatives lost power, and the new Labour administration suspended the operation of the Housing Finance Act. However, something had to be put in its place. In 1975 the Housing Rents and Subsidies Act was enacted as a temporary measure, pending a thorough review of the system. This gave the local authorities back their power to fix rents. It also maintained the subsidies to the local authorities at the levels operating under the transitional arrangements for the implementation of the 1972 Act, and added the following:

> Subsidies towards new investment costs, and towards increases in the costs of servicing old debts [interest rates were rising fast at the time].

Special subsidies to help high cost areas.

Subsidies to enable rents to be kept down as part of the counter-inflationary policies of 1974–1976.

The promised review of the system was completed in 1977 and a 'consultative document' on housing policy was published.[2] This proposed a system that had some features in common with the Housing Finance Act but did not directly interfere with the authorities' power to fix their own rents, and did not entail a gradual phasing out of general-purpose subsidies. The general approach offered a potential for manipulation in a variety of ways determined by the ideology of the government operating it. The consultative document described the approach as follows:

(i) the starting point of the calculation of subsidy would be an authority's entitlement to subsidy in the previous year;

(ii) each year a basis for calculation of the *extra* expenditure admissible for subsidy – including extra costs of management and maintenance assessed on an appropriate formula – would be settled for the coming year in consultation with local authorities;

(iii) each year an appropriate level of increase in the 'local contribution' to costs, from rent and rates, would be determined for the coming year, also in consultation with local authorities;

(iv) if the extra admissible expenditure of an authority exceeded the increase in the 'local contribution', subsidy entitlement would be increased. If on the other hand the extra local contribution exceeded this extra expenditure subsidy entitlement would be correspondingly reduced.[3]

The Labour government fell in 1979 before it could enact this system, but the Conservatives' Housing Act af 1980 essentially took it over. Then, what became crucial, since the new government was committed to reducing as far as possible the central government subsidy to council house rents, was the annual assumptions made under point (iii) above about appropriate levels of rent increases. Loughlin describes what has happened as follows:

Central government subsidy has declined from £1,423 million in 1980–81 to £305 million in 1984–85. As a consequence, council house rents have increased dramatically; using a 1975 index base, council house rents stood at 336.8 in 1983 compared with the a retail price index of 257.6 and a mortgage repayment index of 264.3.[4]

The 1980 Act allows local authorities to make 'profits' on their housing accounts and pay these into the general rate fund. It is not known how many in fact do this, but it may be noted that whereas in 1981–2 350 of the 367 local housing authorities in England (95 per cent) received central government subsidy in 1985–6 only 99 (27 per cent) did so.[5] The authorities remaining in subsidy will tend to be urban authorities which were very heavily subsidized in the past and which had to set up very expensive housing schemes. However, there is one form of subsidy to tenants themselves which remains, that is rebates through the housing benefit scheme. As general subsidy has disappeared and general rents have gone up so housing benefit has tended to go up. To counteract this the DHSS reduced the availabiliy of housing benefits by steepening the rate at which they tapered off with income increases.

The determination of capital expenditure, that is primarily the building of new houses, is also based on a system devised in the late 1970s by the Labour government. Before 1977 local councils determined their home-building programmes without consultation with central government. However, to implement those programmes they had to secure central acceptance both to enable them to undertake such extensive investment and to obtain subsidies (inasmuch as subsidies were linked to specific building projects). Local government proposed, and central government would dispose. The whole system was relatively haphazard since central government tried to link its decisions to national, and relative local, priorities but was dependent upon local initiatives, and did not necessarily have an overall view of the national housing needs. Under the system established in 1977 local authorities are required to submit for annual central scrutiny their 'Housing Strategies and Investment Programmes'. These include not only their plans for the provision of new local authority housing, but also their plans to make loans for house purchase, to give grants for housing improvements, to improve their own stock, to clear unfit houses, to purchase houses and to assist housing associations. Statistical returns from the authorities are required on their own current and future activities, and on their intelligence on local housing needs and problems on private sector building. On the basis of these submissions the local authorities then, after a process of negotiation through the regional offices of the Department of the Environment, receive annual expenditure allocations, not in the form of specific permission for particular projects but in the form of a broad block.

The Thatcher government's impact upon this system in the early 1980s was simply to limit expenditure, particularly on new building. From 1985 onwards, however, there was some relaxation to allow for the improvement of the council housing stock. New building remained low. In the late 1970s local authorities in the United Kingdom built a little over 100,000 dwellings each year. In the early 1980s it was down to a little over 30,000 a year, and in 1985 it was 29,000.[6]

These changes in public housing policy in the 1980s, towards the reduction of subsidies and the restriction of new building need to be seen together with the government's stimulation of the sale of council houses. Local authorities' role in the provision of housing is beginning to be restricted. Legislation before Parliament at the time of writing endeavours to further this process by allowing local authority dwellings to be transferred to private and voluntary association landlords.

In the 1970s the Labour government had argued: 'There is no longer an absolute shortage of houses. Whereas in 1951 there were about 750,000 more households than houses in England and Wales, by 1976 there were 500,000 more houses than households.'[7] It went on to acknowledge that this did not imply a straightforward 'surplus' of houses. A considerable number of houses are temporarily vacant at any time and some people own two houses. However, it particularly emphasized the need to give attention to a range of special housing problems: regional and local imbalances in the supply of houses, the continuing presence of unfit or substandard houses (again unevenly spread across the nation) and the existence of specific groups in the population who have difficulties in securing access to houses adequate for their needs

The Conservatives have more crudely reduced the supply of council houses so that in the area of population pressure around London the numbers of the homeless suggests that a straightforward quantity problem still exists. In other places, however, the central problems concern the deteriorating quality of the housing stock and the existence of local authority dwellings that are difficult or impossible to let. This is an issue to which we will return.

OWNER-OCCUPATION

It has already been suggested that the examination of housing policy raises difficulties for any distinction between social policy and other areas of public policy. It might be imagined that the private market for owner-occupied houses had very little to do with social policy or indeed with government interventions into society. However, such an impression can be readily removed by an examination of the attention housing has been given in the policies of the major parties in the years since the Second World War. A central issue in the general elections of 1950 and 1951 was the performance of the Labour government in 'building' houses, and the claim of the Conservative opposition to be able to 'build' more houses. The argument was about the building of houses, but public authorities were not the only builders. The Conservatives came to power in 1951 committed to 'building' 300,000 houses a year, but many of these were to be built by private enterprise for owner-occupation. Indeed, the Conservatives increasingly encouraged the development of this sector during the 1950s. Both parties have, though in rather different ways, been concerned to assist the development of owner-occupation. They see an aspiration towards owner-occupation as having considerable electoral implications.

How then do public policies influence the owner-occupied housing sector? Of central importance is the large public subsidy to owner-occupiers that is given through the income tax relief available on mortgage interest payments. There has been some political debate as to whether it is appropriate to call relief from taxation a subsidy. What is indisputable is that, with income tax at the standard rate taking – after allowances – about a quarter of most earned incomes, an allowance of this kind reduces the actual rate of interest paid by mortgage borrowers by a quarter.

The value of the tax allowance on mortgage interest is dependent upon several things. Obviously the higher the rate of interest the more valuable the tax concession. This is what has made it so significant in recent years. High rates of interest have enormously increased the sum of money lost to taxation. Indeed, the amounts are now so large that they far exceed the subsidies to public housing. In 1986–7 tax relief to owner-occupiers cost about £4,500 million.[8] It must also be noted that the value of this concession to the individual depends upon his or her tax assessment. Those who pay tax at the higher percentage rates secure a proportionately higher benefit from this form of tax relief. Most important of all, the bigger the amount of the mortgage, the more relief an individual secures. Hence the concession benefits most those who can afford to spend most on housing. This consideration has led the government to restrict it to one house for each individual and to impose a ceiling on the size of mortgages, at the time of writing 30,000, beyond which it will not provide additional relief.

Mortgage interest relief was originally given when owner-occupied houses attracted a tax called Schedule A tax. But Schedule A tax was abolished in 1963. Now, therefore, owner-occupiers are securing help to purchase an asset the real cost of which is, so long as there is inflation, falling throughout the period of the mortgage. The peculiarity of owner-occupied housing today is that considerable financial sacrifices may be necessary to secure a house, but over time initial purchase costs, which of course determine mortgage size, come to be less and less in real terms. Owners have acquired assets that normally depreciate very much more slowly than money. Indeed the very existence of tax relief contributes to their appreciation.

Governments support the aspiration towards house ownership. They therefore want to help more people to become owner-occupiers. However, the peculiar evolution of the system has left them with a device which, while it does help first-time buyers, continues to yield great advantages to owner-occupiers long after they have first started to borrow and concentrates its help upon not low-income but on high-income house-purchasers. Various ideas have been canvassed to reduce what has been called the problem of 'front-loading' of mortgage costs. All require government subsidy to shift the balance of expense. Logically such government expenditure might be offset against some withdrawal of the indiscriminate mortgage subsidy. However, there is a political objection to that (voiced quite plainly in the Labour government's consultative document). This is that people make decisions to borrow money on the basis of certain expectations of tax relief. In other words, any sudden change would be sharply redistributive, would have its most severe impact upon those whose calculations left least margin for variation, and would therefore be very unpopular in a society where over half the householders are owner-occupiers and most of these are still repaying mortgages. The government has developed a number of special ways of helping first-time buyers (which space does not allow us to examne in any detail) but it will not upset the basic structure of mortgage-lending and related income tax relief.

It is not merely through subsidies that the government has influenced opportunities for individuals to secure owner-occupied housing. In the period immediately after the Second World War the government maintained a tight control over building through control over access to building supplies. As it relaxed these controls it stimulated private building. Then, in the 1950s, as it began to reduce the amount of local authority building it thereby encouraged a shift of resources into building for sale. During that period of management of a fully employed economy along Keynesian lines the government came to recognize that one of the ways in which it could most easily influence the economic climate was by influencing the demand for building. While the direct controls of the immediate postwar period no longer exist, there remains a series of factors that influence the scale of building of houses for sale: the extent to which alternative – particularly public sector – opportunities exist for the building industry; the availability of credit – particularly cheap credit – for building enterprises and land speculators; the supply of building workers – particularly skilled workers; the availability of building society funds for home buyers; and the availability of land.

The building societies are interesting financial institutions, with some characteristics not found in many other societies. Their origins lie in nineteenth-century self-help and charitable ventures, and they remain in some sense non-profit-making institutions. They depend for their operation on being able to attract funds at predetermined rates of interest to lend to house-buyers. To be able to continue to be active lenders they must be able to borrow money, yet their borrowing capacity depends heavily upon fluctuations in the attractiveness of other investments. Hence their capacities to lend vary enormously through time in ways that bear no relation to the demands from home-buyers. Futhermore, when money is scarce interest rates to lenders have to be raised to attract funds. Since this implies also the raising of rates to borrowers, this shortage of money can be offset only by a change in policy that makes it harder for house-buyers to afford to borrow. This has become a problem of great concern to the government, which has therefore intervened to try to ensure that excessivley cautious lending policies are suspended when money is scarce, and to try to limit the extent to which the societies raise interest rates. Such a policy can be sustained only if the government itself moves in to supply funds, and on one occasion this was what was done. A development of this kind clearly involves government in housing policy in a new way. Yet there are problems entailed in such *ad hoc* responses. When, because of high inflation, the government sought to protect home-buyers in this way it contributed in a most peculiar way to the redistribution of resources. Lenders to building societies, many of whom were small savers with few other ways of safeguarding funds, were being paid rates of interest well below the inflation rate, and were thus losing money, while borrowers were being protected from high interest rates by the government intervention and were thus receiving inflated subsidies. Such are the problems of government intervention, for political motives, in a mixed economy.

Government encouragement of home ownership naturally entails, now that the proportion of the population with their own houses is so high, a concern to open opportunities to borrow money to those who are regarded by the building societies, who have been naturally cautious in these matters, as 'bad risks'. Hence there has been governmental pressure upon these 'private' organizations to lend to more 'marginal' people or on more 'marginal' properties.

Government intervention in the land market also has an impact upon owner-occupation – both by affecting the availability of building land and by affecting its price. Of course these two are interrelated, and one of the problems for intervention in the land market has been the relative unpredictability of these two effects. A concern about profiteering from land speculation has influenced legislation by all the postwar Labour governments, while the Conservatives have sought to reduce the Labour impact upon a free market for land. The actual impact upon private housing of this long-running political battle – through the Town and Country Planning Act of 1947, the repeal of many of its features by the Conservatives in the 1950s, the 1967 Land Commission Act, the

Community Land Act of 1975 and its repeal in 1980 – is unclear, and cannot be considered here. This issue is mentioned, however, because it is important not to overlook the significance of land legislation for the housing market.

## THE PRIVATE RENTED SECTOR

The private-rented sector (excluding the housing association sector – see later sector), which now houses only about 9 per cent of the population, is increasingly seen as the 'residual' sector. Since, however, its decline to this position is a relatively recent phenomenon (in 1951, over half of the households in England and Wales were in this sector and in 1918 probably about 90 per cent were renting privately), it is important to register the impact of its decline. It is also important to acknowledge that the decline may continue, in which case an absence of accommodation of this kind, which is beginning to be the case in some areas, will have important implications for other sectors, and particularly for the local authorities.

There has been a political, but now rather academic, argument about the causes of the decline. Was the decline of the private rented sector inevitable, as better outlets for investment opened up, or was its decline produced by public intervention in the housing market? What we can say now is that, except in certain very special markets (high class flats in central London), the rent levels that would be required to attract investment of this kind would probably be publicly unacceptable. The remaining rented property is either very old, and much of this will either be sold as tenants die or be acquired by local authorities as it becomes unfit, or owned by people who have special reasons for not wanting to sell.

Political controversy has raged over the protection of private tenants from both eviction and high rents. The fair rent principle adopted for most forms of private tenure represents a political compromise based on a comparatively nonsensical formula in which rent officers are expected to assume that properties are let in a market in which there is no scarcity. The first lesson any student of economics learns is that market prices are determined by the balance between supply and demand. However, fair rents are determined by a system of comparisons at levels some way below what the market may be expected to bear.

Private tenants may acquire housing benefits when their incomes are low. The Thatcher government seems to be unhappy about the system of rent control. The use of loopholes in the law by private landlords – notably the system of granting 'licences to occupy' rather than tenancies

– has been tolerated, and at the time of writing much greater relaxation of control is envisaged in legislation before Parliament. It may be presumed that in this sector, as in council housing, the housing benefit scheme will be allowed to grow as a form of subsidy to allow low income people to take on high rented property. Such a shift from rent control to rent subsidy could possibly lead to some revival in the private sector. However, as was shown in chapter 5, housing benefits for private tenants tend to have a low rate of take up. Moreover there are rules in the housing benefit scheme to enable authorities to resist demands for them to rebate in full rents which are regarded as unreasonably high. We have another example here, as there has been with council house rents, of one government department, Environment, adopting policies which force rents up while another, DHSS, resists the implications of these policies for housing benefit expenditure and passes the cost on to low income tenants.

The private rented sector is unevenly distributed across the country. In some areas, and particularly in the North, there are still old, poor-quality houses occupied by elderly tenants who have been in them for very many years. With this property the main public concern has been about conditions. Local authorities have included many such houses in their slum clearance programmes. As they have removed the worst houses it has been increasingly questioned whether improvement is not preferable to demolition. A feature of the better estates of old houses has been the piecemeal extension of owner-occupation among the rented property. Owner-occupiers have been more ready to make use of improvement grants than landlords. The consequence has been the patchy regeneration of such areas. To further this process therefore local authorities have been able to designate 'general improvement areas' or 'housing action areas' where they can better the overall environment and pressurize or buy out private landlords in order to secure the improvement of the remaining houses.

Elsewhere the private sector may have rather different characteristics. In London in particular, but also in many other big cities, much of this accommodation is in the form of flats created out of large old houses. Local authorities may again tackle the problems of these areas through compulsory purchase or improvement, but they are often reluctant to go beyond the more limited powers they possess to curb the worst abuses of 'slum landlordism'. In the 1980s there has been a lack of support from central government for the 'municipalization' of private rented housing. These areas tend to accommodate people whom local authorities do not see as their responsibility (or at least place very low on their scales of priorities): in particular, newcomers to the area and the young single. The concentration of housing problems in areas of this kind, therefore, offers a challenge for the development of more comprehensive local authority policies. As other housing problems have been solved the gap between the good housing conditions of the majority and the often very poor conditions experienced in this part of the private sector has become increasingly evident.

## HOMELESSNESS

It is appropriate to follow a discussion of the most problematical part of the private sector with an examination of the issue of homelessness, because those who seek a local authority's help because they are homeless often come from that sector and must often return to it if they are refused public help. It is the decline in availability of even this very poor form of accommodation that has increased the need for effective local authority response to the problem of homelessness. The paradoxical growth in homelessness against a background of diminishing housing scarcity is closely linked with this decline in privately rented accommodation, and the importance of barriers to access provided by income requirements in the owner-occupied sector and bureaucratic rules in the public sector. These problems particularly arise in the high housing pressure, high cost environment of Greater London.

In 1977 the Housing (Homeless Persons) Act imposed a duty upon local housing authorities to provide accommodation for homeless persons in certain 'priority' groups. These priority groups are, broadly, families containing children or elderly or sick persons, together with those made homeless by disasters such as flood or fire. However, authorities need not help families who are deemed to have become homeless 'intentionally'. This controversial provision was added to the Act by an amendment and may be used to justify refusal of help to someone who is evicted for not paying rent.

This Act is an interesting one, since for many years there had been uncertainty about the relative responsibilities for helping the homeless of the housing and the social services authorities. In 1974 a government circular urged housing authorities to provide adequate help for the homeless. The resulting patchy response intensified the conflict between housing and social services in some areas, and created anomalies where neighbouring authorities treated the homeless very differently. The government decided, under strong pressure from some of the housing charities, to rectify this by legislation. However it could not find time for this in the 1976–7 parliamentary session. But when a Liberal member, Stephen Ross, promoted a private member's Bill they gave full governmental support. Hence the law was changed in an unusual way. The new legislation aims to secure a more uniform response and, by making it mandatory for any authority to give temporary help and for more permanent help to be given where a homeless person has a (carefully defined) local connection, to end the buckpassing between authorities that caused great distress and hardship. The other important aspect of the clear shift of responsibility is that it is implicit within the Act that the homeless must be rehoused, except on a very temporary basis, in permanent homes, and not herded into the inadequate accommodation that was so often provided by the social services departments. In this sense they are in competition with those rehoused by the housing departments from their waiting lists. In practice many authorities, particularly in London, use poor quality temporary accommodation for housing homeless people for long periods of time.

HOUSING ASSOCIATIONS

It has already been noted that there is a housing association sector owning around half a million homes (around 2 per cent of the housing stock). Housing associations were important in the nineteenth century, as voluntary, charitable bodies, but declined with the growth of the public sector in the twentieth. But over the last twenty years housing association growth has begun to be given government envouragement, being seen as an alternative form of 'social' housing to the large and bureaucratic local authority sector. Housing associations may receive grants and subsidies from government, through the Housing Corporation. The legislation which will enable local authority tenants to opt to have their houses shifted out of local authority control may greatly enhance the housing association sector. Housing associations vary widely in size, scope and character. Some differ little in their characteristics from private companies, many have district charitable aims and objects, and a small number are cooperatives.

LOCAL AUTHORITY ALLOCATION PROCEDURES

Wherever there is competition for local authority housing the determination of rules to govern priorities is an emotive matter. As local authority housing began to become big business most authorities changed from systems that depended upon the judgements, or whims, of councillors or officials to waiting lists based upon some queuing principles. The main issues were first, to what extent the simple queuing approach should be modified by the development of 'points systems' which enabled individual priorities to be weighted; second, what the balance should be in such systems between needs and waiting time; and third, whether any preference should be extended to those who had resided in the area for some time.

Central government has become increasingly critical of local schemes that do not give overwhelming importance to need. Local authorities have also been urged to abandon residence requirements, both because they may have an impact upon labour mobility and because they may facilitate a covert form of racial discrimination. An official committee, the Cullingworth Committee,[9] strongly urged the adoption of need based points schemes in a report published in 1969. There has been a distinct move towards the development of points schemes; this was particularly enhanced by the abolition of many smaller housing authorities when local government was reformed in 1974. However, local commitments to residence rules die hard. On this issue, together with the issue of secrecy about the nature of points schemes, the 1977 consultative document promised a tougher line from central government. It asserted that the government:

> believe that proposals to control local authorities' allocation policies centrally
> – for example by laying down a statutory framework of allocation schemes –
> should be rejected with the following two exceptions:
> – ending the practice of imposing residential or other qualifications on a housing list;
> – requiring publication of allocation schemes.[10]

However much a local authority endeavours to govern its allocation policies by fair and open points schemes, it has also to make allowance for housing priorities that do not fit those schemes. Homelessness has already been mentioned as one example of this. Slum clearance schemes bring re-housing responsibilities that may cut across waiting list allocation in a significant way. On some occasions in the recent past authorities' commitments to major schemes have brought other movement from waiting lists almost to a standstill. Individual unfit houses may also require immediate responses, unanticipated by waiting list procedures. Finally, some authorities recognize special categories of need, which cannot readily be translated into housing 'points', determined by health or social work priorities, and allow other agencies to make special recommendations. These call for discretionary judgement by housing officials and by doctors or social workers, and there is also an inevitable tension between the maintenance of rules and special arguments for 'queue-jumping'.

## HARD-TO-LET HOMES

Allocation of council houses involves achieving a balance between what people want, what they are deemed to need, and what is available. In the past, under conditions of housing scarcity, individuals were, unless their co-operation was required with a redevelopment scheme, in a weak position to assert their wants. Housing authorities allocated on the basis of assessments of need, attempting to make the most efficient use of the housing stock. But they often gave attention to capacity to pay, and many were also disposed to make judgements about potential tenants' suitability for 'good' houses. Elizabeth Burney portrayed this decision making as follows:

> The principle is simple: a clean person gets a clean house and a dirty person gets a dirty house. In between are all kinds of subtle gradings which are the everyday material of housing management. Quiet, clean, steady-earning families with not more than three children are highly prized because they make life easy for management and their neighbours. They are usually repaid by being put near other 'good' families in better houses. The most unsatisfactory tenants may only get old terraced property awaiting demolition, or rehabilitated as part of the council's permanent stock; or simply one of the shabbier inter-war houses.[11]

The Cullingworth Committee also attacked this aspect of housing management. Housing authorities have become increasingly sensitive to the problems entailed in, and following from, policies of this kind. However, as in some areas the numbers of families who are desperate for help declines, so the balance of power between housing officers who judge needs and potential tenants who express their demands inevitably shifts. Now, poorer houses are often only easily allocated to, for example, the homeless. However, a reshuffling of tenants proceeds all the while, and those allocated the 'bad' houses seek transfers to better ones. Often they secure such transfers only if they have been 'good' tenants, and in particular if they have been regular rent-payers. The only people who shift in the opposite direction are those who are punished for rent arrears, or strikingly non-conforming behaviour, by being evicted from 'good' houses into 'bad' ones.

Local authorities now have stocks of houses and flats of various kinds, in particular, prewar semis, postwar semis built when standards were very low, modern houses built to very high 'Parker Morris' standards,[12] flats in blocks of various sizes, good old houses acquired from private owners, and patched houses with short lives pending demolition. Of course these dwellings vary in popularity, with perhaps high flats and short-life houses as the least popular. If through allocation and transfer policies there are various forms of segregation within an authority's housing stock, then the 'hierarchy of popularity' will have been influenced by social as well as architectural considerations. Indeed, these social factors may well complicate the hierarchy as certain estates, not necessarily characterized by severe design problems, also acquire reputations as 'rough' or 'respectable', perhaps as a result of some really rather complex accidents of history. The sale of council houses (see next section) further complicates the picture, since houses on popular estates and estates in which the more prosperous tenants live will be more likely to be sold.

As a result of this mixture of factors local authorities now find that, where the demand for housing is falling, they have 'hard-to-let houses'. Families still in quite poor conditions in the private sector regard their existing situations as preferable to rehousing in, for example, a badly vandalized tower block. Authorities' problems may be compounded moreover, by the fact that those families least able or likely to object to these undesirable dwellings may be the very families who, rightly or wrongly, are identified in the eyes of others as contributing to the stigma attached to them. Moreover, some aspects of this vicious circle have already been identified above. What do the authorities do about applications for transfers out of unpopular dwellings? And if an authority does not want to create homelessness, what weapon can it use against bad rent-payers but 'demotion' to less desirable accommodation?

Authorities resort to a variety of devices in these situations. Some do halt transfers, and seek to allocate unwary 'good' tenants to unfavourable property, but this is unpopular and may have political repercussions. In some cases architectural and environmental improvements may help. In some areas a group whom hitherto local authorities have largely ignored, the young single, are accommodated in unpopular properties, particularly high flats. Some authorities have sold some blocks of flats cheaply to private owners. But in some cases demolition, even of relatively modern property, has been seen as the only answer. In many places local authorities are worried about the extent to which they are becoming new kinds of 'slum landlords'.

## THE SELLING OF COUNCIL HOUSES

The Conservative party has advocated the selling of council houses to their occupiers for some years. While Labour generally, and particularly Labour local authorities, resisted this policy, their line on this issue was modified in the 1970s.

The Conservatives came to power in 1979 determined to stimulate the sale of council houses. Table 10.1 charts the success of the government's sales policy in the 1980s.[13] Its Housing Act of 1980 provided a statutory right to tenants to buy their own houses, at market prices less a discount based on length of tenancy ranging from 33 to 50 per cent. Subsequently the government put pressure on Labour-controlled authorities which dragged their feet in implementing this provision, going so far in one case, Norwich, as to secure legal intervention to enable it to put in a special commissioner to do the job.

TABLE 10.1   Sales of dwellings owned by local authorities and new towns, 1980–1985

| Year | Dwellings |
| --- | --- |
| 1980 | 92,140 |
| 1981 | 124,275 |
| 1982 | 227,720 |
| 1983 | 170,130 |
| 1984 | 129,780 |
| 1985 | 116,165 |

Since council tenants are, generally speaking, low income people, and the 1980s has been a time of high unemployment and increasing poverty, there must be a tendency for council house sales to fall away over time. Table 10.1 suggests this is beginning to happen. It is also the case that the success of the policy varies markedly from area to area, according to levels of prosperity. The government continues to seek ways to encourage purchase by tenants, but is now, as we have seen, exploring other ways of distributing local authority housing to new owners, such as housing associations.

The debate about the selling of council houses is partly a technical one about the actual effect of such a sale upon the housing effort as a whole, and partly an ideological one about council tenants' rights. Even if it believes that a council house sale diminishes its capacity to respond to unmet needs – this is a complex issue which we cannot go into here – a Labour local authority is faced by a peculiar dilemma about putting the interests of potential future tenants above those of actual present ones.

This debate must also be seen in the light of what was said in the last section about hard-to-let houses. The houses that tenants are likely to buy will be in 'good' popular estates. The developmentwithin these of a mixture of owner-occupation and renting may be seen as desirable for the future of such estates, in the long run extending social mixing and social diversity to those estates. But such a development reinforces the growing gap between the 'good' estates and the 'bad'. In this way it reinforces a future for local authority housing, in a society in which owner-occupation is continuing to grow, in which public renting will be seen as a much inferior option to ownership. The political problem is that owner-occupation is popular, and its growth seems therefore desirable, but this growth leaves a minority behind in possibly decreasingly satisfactory circumstances.

It is significant that in order to enhance the sale of council houses the government has been forced to provide large discounts. The fact is that for several years already the greater desirability for prosperous working-class people of owner-occupation as against council housing has been so clear that few who can readily afford mortgages for full-cost house purchase are left on council estates. Many who have incomes high enough to buy are already too old to take out a mortgage of normal length. The provision of discounts weakens the economic arguments for sales; older houses that are, perhaps quite reasonably, sold to long-term sitting tenants at low prices still have to be replaced, if there is outstanding housing need, by new highly expensive houses. The issue draws our attention to a variation of the same anomaly as exists within the owner-occupied sector: there is a vast gap between the original 'historic' costs of housing and modern 'replacement' costs. In the owner-occupied sector someone who bought a house, say in the 1960s, for £2,000 may today be repaying a minute (by modern standards) mortgage. If he or she dies heirs will receive as asset worth over ten times the original price. In the local authority sector a similar house may, assuming rents have moved in line with prices, today be yielding the local authority a 'profit', which it returns to the rent pool to subsidize newer houses. What is a fair rent (in the true sense – not in the sense in which it is used in the Rent Acts) for such a house? And if the occupier wants to buy, what is a fair price? There are no right answers to these questions; the whole situation is riddled with anomalies. To treat such a tenant well is to give a privilege relative to those who are still seeking local authority accommodation. To treat him or her harshly is to emphasize his or her disadvantage relative to the long-term owner-occupier.

## CONCLUSIONS

The latter part of this chapter has particularly emphasized the issues that arise from the interaction between Britain's three major housing sectors as pressure of demand begins to fall, and as the growth of owner-occupation and the decline of the private sector continue. The interactions here are complex. Recent studies of housing have given attention to·movement between the sectors, examining the filtering hypothesis which suggests that the benefits of new houses, even at the top of the owner-occupier market, filter down to contribute to the reduction of housing need. Superficially this seems plausible. However, the 'chains' that have been traced resulting from new houses at the 'top' end of the system are often short. Typically they extend down only to a young new entrant to owner-occupation, perhaps from that special part of the private sector where the needs of the young mobile middle class are met, perhaps merely forming a new separate household for the first time.[14]

In this concluding section it is intended neither to overload the argument that can be developed from this sort of example nor to elaborate at any length the findings of the research from which it is drawn. What must be stressed is that three very different kinds of housing 'career' can be detected. Many involve movement into or entirely within the owner-occupied sector as described above. Some involve movement, either on separation from a parental home or via the private rented sector, to council housing, but then stop there for the rest of life. And some, of diminishing significance, involve difficulty in moving from the private rented sector to either of the other more privileged sectors. The argument in this chapter has involved acceptance that the last of these 'careers' is likely to die out. If this is correct, then some of the peculiar problems we have identified about the different expectations within the two major sectors become of increased importance. At the moment interchange between them takes the form of movement out of local authority housing (often by purchase of a council house).

What are the implications for social segregation in Britain if this remains the case? But equally, what are the implications of those interchanges that do occur, since they may, as the examination of the issue of the sale of council houses implied, reinforce this new form of social segregation? It is a division in our society that does not precisely correspond with the social class division between manual and non-manual work which has received so much attention in the past. Yet it is a division that may have equally serious implications for the allocation of opportunities and for territorial justice in our society. Perhaps too little attention has been given so far to aspects of the interaction of housing policies and other policies – in particular employment and education policies. The progressive reshaping of our housing system over the past twenty to thirty years emphasizes the need for attention to this issue.

SUGGESTIONS FOR FURTHER READING

Donnison and Ungerson's *Housing Policy* provides an overview of British housing policy which puts it in a European context.[15] The many issues about housing finance are well discussed in Lansley's *Housing and Public Policy*,[16] while Merrett's *State Housing in Britain* provides an historical analysis of British housing policy rooted in a Marxist theoretical framework.[17] Two books which deal with contemporary developments such as the sale of council houses are Malpass and Murie's *Housing Policy and Practice* and Malpass's edited collection, *The Housing Crisis*.

# CHAPTER 11

# Social Policy and Society

## INTRODUCTION

This book has given attention to the major policy areas that are conventionally labelled 'social policy'. It has shown that within these areas the state is responsible for a wide range of activities. In the chapters on individual policies a number of weaknesses were noted in the pattern of provision. Yet it is widely suggested today that the state takes on too much, and that the public service sector, of which the social policy areas account for a large proportion, is too large. We need therefore to look, in this final chapter, at some of the general issues about the role of social policy in society and at some of the attempts to make social policy, as a whole, more effective and more responsive to popular needs and attitudes.

First, however, some figures must be considered to place social policy expenditure in the context of national expenditure.

Table 11.1 provides figures setting out expenditure under the main functional headings with which this book has been concerned together with some other functions, for the purposes of comparison. It compares expenditure in the first full year of Conservative rule in the 1980s with 1986–7, using what are described as 'real terms' figures. These are figures adjusted to common price levels, in this case those prevailing in 1984–5, to try to eliminate the distorting impact of inflation.

The total amount of public expenditure is about 43 per cent of the 'gross domestic product' (GDP). The latter is defined as 'the value of goods and services produced by United Kingdom residents'.[2] It has fallen to this level from about 45 per cent in the early 1980s. Of course, the relationship of public expenditure to the GDP depends upon both the level of public expenditure and the level of productive output. Politicians pay attention to the relationship between public expenditure and GDP, and some critiques of the welfare state suggest that it is dangerously high. However, much public expenditure involves no more in practice than transfers between citizens (as in social security

TABLE 11.1  Public expenditure by function (£ million in real terms, with proportion of total public expenditure in brackets)

| Function | 1980–1 | 1986–7 | Rate of growth 1980–1 to 1986–7 (%) | Average annual rate of growth (%) |
|---|---|---|---|---|
| Housing | 7,308(6.1) | 3,558(2.8) | –51.3 | –8.6 |
| Education and Science | 17,099(14.3) | 15,955(12.6) | –6.7 | –1.1 |
| Health and personal social services | 18,194(15.3) | 20,065(15.8) | 10.3 | 1.7 |
| Social security | 31,086(26.1) | 40,365(31.8) | 29.8 | 5.0 |
| Industry, energy, trade and employment | 7,440(6.2) | 6,037(4.8) | –18.9 | –3.1 |
| Defence | 14,388(12.1) | 16,883(13.3) | 17.3 | 2.9 |
| Law, order and protective services | 4,894(4.1) | 6,132(4.8) | | |
| Total national public expenditure | 119,196 | 126,735 | 6.3 | 1.1 |
| Total local authority expenditure (within the national total) | 32,044(26.9) | 32,001(27.5) | –0.1 | –0.0 |

payments). Hence the notion, sometimes expressed, that a large part of the output of the nation is absorbed into the 'unproductive' public sector is rather misleading.

Some points about the data in table 11.1 are worth underlining. If we treat the first four rows in the table as representing 'social expenditure', that is leaving out employment and including some items in the education budget which have not been considered (scientific research and library expenditure, particularly), we find that it represents 63 per cent of public expenditure. Between 1980–1 and 1986–7 social expenditure has grown slightly faster than public expenditure as a whole, largely because of the large increase in social security expenditure. It is the comparative absence of this item from local expenditure (only the housing benefit scheme is locally administered) that accounts for the fact that the government has been able to curb the growth of spending by local authorities whilst it has failed to check its own expenditure increase. The Thatcher government has been committed to public expenditure cuts but has not achieved them. We will come back to this, and discuss a little more the detailed changes to expenditure on the various services, but let us first digress a little to examine the ideological perspectives which may influence the way we assess the performance of the so-called 'welfare state'.

ALTERNATIVE PERSPECTIVES ON SOCIAL POLICY AND THE STATE

The financing of extensive public expenditure requires heavy taxation. It is argued that the size of the redistributive exercise via taxation into public expenditure undertaken by the British government has a disincentive impact upon private initiative and has contributed towards low productivity. It is also suggested that the scale and the scope of the state 'bureaucracy' is such that public resources are inevitably used inefficiently. The British people are alleged to be overtaxed and overgoverned. These are propositions about public expenditure found in the attack upon the welfare state which comes from the political Right.[3]

One way of examining propositions of this kind is to compare Britain with other countries. Newspaper articles regularly attempt to do this, skating cheerfully over the many problems about making such comparisons, in particular different definitions of public expenditure and the gross domestic product. Nevertheless such comparisons tend to show that, while in the United States public authorities proportionately tax less and spend less, Britain's position in league tables of comparable European countries is not particularly exceptional. Perhaps this merely proves that 'overgovernment' is a shared European problem. Alternatively, it may be suggested that the important comparisons concern not overall taxation and expenditure but kinds of taxation, in particular differences in the use made of direct and indirect taxation, and kinds of expenditure. There are some very clear differences in the extent to which different nations use insurance devices in relation to expenditure on social security and health; and widely differing uses are made of means tests to control spending on all the major services.

Hence while attention to comparison between overall levels of public expenditure may not be very revealing, the more detailed examination of ways of providing social policies introduces us to some of the main standpoints in political debate. Government in modern industrialized societies is unlikely to be indifferent to the need to provide cash for those unable to earn, education for the young and health care for all, but it may choose various options for their provision. It may seek to encourage, regulate and strengthen broadly private provisions. It may devise very mixed forms of private and public services. Or it may lay its emphasis on public services, and in so doing endorse the possibility of extensive social engineering towards egalitarian goals.

Certainly political theorists on the Right see the provision of health and social care, housing and education, together perhaps with social security (beyond some bare minimum), as the responsibility of the individual. It is asserted that instead of depending upon a paternalistic state people should be free to make choices about amounts and kinds of social benefits just as they make choices about the purchase of ordinary consumer goods. This perspective is likely to embrace the view that a protective welfare state is undesirable, and that individual initiative and independence are desirable characteristics of society which are undermined by welfare measures. People of this persuasion generally regard the existing range of social policies as already too developed in this respect. They argue, therefore, in favour of the maintenance of private sectors in health and education, and of the rationing of services through charging policies.

The advocates of less government involvement, and of the extension of the role of the market, generally have a stance on social equality too. While it could be the case that bureaucratic rigidity and the lack of choice in the present social welfare system might be reduced by an extension of the free market system, changes to such a system might leave vulnerable low income groups unprotected. In theory such problems might be countered by government interventions to enhance the incomes of the poor and decrease inequality. Hence the poor would gain both more income and more choice. Their difficulty with such compensating changes is that they would entail very extensive government interventions to equalize incomes. These would be anathema to those who expound the virtues of free enterprise. They require instead the distribution of incomes to be determined by the 'hidden hand' of the market. Modern British society is today an enormous distance away from such a free market. Clearly political realists among the exponents of this view have a gradual programme of moves towards their ideal society. They look to means of enhancing private social policies, with state policies playing underpinning roles.

The most clear alternative to this perspective sees social policies as potentially able to contribute to the redistribution of income in Britain. As Titmuss and his colleagues developed the study of social policy in

Britain in the 1950s they were concerned to attack the complacent belief that the creation of a 'welfare state' has occurred, particularly through the social policy reforms of the 1940s, in which state-promoted policies had secured a very much more equal society. It was pointed out that the main beneficiaries of some of the key reforms were the relatively well-to-do. The free health service extended benefits to all, but was more used by the higher social classes. The middle classes could now send their children to grammar schools without having to pay fees. Even the main extensions of the social security system gave the better-off access to benefits from which they were previously excluded. At the same time, while it was true that the tax burden had considerably increased for higher earners, a wide range of concessions and untaxed fringe benefits offset this or provided compensating benefits.[4]

Towards the end of the 1950s researchers, including notably Abel-Smith and Townsend,[5] showed that extensive poverty was still present in Britain. Not only were there large numbers of people dependent upon that subsistence level guaranteed by national assistance, but there were also many – a considerable proportion of whom were in families containing a full-time wage-earner – with incomes below or only a little above that level.

Hence it was argued that the 'welfare state' was neither markedly redistributive nor particularly effective at eradicating poverty. Studies of the overall distribution of income and wealth suggest that the degree of equalization that has occurred in the course of the twentieth century has been comparatively slight.[6]

But should social policy be redistributive? Is the prevailing degree of inequality acceptable? And is the extent and nature of poverty tolerable? Students of poverty have tended to shift their attention away from consideration of an absolute definition, in terms of the minimum income necessary to sustain life, to a relative one.[7] While it is accepted that of course the poor in Britain are very much better off than the poor in, for example, India, it is argued that poverty needs to be interpreted in terms of the standard of life attained by others in the same society. Probably most people in Britain today, no matter how tough their attitude to poverty, would accept some version of this thesis. Few would argue for a 'bowl of rice a day' level of nutrition or be content to see the children of the poor in our society without shoes. However, what is clearly more controversial is how a relative poverty 'standard' is to be identified. Should the politically determined 'income support' level, which was described in chapter 5, be such a standard? Should the standard be related to average wages? Should the lowest quartile in the income distribution be deemed to be in poverty, whatever the nature of that distribution? In short, are the key political questions about poverty or about inequality?

Clearly the way you answer these questions will determine your answers to the wider questions about the success of the government's interventions into social policy. They will determine whether you regard it as sufficient to ensure that all citizens secure access to free education, free primary health care and subsistence-level benefits when they are unable to work; or whether you believe that social policy should be a really powerful engine for social equality. It is quite likely that neither of these extreme statements fits your requirements for social policy, in which case you will be faced by rather more complicated questions about policy adequacy and the extent to which an element of redistribution should be built into social policy.

Here then are two rather different perspectives on the role of social policy in society. On the Right are those who see the provision of social services as the responsibility of the individual and who reject the idea that such services should be redistributive. The role of the state is merely to alleviate the most extreme forms of hardship, but otherwise to stand back from interfering in the market.

Alternatively, on the Left are those who evaluate social policy in relation to its commitment to equality. But there is also a 'Centrist' position of considerable importance for British politics. Not only does it have its adherents in both major parties, but there are also strong political forces which influence the adoption of this stance by governments regardless of their initial ideological inclinations. Labour governments have become inhibited from developing policies that expand the public sector, and particularly the social policy sector, for fear of its impact upon either inflation or taxation. It has been argued that public expenditure draws in so many resources that it inhibits investment in industry.[8]

The Conservatives came to power in 1979 committed to cuts in public expenditure, other than defence and law and order, claiming that this would enable the economy to recover. They have, apparently, been successful in curbing public expenditure on housing, but even that is misleading because (a) housing support for low income people has increasingly been given through the housing benefit scheme (which is classified under social security expenditure) and (b) tax relief for mortgage interest payers has risen sharply. Expenditure on education has fallen in real terms. Expenditure under the other two social policy headings has increased, markedly so in the case of social security. As far as health expenditure is concerned the government is inhibited from cutting by the continuing popularity of that service. Nevertheless, as was suggested in chapter 7, the actual growth level has been sufficiently low for it to be regarded in many quarters as involving a decline in the standard of service provided.

Hence, while the government has seen itself, and been seen, as engaged in an attack on social expenditure, what we actually find is some rather confusing changes. The government has gone to considerable lengths to cut social security benefits, but demographic trends (increased numbers of the elderly), economic trends (increased unemployment) and a tendency to shift other social expenses on to income maintenance (housing support, in particular, but also some of the costs of care of the elderly – see chapter 6) has sharply increased expenditure under this heading. Education and health expenditure have been attacked, but an actual fall in real expenditure has only occurred in the first case. The one big success has been in cutting *direct* expenditure on *public* housing. At the time of writing the squeezing process continues.

Inevitably, in a situation in which social policy expenditure consumes a high proportion of national income and provides little room for political manoeuvre, yet leaves ample scope for dissatisfaction about what is provided, there is a search for better ways of delivering the social services. Political parties unable markedly to influence the overall pattern of public services will seek other ways of modifying their performance and enhancing the 'value for money' provided. The various forms this search has taken are the subject of the next section.

THE QUEST FOR EFFICIENT AND RESPONSIVE MODES OF SOCIAL POLICY DELIVERY

The view that social policy interventions have not achieved the success that might be expected from the effort put into them has been accepted by many politicians and public servants. It has been recognized that a complex bureaucracy has been developed to provide social services, and that efforts are therefore needed to overcome the resulting institutional and professional divisions within the system.

In the 1960s and 1970s governments devoted a considerable amount of attention to the organization of both central and local government. There was a search for the most rational form of organization. The search was always made difficult by a wide range of political considerations; reorganization may change the balance of power and alter individual opportunities and career prospects. Moreover, established patterns of organization develop supporting sentiments and loyalties. In any case, the rationalization of government is not an easy process. There are often competing criteria for rationalization which are hard to evaluate. For example, there is a conflict between the achievement of uniformity through centralization and the the maximization of flexibility through decentralization. The close integration of particular services – for example health and the personal social services – may weaken links between those services and other related activities – for example the provision of housing and the achievement of high environmental standards. Rationalization seems to involve a search for the best arrangement, when perhaps in reality there are merely alternative arrangements, each carrying costs and benefits. These are hard to evaluate. Finally, there are 'informal' aspects to organizational arrangements which develop within formal structures. While in theory formal arrangements may be sought to maximize effective informal links, these are particularly hard to predict. Moreover, one of the effects of a formal reorganization is to distort and perhaps undermine informal links operating prior to reorganization.

At central government level there was, between the mid-1960s and the mid-1970s, a move towards super-departments embracing many different policy areas, offset very slightly in the early 1970s by an effort by the Conservatives to create 'hived-off' separately managed units for the implementation of specific policies. In the policy areas with which this book is concerned, therefore, the integration of the government responsibility for health, social security and the personal social services within the DHSS illustrates the main theme, and the creation of the Manpower Services Commission the minor theme.

Despite the fact that the DHSS has proved to be a juggernaut department in which the relationship between the social security part and the health and personal social services part is often very tenuous, it can still be argued that, as far as the relationship between central and local government is concerned, there is a lack of integration between DHSS links with the local social services departments, DES links with the local education service and DOE concerns about local housing policies and its general responsibilities for local government as a whole. This is not an argument for some further aggregation of departments; it is merely to illustrate the limits to integration by way of the creation of super-departments. Indeed, there are other kinds of divisions in government, for example between the 'economic' and the 'social' policy departments, which the integration of the latter would increase.

One other way of tackling the issue of policy integration is to abandon the notion of combination at the centre in favour of forms of decentralization which enable policy responsibilities to be integrated locally in smaller, more manageable units. The creation of the local social services departments seemed to be a move in this direction, particularly as it was accompanied by the ending of the relatively rigid control over the children's services exercised by the Home Office. However, there were few other senses in which responsibilities were devolved in this case; central fiscal controls have if anything increased, and the thrust towards greater co-ordination between the personal social services and the health service has inevitably complicated the situation.

During the late 1960s local authorities developed an interest in corporate management, involving the co-ordination of all local services under a chief executive. Central government certainly sought to encourage this development, though it lacked a form of organization of its own that could effectively relate to it. Moreover, the form of local governmemt reorganization adopted in 1971, far from assisting the integration of departments at the local level, maintained a two-tier system. Indeed, in many urban areas integrated authorities, the former county boroughs, found their powers split between counties and districts. The Royal Commission on Local Government in England recommended a more unified system.[9] There were strong political reasons why the Conservative government preferred to preserve a two-tier structure which did not depart too radically, apart from the elimination of the often Labour-controlled county boroughs, from the existing system. The abolition of the metropolitan counties in the 1980s did, however, represent a Conservative shift on this issue, for rather different political reasons (a hostility to the Labour-controlled metropolitan counties and a concern about their 'extravagances').

However, probably the most important limitation upon local integration of services lies in the central government reluctance to devolve powers, and the corresponding continuing importance of two central departments (DES and DHSS) in which specific interests in particular services are strongly protected. Indeed it has also already been suggested in chapter 3 that central controls – particularly of a financial kind – have been increased rather than decreased in the last few years.

There has been one policy area in which some policy unification has been achieved: the health service. Here the main changes in the early 1970s were the integration of the local authority community health services with the hospital services, and the adoption of a structure that did a little more to tie in the family practitioner services with the rest of the service. This is a good exmple of a change that strengthened one kind of link – hospital and community health services – at the expense of another – community health and social services. There is certainly no easy way of determining which link matters most.

The general observations on organizational relationships at the beginning of this discussion suggested that there may be limits to the extent to which policy integration may be facilitated by institutional reorganization. An alternative response long popular in government is to seek to achieve integration by special administrative devices. Perhaps the most widely used of these is inter-departmental or inter-agency committee. In central government such committees are of considerble importance, though much of their work is invisible to the outside world. Clearly such devices are also used in local government, particularly in relation to corporate management. At the local level committee structures have also been developed to link the health service to local government and to foster joint planning. In chapter 6 a comment was made on the part played by the availability of 'joint finance' in stimulating joint planning between the health service and the social services departments.

In central government efforts have been made to secure the examination of the impact of groups of policies upon particular groups in the population, even when responsibilities for those policies lie with more than one government department. The consultative document on policies for the elderly published in 1978 is an example of this.[10] Some efforts were made to examine policies for the family in the same way. The Audit Commission's report on community care,[11] and the government's response to it (see chapter 6) can be seen in a similar light.

In the middle of the 1960s concern developed about the concentration of social problems in certain inner-urban areas. This was not, at that stage, primarily a concern about economic decline in urban areas – that was to come in the mid 1970s. Rather it was made clear that people with considerable needs – for social security, social services, health care and help with the educational problems of their children – were concentrated in particular areas, and that often the levels of service provision in those areas were below the national average. Those who drew politicians' attention to these urban problems were a mixed group of people; for some the central problems were deprivation and poor public facilities, while for others they were individual behaviour and motivation, levels of crime and the incidence of 'problem families'. The whole policy response was complicated by the extent to which race relations problems were concentrated in deprived inner-city areas. A special response to urban problems enabled politicians to offer resources at the same time both to minority groups who were victims of discrimination and to some of the deprived white people who (if some of the interpretations of election results and public opinion polls were correct) were most prone to blame their intensifying problems upon immigrants. Compensating resource distribution towards areas was preferable to 'positive discrimination' towards selected individuals.

The American 'urban programme' offered a largely undigested model for this British intervention. A combination of new resources, encouragement to community organization and personalized assistance for demoralized individuals was seen as appropriate. The first British initiatives were concerned solely with education. 'Educational priority areas' were designated where new capital investments and compensatory education experiments were backed up by special allowances to teachers. Then in 1968 the government developed an 'urban programme' of more varied aid to deprived urban areas. Local authorities could seek central government support for three-quarters of the cost of a variety of policy initiatives in specified deprived areas.

In 1969 it was decided that this new urban programme should be supported by a number of community development projects (CDPs).

These were 'action research' projects concerned to find 'ways of meeting, more effectively, the needs of individuals, families and communities, whether native or immigrant, suffering from many forms of social deprivation'.[12] Hence there was an attempt to concentrate efforts to improve social conditions in small areas, most of them only segments of the local authority areas in which they were based, and to monitor those efforts.

The history of the CDP initiative ia a curious one. The various local projects ran for fixed periods during the next nine years, although most of them changed course at least once during their lives and many had very stormy existences. Neither central government nor the loacl authorities were very sure what CDP teams should do, and both were often unhappy about what they decided to do. The teams, and particularly their research components, attracted young radical social scientists who moved the projects very clearly away from policies implied by the individual pathology explanation of urban deprivation. Several of the CDP teams set out to demonstrate that the central causes of the problems in their areas lay in the national, or even the international, economy. Some of their publications therefore proclaim the limitations of solutions based on local action and stress the very much wider determinants of social welfare.[13]

After the demise of CDPs, in an atmosphere of fierce controversy about these very political initiatives, the urban programme developed in a more limited and centrally controlled way. At the end of the 1970s there was a distinct shift, clearly influenced by growing unemployment, towards local initiatives more concerned with employment creation. In a White Paper published in 1977 the Labour government announced a considerable increase in money for the urban programme and invited some inner-urban local authorities to join with it in 'partnership' arrangements to co-ordinate the activities of both central and local government and the health service.[14]

On coming to power in 1979 the Conservatives continued these initiatives, and added new approaches motivated by a concern about local economies. They set up a number of 'enterprise zones' where business initiatives might be set up with a minimun of planning controls and relief from local rates. Local authorities also showed increased concern at this time to engage in employment creation. Some Labour authorities argued the case for socialist local economic strategies: using co-operatives, stressing equal opportunities and aiming to increase welfare at the local level. Central government hostility to these initiatives fuelled its concern to curb local expenditure. The Thatcher government's perspective was that local taxes and local authority controls were inhibiting economic initiatives in the urban areas. It added new Urban Development Corporations to its battery of measures, to stimulate economic activity in specific areas without local government interference.

Riots in inner city areas in summer 1981 have helped to keep urban problems on the political agenda. While political approaches may differ, with the Conservatives more clearly committed to free enterprise 'solutions', there is consensus about the economic roots of these problems. This issue was highlighted in the late seventies by some 'inner area studies' carried out by consultants in parts of London, Liverpool and Birmingham.[15] They gave a new ingredient to planning for the inner cities which had not been, or had not been perceived to be, important when the urban programme was first initiated. However, the CDP observation about the importance of economic factors outside local control would seem to be specially pertinent where the central problem is diagnosed to be the decline of employment opportunities. Small area initiatives certainly facilitate a relatively precise form of inter-agency co-operation, and the central government role in the 'partnerships' is very explicit (by contrast with the CDP projects). Yet is this the critical level for policy co-ordination? To what extent can inner-urban decline be halted in a context of national economic change and decline?

With the partial exception of the CDP projects, all of the initiatives discussed above were very largely 'top–down' in character; their development did not entail any close examination of the attitudes of those for whom policies are designed. They were motivated primarily by a concern to build better organizational systems. The alternative way of looking at weaknesses of policy, and of seeking to adopt policy better to public needs, is perhaps incompatible with the development of rational policy delivery systems. People demand individualized policies; they do not fit readily into 'systems'. Moreover, attempts to develop better policy integration have been linked with concerns about political control. In chapter 3 some of the problems about the relationship between overall political control and the responsiveness of politicians to the interests of members of their electorate were explored. Accordingly it is realistic to look elsewhere for situations in which the relationship between social policy and the individual citizen is more meaningful. Hence the author has earlier argued:

> Involvement in politics in any way is very slight. By contrast everyone is engaged in a series of often very active relationships with public administration. We pay rates and taxes, apply for social security benefits, have to take note of many administrative regulations, send our children to school, make use of the National Health Service and so on. . . . If you ask a sample of people about their relationship with the State, once you have explained your question – which will merely baffle many in the first instance – they will surely tell you about these kinds of contacts rather than about the matters that have been the traditional concerns of political scientists.[16]

In the course of implementation, as was argued in chapter 4, relationships between field-level administrative and professional staff and the public may influence the impact of policy. This is a general background issue for this discussion but is not the main concern here. For what have been so far largely neglected in this book are devices to facilitate the redress of individual grievances against the administration. These have developed quite markedly in recent years and have a considerable indirect impact upon social policy.

In principle, the two categories into which grievance procedures fall are nearly as old as the nation-state itself: appeals to courts and complaints to elected representatives. In practice, they take modern forms very different to these traditional grievance procedures. In centuries past litigation about dissatisfaction with an administrative agency depended upon an elaborate and costly legal procedure whereby the royal prerogative was invoked on behalf of the aggrieved citizen. These 'prerogative remedies' are still used from time to time, and today individuals may secure legal aid or the assistance of a powerful voluntary organization to enable them to take grievances against public authorities to the High Court. But for everyday purposes what is much more important is that a large number of lower 'courts', generally known as 'tribunals', have been set up to deal with appeals against decisions of public agencies.

The area of social policy in which tribunals are most important is social security. Individuals may appeal against most decisions taken by DHSS officials. There is a two-tier appeal system for social security benefits, with commissioners who operate at the top level and whose decisions are regarded as precedents for lower-tier decisions. Special systems, less detached from day-to-day decision makers, exist to deal with claimants dissatisfied with Social Fund and housing benefit decisions.

In the housing sector there are tribunals to deal only with disputes over rent levels and security of tenure in the private sector. Disputes between tenants and local authorities are not covered. Family practitioner committees in the National Health Service are required to set up what are, in effect, tribunals to hear complaints against doctors, dentists and pharmacists. There are also tribunals that review cases of compulsory detention under the Mental Health Acts. Parents may appeal against a local authority decision on allocation of a child to a school, and a tribunal exists to hear appeals by private schools against ministerial decisions that they should be closed.

It will be seen, therefore, that only in the social security field do tribunals play a really major part in policy implementation. There is scope for considerable extension of tribunal activity, particularly in areas where local authorities are the decision makers. This has happened recently to some degree in relation to school allocation decisions and housing benefit decisions, but in both cases the new adjudication bodies consist of local councillors who may be considered to be less than independent.

The case for tribunals is that they provide for the independent review of decisions, particularly where they involve official discretion. They are less important for the control of policy itself; it is comparatively rarely that tribunal decisions indicate a significant defect in policy. To aggrieved individuals they offer not so much a chance to change policy as an opportunity to check a controversial application of policy.

The system of tribunals in Britain has been improved considerably in recent years. As a result of the Franks Committee,[17] which reported in 1956, attempts have been made to make tribunal proceedings more consistent and impartial. There is, nevertheless, still a suspicion that some tribunals are too closely identified with the government agencies whose decisions they are expected to examine. The tribunals for supplementary benefits, for example, have members selected by the DHSS and their clerks are officials from that department. Similarly, the committees that adjudicate on complaints against doctors have been seen as rather too closely identified with the administration of the family practitioner services.

In the Scandinavian countries there are officials known as 'ombudsmen' who investigate complaints against the administration. When the appointment of such officials was first proposed for Britain one of the arguments used against it was that elected representatives perform this function. Eventually in 1967 the office of parliamentary commissioner was set up, but only to investigate individual public grievances passed on to him by members of Parliament. Later, when local government and the health service were reorganized, local government and health service commissioners were appointed. Complaints against local authorities were to be presented by councillors, but a provision was included to enable the local government commissioners to investigate direct complaints when they were satisfied that a member of the public might have had difficulty in securing a councillor's backing (presumably because of involvement in the decision at issue). However, in the absence of elected representatives within the health service direct access was allowed to the health service commissioners. Hence there is a curious mixture of direct and indirect access to these British 'ombudsmen'. Perhaps in due course direct access will become the rule for all.

The commissioners are solely concerned with maladministration. They do not deal with policy, so long as that policy has a clear statutory foundation. Nor do they deal with decisions that involve statutorily legitimate discretion or professional judgement. They provide, therefore, like the tribunals, only a limited protection for citizens against the worst abuses of administrative behaviour, and not an opportunity to participate in policy formulation or to comment upon its overall implementation.

During the last twenty years, however, there has been interest in the development of forms of participation that enable citizens to become more closely involved in policy issues. Arguments for greater participation have developed against the backcloth of the elimination of the smaller organs of local government and the increased centralization of decision making. Accordingly, in those areas where governments, or local authorities, have been willing to countenance the development of participatory devices, there have been grounds for regarding this as tokenism designed to disguise the retreat of the real locus of power. To put it a little more neutrally, there is a significant conflict between the desire for centralized uniformity and the suspicion of particularistic local interests on the one hand and real local accountability on the other.

Perhaps the most significant area in which participatiom rights have been extended is in strategic and local land use planning, areas of policy outside the scope of this book. Within social policy two examples have been discussed in earlier chapters: community health councils (CHCs) in the health service, and school governors and managers in education. In the first of these cases actual power is very limited; CHCs are officially supported pressure groups. In the case of school management significant steps are being taken to ensure parents' representatives an equal share with local authority nominees in a context of increasingly devolved powers over school arrangements but not over the curriculum.

This discussion highlights the extent to which we have a political and administrative system in which it is generally difficult to conceive of meaningful participation, except through representative political institutions, for consumers of social services. The representation of the staff of those services is by contrast rather more significant since increasingly strong professional and trade union organizations provide opportunities for influence both upon policy delivery and upon policy content. Social policy consumers, by virtue of the fact that they very largely need the help of the system more than it needs them, are in a very weak position to participate except as passive recipients.

While the concern about participation continues in the 1980s it can be seen to tend to divide into two, often distinct, ideological branches. For some the key to control lies in the market place. Services should be privatized, and consumers put into a position in which they can make choices as the free purchasers of services. For others decentralization of public provision to the local level, breaking up big bureaucracies and offering local participation in service control, is the preferred approach to this problem. Given the ideological dispositions of a Conservative central government on the one hand, and many Opposition controlled urban local governments on the other, it is not hard to see that the search for ways to privatize have come from the more powerful centre and that experiments in decentralization are more fragile developments at local level. Examples of the former have been discussed at various points in this book.[18] Examples of the latter involve the setting up of local teams, committees and community participation arrangements bringing together social services and housing with other local services, but not involving education.[19] In education, of course, the school is the crucial local unit, and in this case central government has been the driving force towards decentralization.

CONCLUSIONS

This chapter has looked at the issue of social policy and society by considering first some of the political perspectives on the level and character of social service expenditure, and then some government or local authority-inspired attempts to improve social policy co-ordination, or to enable citizens to have some slight influence on the impact of policy upon themselves. It has thus concentrated primarily on some of the more detailed questions about the relationship betweeen policy and society. It could, however, have developed an entirely different level of analysis in which attention was focused upon the functions of social policy in British society and its relationship to social structure.

Many of the propositions discussed in this chapter presuppose that social policy has developed out of a concern to protect, and to offer services for, weak and vulnerable groups in society. For some writers on social policy such state activities have an integrative function, serving to unite us in one mutually dependent community. Within such a community developments to enhance social equality may occur. A 'welfare state' advances a nation towards a 'welfare society'. But the development of social policy may also be seen very differently. Perhaps the clearest alternative view is provided by Marxists (as was suggested in chapter 1). Of course. they argue, various social benefits have been extended to the poor. These are designed to increase their productive efficiency, by educating them and keeping them in good health, and to stave off revolution by meeting their most salient grievances. But such benefits are never likely to advance a capitalist society far along the road to social equality. In this sense democratic socialists are likely only to secure social policies that help to preserve the status quo, while the radical free marketeers on the Right are likely to be restrained by the fact that a return to the open market place would accelerate the drift towards the class warfare that Marx originally predicted. This modern

Marxism rejects historical inevitability, arguing instead about capitalism's capacity to retain its dominance in a changing society.

This argument secures credence from the fact that social policy has not so far been proved to be a powerful source of social change. It must be analysed in relation to political motives, and in terms of social structure. At the level of the interpretation of political motives and political behaviour the Marxist position cannot be disregarded. Most political conflicts in a society like our own are battles between those who seek to gain from social change and those who benefit from the status quo. Those who seek change are always likely to be most successful when the defenders of the existing order see advantages in making concessions. Conservative politicians have at various times in the past spoken openly of the need to win popular support through specific measures. Countless government reports have drawn attention to the inefficiency of a society which is insufficiently fit to work hard, or fight wars, and insufficiently educated to provide the skills needed for industry. Social reformers with unquestionable humanitarian and altruistic motives have always fought alongside politicians who see new policies as expedient to protect the status quo and to win popular support.

The most difficult part of this argument to evaluate is that which deals with the role played by mass political movements. Marxist theorists have long been split between those who believe that the working class can force capitalism to change peacefully and gradually, and those who believe real change will be achieved only by revolution. Clearly, in twentieth-century Britain the organized working class has sought to secure gradual social change. How successful has it been? And how much more success is it likely to achieve?

These are questions to which readers will want to choose their own answers. Clearly they raise issues that go far beyond the scope of the policies discussed in this book. However, there is one rather complicated answer to these questions which has a considerable bearing upon the interpretation of the making of social policy. This is that the organized working class has achieved quite considerable political success in Britain, forcing concessions from capitalism that nevertheless fall short of the transformation of Britain into a 'socialist society'. However, those concessions are much more marked in some areas of social life than in others, and serve to benefit the better organized segments of the working class more clearly than anyone else. Hence while it is true that the overall distribution of income and wealth has been affected but little, and particularly has changed little at the extremes, some groups of manual workers have advanced significantly in income relative to some groups of non-manual workers and small entrepreneurs. These new middle-income workers are also significant beneficiaries from the advancements in the health and education services, and from income maintenance reforms which provide good short-term benefits. However, their gains have done very little to benefit those who are less well organized, who remain low-paid and highly vulnerable to unemployment. The more powerful groups of workers also have relatively little interest in some of the problems for social policy that have been described in this book (such as homelessness, mental handicap, racial disadvantage). Those most in need of help from the 'welfare state' are likely to be correspondingly ill-equipped to secure concessions from it.

That is a personal, and inevitably contentious, suggestion of the way in which an interpretation of the development of social policy that has its roots originally in the Marxist perspective may be of relevance. It is an argument about power in the social structure, seeing capitalist interests as still of considerable importance but being forced to compromise with sections of the organized working class. It is important to recognize that political action in our complex society is enormously complicated. In no way is it a simple confrontation between twin forces of capital and labour. Both of these forces tend to be segmented in various ways. In addition, the role of the state has grown to such an extent that it employs, at various levels and with various interests, a great army of people who are not necessarily readily aligned with any other forces in British society. In explaining social policy the impact of such groups of state employees as doctors, teachers, central administrators,[19] and to a lesser extent groups of publicly employed manual workers who are growing in political awareness, need to be brought into the equation. In sum, readers are being asked to accept that social policies are not merely derived from humanitarian aspirations, but are also products of power conflicts in our society.

An understanding of social policy depends upon taking into account this balance between conflict and humanitarianism; it also depends upon relating to it a comprehension of the much more detailed factors that influence individual policies. This book certainly cannot claim to have made all the key connections in this complex field, but it is hoped it has introduced readers to many of the more important ones.

SUGGESTIONS FOR FURTHER READING

The government's 'public expenditure White Papers' are the most thorough up-to-date sources on expenditure patterns. They are published early in each calendar year. In fact, the author used in the chapter another annual government publication which had provided a rather better summary of the data, *Social Trends*. This is a most valuable collection of official statistics, much used in this book. The two sides in the debate on social policy provision are represented in the writings cited in notes 3 and 4. In addition other important recent contributions to this debate are Bosanquet's *After the New Right*,[20] and Deakin's *The Politics of Welfare*.[21] The book by Higgins cited in n.12 discusses the earlier urban programme, and its development up to 1983 is explored in Higgins et al.'s *Government and Urban Poverty*.[22]

The author's own *The State, Administration and the Individual* (see n. 16) deals with the relations between individuals and the administration. On tribunals the standard work is by Wraith and Hutchesson.[23] Developments in administrative law are well discussed in Harlow and Rawlings' *Law and Administration*.[24]

Further reading on the wider debate on social policy is suggested at the end of chapter 1.

# Notes

## CHAPTER 1  WHAT IS SOCIAL POLICY?

1  T. H. Marshall, *Social Policy* (3rd edn), London, Hutchinson, 1970.
2  See J. Carrier and I. Kendall, 'Social Administration as Social Science', in H. Heisler (ed.), *Foundations of Social Administration*, London, Macmillan, 1977.
3  F. F. Piven and R. A. Cloward, *Regulating the Poor*, London, Tavistock, 1972, p. xiii.
4  See J. O'Connor, *The Fiscal Crisis of the State*, New York, St Martin's Press, 1973 and I. Gough, *The Political Economy of the Welfare State*, London, Macmillan, 1979.
5  J. Higgins, *The Poverty Business*, Oxford, Blackwell, 1978.
6  R. M. Titmuss, 'War and Social Policy', in *Essays on the Welfare State*, London, Allen and Unwin, 1958, p. 86.
7  See, in particular, his *Essays on the Welfare State*; *Commitment to Welfare*, London, Allen and Unwin, 1968; and *Social Policy: An Introduction*, London, Allen and Unwin, 1974.
8  J. Kincaid, *Poverty and Equality in Britain*, Harmondsworth, Penguin, 1973.
9  R. M. Titmuss, *The Philosophy of Welfare*, London, Allen and Unwin, 1987.
10  R. Mishra, *Society and Social Policy*, London, Macmillan, 1977; and *The Welfare State in Crisis*, Brighton, Wheatsheaf, 1984.

## CHAPTER 2  THE HISTORY OF SOCIAL POLICY

1  See D. Bell, *The Coming of Post Industrial Society*, New York, Basic Books, 1973.
2  These developments are explored in chapter 1 of the author's *The State, Administration and the Individual*, Glasgow, Fontana, 1976.
3  See H. Wilensky and C. Lebeaux, *Industrial and Social Welfare*, New York, Free Press, 1965; G. Rimlinger, *Welfare Policy and Industrialization in Europe, America and Russia*, New York, John Wiley, 1971; P. Kaim Caudle, *Comparative Social Policy and Social Security*, London, Martin Robertson, 1973; R. Mishra, 'Welfare and Industrial Man: A Study of Welfare in Western Industrial Societies in Relation to a Hypothesis of Convergence', *Sociological Review*, 21 (November 1973), pp. 535–60; and J. Carrier and I. Kendall, 'The Development of Welfare States: The Production of Plausible Accounts', *Journal of Social Policy*, 6 (July 1977), pp. 271–90.
4  See H. Heclo, *Modern Social Policies in Britain and Sweden*, New Haven, Yale University Press, 1974.
5  D. Roberts, *Victorian Origins of the British Welfare State*, New Haven, Yale University Press, 1960.
6  A. V. Dicey, *Lectures on the Relations between Law and Public Opinion in England*, London, Macmillan, 1905.
7  C. Booth, *Life and Labour of the People in London*, provided, in 17 volumes published between 1889 and 1903, a detailed account of poverty in the metropolis. Booth's work is described in T. S. Simey and M. B. Simey, *Charles Booth: Social Scientist*, London, Oxford University Press, 1960. Another important contribution was a study of poverty in York: B. S. Rowntree, *Poverty, A Study of Town Life,* London, Macmillan, 1901.

8  See B. Semmel, *Imperialism and Social Reform*, London, Oxford University Press, 1961.

9  D. Fraser, *The Evolution of the British Welfare State*, London, Macmillan, 1973.

10  Heclo, *Modern Social Policies*; see also J. Harris, *William Beveridge: A Biography*, London, Oxford University Press, 1977.

11  B. Abel-Smith, *Value for Money* in Health Services, London, Heinemann, 1976, ch. 2.

12  See J. Harris, *Unemployment and Politics*, London, Oxford University Press, 1972; and also her *William Beveridge*.

13  D. Lloyd George, budget speech, 1909.

14  D. Lloyd George, speech at Limehouse, 30 July 1909.

15  B. B. Gilbert, *British Social Policy 1914–39*, London, Batsford, 1970.

16  See A. Deacon, *In Search of the Scrounger*, London, Bell, 1976.

17  See H. Eckstein, *Pressure Group Politics*, London, Allen and Unwin, 1960; and M. Foot, *Aneurin Bevan*, vol. 2: *1945–60*, London, Davis-Poynter, 1973.

18  See J. Packman, *The Child's Generation*, Oxford, Blackwell, 1975, ch. 1.

19  J. M. Keynes, *The General Theory of Employment, Interest and Money*, London, Macmillan, 1936.

20  B. Abel-Smith and P. Townsend, *The Poor and the Poorest*, London, Bell, 1965; D. Cole and J. Utting, *The Economic Circumstances of Old People*, London, Codicote, 1962; and T. Lynes, *National Assistance and National Prosperity*, London, Codicote, 1962.

21  The need to see poverty in relative terms, rather than in the absolute terms principally used in the Rowntree studies of poverty, was first effectively argued in P. Townsend, 'Measuring Poverty', *British Journal of Sociology*, 5 (June 1954), pp. 130–7. More recent statements of this argument are contained in P. Townsend (ed.), *The Concept of Poverty*, London, Heinemann, 1970; and R. Holman, *Poverty*, London, Martin Robertson, 1978. Rowntree replicated his original York study (see n. 7 above) twice, in 1936 and 1950. The report of the latter study (B. S. Rowntree and G. R. Lavers, *Poverty and the Welfare State*, London, Longmans, 1951) reached, by maintaining a very rigorous definition of adequate income, very complacent conclusions about the incidence of poverty. However, readers may like to note a recent article which shows that Rowntree was more open minded than Townsend suggests on the case for an absolute definition, this is J. H. Veit-Wilson 'Paradigms of Poverty: A Rehabilitaton of B. S. Rowntree', *Journal of Social Policy*, 15 (January 1986), pp. 69–99.

22  *Proposals for a Tax-Credits System*, Cmnd 5116, London, HMSO, 1972.

23  *Reform of Social security: Programme for Action*, Cmnd 9691, London, HMSO, 1985.

24  Report of the Central Advisory Council for Education, *Early Leaving*, London, HMSO, 1954.

25  Report of the Central Advisory Council for Education, *Fifteen to Eighteen* (Crowther Report), London, HMSO, 1959.

26  Report of the Central Advisory Council for Education, *Half our Future* (Newsom Report), London, HMSO, 1963.

27  *Higher Education* (Robbins Report), Cmnd 2154, London, HMSO, 1963.

28  Report of the Central Advisory Council for Education, *Children and their Primary Schools* (Plowden Report), London, HMSO, 1967.

29  *The Administrative Structure of Medical and Related Services in England and Wales*, London, HMSO, 1968; and *The Future Structure of the National Health Service*, London , HMSO, 1967.

30  *Report of the Royal Commission on the National Health Service* (Merrison Report), Cmnd 7615, London, HMSO, 1979.

31  *NHS Management Inquiry* (Griffiths Report), London, DHSS, 1983.

32  *Report of the Working Party on Social Workers in the Local Authority Health and Welfare Services* (Younghusband Report), London, HMSO, 1959.

33  *Report of the Committee on Local Authority and Allied Personal Social Services* (Seebohm Report), Cmnd 3703, London, HMSO, 1968.

34  See National Institute of Social Work, *Social Workers: Their Roles and Tasks: Report of a Working Party*, known as the Barclay Report, London, Bedford Square Press, 1982.

35  For an account of these developments, up to the emergence of the 'community charge' idea see T. Travers, *The Politics of Local Government Finance*, London, Allen and Unwin, 1986.

36  For recent expositions of this view, see M. Wicks, *A Future for All*, Harmondsworth, Penguin, 1987; and N. Deakin, *The Politics of Welfare*, London, Methuen, 1987.

37  S. Brittan, *Steering the Economy*, Harmondsworth, Penguin, 1971.

38  The leading monetarist theorist is an American, Milton Friedman. His best-known book is *Capitalism and Freedom*, Chicago University Press, 1962. For an analysis of this and other 'new

Right' arguments see N. Bosanquet, *After the New Right*, London, Heinemann, 1983.
39 See S. Mukherjee, *Making Labour Markets Work*, London, PEP, 1972.
40 P. Thane, *The Foundations of the Welfare State*, London, Longman, 1982.
41 K. O. Morgan, *Labour in Power*, London, Oxford University Press, 1984.
42 N. Deakin, *The Politics of Welfare*, London, Methuen, 1987.

## CHAPTER 3   THE MAKING OF SOCIAL POLICY

1 Perhaps the most important modern exposition of this theory of democracy is by J. Schumpeter in *Capitalism, Socialism and Democracy*, New York, Harper and Row, 1950.
2 R. H. S. Crossman, *Diaries of a Cabinet Minister* (3 vols), London, Hamish Hamilton and Jonathan Cape, 1975, 1976 and 1977.
3 See ibid. vol. 2, on Crossman's experience as Lord President of the Council.
4 For a further discussion of these issues see T. Travers (n. 35 in ch. 2); and M. Loughlin, *Local Government in the Modern State*, London, Sweet and Maxwell, 1986.
5 *Paying for Local Government*, Cmnd 9714, London, HMSO, 1986.
6 See G. Bramley, 'Paying for Local Government', in M. Brenton and C. Ungerson (eds), *Yearbook of Social Policy 1986–7*, London, Longman, 1987, pp. 178–95.
7 See P. Taylor-Gooby, *Public Opinion, Ideology and State Welfare*, London, Routledge and Kegan Paul, 1985.
8 In particular see S. E. Finer, *Anonymous Empire*, London, Pall Mall, 1958; G. Wootton, *Interest Groups*, Englewood Cliffs, NJ, Prentice-Hall, 1970; and G. K. Roberts, *Political Parties and Pressure Groups in Britain*, London, Weidenfeld and Nicolson, 1970.
9 See, in particular, R. A. Dahl, *Who Governs?*, New Haven, Yale University Press, 1961.
10 See E. E. Schattschneider, *The Semi-Sovereign People*, New York, Holt, Rinehart and Winston, 1961; and P. Bachrach, *The Theory of Democratic Elitism*, London, London University Press, 1969.
11 For a view of the theoretical literature on elites see T. B. Bottomore, *Elites and Society*, London, Watts, 1954. The best reviews of the evidence on elites in Britain are contained in J. Urry and J. Wakeford (eds), *Power in Britain*, London, Heinemann, 1973; and P. Stanworth and A. Giddens, *Elites and Power in British Society*, Cambridge University Press, 1974.
12 See Harris, *William Beveridge* (n. 10 in ch. 2).
13 See M. Gowing, *Richard Morris Titmuss* (Proceedings of the British Academy, vol. LXI), London, Oxford University Press, 1975.
14 This is fundamental to the approach to the study of politics in Dahl, *Who Governs?* and his followers in the United States. For an application to Britain see S. H. Beer, *Modern British Politics*, London, Faber, 1975.
15 J. Stalin, attrib.
16 M. J. Hill, *The Sociology of Public Administration*, London, Weidenfeld and Nicolson, 1972.
17 J. M. Lee, *Social Leaders and Public Persons*, London, Oxford University Press, 1963, p. 214.
18 J. K. Friend, J. M. Power and C. J. L. Yewlett, *Public Planning: The Inter-Corporate Dimension*, London, Tavistock, 1974, p. 40.
19 W. I. Jenkins, *Policy Analysis*, London, Martin Robertson, 1978.
20 B. Smith, *Policy Making in British Government*, London, Martin Robertson, 1976, p. 13.
21 See H. Heclo and A. Wildavsky, *The Private Government of Public Money*, London, Macmillan, 1974.
22 See D. Braybrooke and C. E. Lindblom, *A Strategy of Decision*, New York, Free Press, 1963.
23 A. H. Hanson and M. Walles, *Governing Britain*, Glasgow, Fontana, 1970.
24 T. C. Hartley and J. A. G. Griffith, *Government and Law*, London, Weidenfeld and Nicolson, 1975.
25 J. Jowell and D. Oliver (eds), *The Changing Constitution*, Oxford, Clarendon Press, 1985.
26 T. Byrne, *Local Government in Britain*, Harmondsworth, Penguin, 1981.
27 J. Gyford, *Local Politics in Britain*, London, Croom Helm, 2nd edn, 1984.
28 P. Hall, H. Land, R. Parker and A. Webb, *Change, Choice and Conflict in Social Policy*, London, Heinemann, 1978.
29 K. G. Banting, *Poverty, Politics and Policy*, London, Macmillan, 1979.
30 C. Ham, 'Approaches to the Study of Social Policy Making', *Policy and Politics*, 8 (1980), pp. 55–72.

31  C. Ham and M. Hill, *The Policy Process in the Modern Capitalist State*, Brighton, Wheatsheaf, 1985.

CHAPTER 4    IMPLEMENTATION

1  M. J. Hill, 'The Exercise of Discretion in the National Assistance Board', *Public Administration*, 47 (1969), pp. 85–6. See also T. Prosser, 'The Politics of Discretion: Aspects of Discretionary Power in the Supplementary Benefits Scheme', in M. Adler and S. Asquith (eds), *Discretion and Welfare*, London, Heinemann, 1981.
2  A. Deacon, *In Search of the Scrounger*, London, Bell, 1976.
3  J. Jowell, 'The Legal Control of Administrative Discretion', *Public Law*, Autumn 1973, pp. 178–220. See also his *Law and Bureaucracy*, New York, Dunellen, 1975.
4  E. Bardach, *The Implementation Game*, Cambridge, Mass., MIT Press, 1977.
5  E. L. Trew, 'Organisation and Management of Social Security Services', in *Social Security Research*, papers presented at a DHSS Seminar on 7–9 April 1976, London, HMSO, 1977, p. 79.
6  J. Pressman and A. Wildavsky, *Implementation*, Berkeley, University of California Press, 1973.
7  D. Schon, *Beyond the Stable State*, London, Maurice Temple Smith, 1971.
8  This is a strong theme in American policy studies literature going right back to P. M. Selznick's *TVA and the Grass Roots*, Berkeley, University of California Press, 1949. It is emphasized as a crucial problem for the 'poverty program' (see D. P. Moynihan, *Maximum Feasible Misunderstanding*, New York, Free Press, 1969).
9  This is of course one of the main issues discussed in C. C. Hood, *The Limits of Administration*, Chichester, Wiley, 1976 and Hill, *The Sociology of Public Administration* (n. 16 in ch. 3). The importance of this preoccupation in organization theory is discussed in D. J Hickson, 'A Convergence in Organisation Theory', *Administrative Science Quarterly*, 11 (1966), pp. 224–37. Key texts on theoretical contributions on this theme are C. Argyris, *Understanding Organisational Behaviour*, London, Tavistock, 1960; T. Burns and G. M. Stalker, *The Management of Innovation*, London, Tavistock, 1961; and M. Crozier, *The Bureaucratic Phenomenon*, London, Tavistock, 1964.
10  The literature on the police is discussed in A. K. Bottomley, *Decisions in the Penal Process*, London, Martin Robertson, 1973. Studies of other rule enforcers include N. Gunningham, *Pollution, Social Interest and the Law*, London, Martin Robertson, 1974; and W. G. Carson, 'White Collar Crime and the Enforcement of Factory Legislation', *British Journal of Criminology*, 10 (1970).
11  A. Etzioni, *A Comparative Analysis of Complex Organizations*, New York, Free Press, 1961.
12  For an exploration of the role of 'trust' in superior–subordinate relations see A. Fox, *Beyond Contract: Work, Power and Trust Relations*, London, Faber, 1974.
13  On this see ibid. and E. Jacques, *Equitable Payment*, Harmondsworth, Penguin, 1967. The interaction between the various sources of discretion is discussed in M. J. Hill, *The State, Administration and the Individual*, Glasgow, Fontana, 1976.
14  M. Lipsky, *Street-Level Bureaucracy*, New York, Russell Sage Foundation, 1970.
15  Etzioni, *A Comparative Analysis of Complex Organizations*.
16  See A. Etzioni (ed.), *The Semi-Professions and their Organization*, New York, Free Press, 1969.
17  C. Desborough and O. Stevenson, *Case Conferences: A Study of Interprofessional Communication concerning Children at Risk*, 1977, available from Department of Social Policy and Social Work, University of Keele.
18  For example H. Eckstein, *Pressure Group Politics*, London, Faber, 1960; P. Draper et al., 'The Organisation of Health Care: A Critical View of the 1974 Reorganisation of the National Health Service' in D. Tuckett (ed.), *An Introduction to Medical Sociology*, London, Tavistock, 1976; and C. Ham, *Health Policy in Britain*, London, Macmillan, 1982.
19  J. Packman, *The Child's Generation*, Oxford, Blackwell, 1975.
20  P. Hall, *Reforming the Welfare*, London, Heinemann, 1976.
21  B. R. Clark, 'Organizational Adaptation and Precarious Values', *American Sociological Review* 21 (1956), pp. 32–6. See also his *Adult Education in Transition*, Berkeley, University of California Press, 1956.
22  This example is drawn from D. Marsden, *Mothers Alone* (revised edn), Harmondsworth, Penguin, 1973.
23  See the essay by Adrian Webb in R. Berthoud (ed.), *Challenges to Social Policy*, Aldershot, Gower, 1985.

24  R. Titmuss, 'The Social Division of Welfare' in *Essays on the Welfare State*, London, Allen and Unwin, 1958.
25  A. Sinfield, 'Analysis in the Social Division of Welfare', *Journal of Social Policy*, 7 (1978), pp. 129–156.
26  P. Townsend, *Poverty in the United Kingdom*, Harmondsworth, Penguin, 1979, ch.5.
27  H. Rose, 'Rereading Titmuss: The Social Division of Welfare', *Journal of Social Policy*, 10 (1981), pp. 477–502, and H. Land and H. Rose, 'Compulsory Altruism for Some or an Altruistic Society for All', in P. Bean, J. Ferris and D. Whynes (eds), *In Defence of Welfare*, London, Tavistock, 1985.
28  M. Weber, *The Theory of Social and Economic Organization* (trans. A. M. Henderson and T. Parsons), Glencoe, Ill, Free Press, 1947.
29  M. Hill and G. Bramley. *Analysing Social Policy*, Oxford, Blackwell, 1986.
30  S. Barrett and C. Fudge (eds), *Policy and Action*, London, Methuen, 1981.
31  D. S. Van Meter and C. E. Van Horn, 'The Policy Implementation Process: A Conceptual Framework', *Administration and Society*, 6 (1975), pp. 445–88.
32  K. C. Davis, *Discretionary Justice*, Louisiana State University Press, 1969.
33  M. Adler and S. Asquith (eds), *Discretion and Welfare*, London, Heinemann, 1981.

CHAPTER 5  SOCIAL SECURITY

1  *Social Insurance and Allied Services*, (Beveridge Report), Cmnd 6404, London, HMSO, 1942.
2  *Reform of Social Security: Programme for Action*, Cmnd 9691, London, HMSO, 1985.
3  *The Government's Expenditure Plans* 1987–88 to 1989–1990, Cm 56, vol II, London, HMSO, 1987, p. 243.
4  Particularly B. S. Rowntree and G. R. Lavers, *Poverty and the Welfare State*, London, Longman, 1951.
5  P. Townsend, *Poverty in the United Kingdom*, Harmondsworth, Penguin, 1979.
6  Ibid.
7  J. Mack and S. Lansley, *Poor Britain*, London, Allen and Unwin, 1985.
8  See N. A. Barr, 'Empirical Definitions of the Poverty Line', *Policy and Politics*, 9 (1981), pp. 1–21.
9  For a fuller discussion of these issues see ch. 6 of J. Dale and P. Foster, *Feminists and State Welfare*, London, Routledge and Kegan Paul, 1986.
10  For a discussion on these alternatives see A. Deacon and J. Bradshaw, *Reserved for the Poor*, Oxford, Martin Robertson, 1983, and A. W. Dilnot, J. A. Kay and C. N. Morris, *The Reform of Social Security*, Oxford, Clarendon Press, 1984.
11  National Consumer Council, *Means-tested Benefits*, London, NCC, 1976.
12  Social Security Consortium, *Of Little Benefit*, London, AMA, 1986 (a revised edition of this is due out at the end of 1987).

CHAPTER 6  THE PERSONAL SOCIAL SERVICES

1  See DHSS, *Priorities for Health and Personal Social Services*, London, HMSO, 1976.
2  Central Statistical Office, *Social Trends 17*, London, HMSO, 1987, p. 133, table 7.34.
3  Ibid.
4  Audit Commission, *Making a Reality of Community Care*, London, HMSO, 1986, p. 3.
5  DHSS, *Health and Personal Social Services Statistics*, London, HMSO, 1987.
6  B. Davies and D. Challis, *Matching Resources to Needs in Community Care*, Aldershot, Gower, 1986.
7  Source for statistics, *Social Trends 17* p. 134, table 7.37.
8  Ibid., p. 55, table 3.1.
9  Audit Commission, *Making a Reality*, p. 19
10  Ibid., p. 24.
11  See DHSS, *Social Work Support for the Health Service*, London, HMSO, 1974.
12  As in *Priorities for Health and Personal Services* and *The Way Forward*, London, HMSO, 1977.
13  These issues are discussed in K. Judge, *Rationing Social Services*, London, Heinemann, 1987. For

a strong pro-pricing line see R. Harris and A. Seldon, *Pricing or Taxing*, London, Institute of Economic Affairs, 1976.

14  Z. T. Butrym, *The Nature of Social Work*, London, Macmillan , 1976, pp. 10–11.

15  British Association of Social Workers, *The Social Work Task*, Birmingham, BASW, 1977.

16  National Institute of Social Work, *Social Workers: Their Roles and Tasks: Report of a Working Party*, London, Bedford Square Press, 1982 (known as the Barclay Report).

17  See B. Wootton, *Social Science and Social Pathology*, London, Allen and Unwin, 1959; and R. A. Sinfield, *Which Way for Social Work?*, London, Fabian Society, 1969.

18  See H. Specht and A. Vickery, *Integrating Social Work Methods*, London, Allen and Unwin, 1977.

19  These issues are explored in *Social Services Teams: The Practitioner's View*, London, HMSO, 1978.

20  See R. Hadley and M. McGrath, *Going Local: Neighbourhood Social Services*, London, Bedford Square Press, 1981.

21  The relationship between ideal and reality is discussed very fully in B. Jordan, *Poor Parents*, London, Routledge and Kegan Paul, 1974; and in M. J. Hill and P. Laing, *Social Work and Money*, London, Allen and Unwin, 1979.

22  See R. Holman, *Poverty*, London, Martin Robertson, 1978.

23  See Jordan, *Poor Parents*.

24  Ibid.; also J. Handler, *The Coercive Social Worker*, Chicago, Rand McNally, 1973.

25  See A. Holme and J. Maizels, *Volunteers in Social Work*, London, Allen and Unwin, 1978.

26  See C. Hallett and O. Stevenson, *Child Abuse: Aspects of Interprofessional Communication*, London, Allen and Unwin, 1979.

28  Audit Commission, *Making a Reality*.

29  C. Hallett, *The Personal Social Services in Local Government*, London, Allen and Unwin, 1982.

30  A. Webb and G. Wistow, *Social Work, Social Care and Social Planning: The Personal Social Services since Seebohm*, London, Longman, 1987.

31  T. Booth (ed.), *Planning for Welfare: Social Policy and the Expenditure Process*, Oxford, Blackwell, 1979.

32  E. M. Goldberg and R. W. Warburton, *Ends and Means in Social Work*, London, Allen and Unwin, 1979.

33  D. N. Thomas and R. W. Warburton, *Community Workers in a Social Services Department*, London, National Institute for Social Work, 1977.

34  K. Judge, 'The Public Purchase of Social Care', *Policy and Politics*, 10 (1982).

35  A. Webb and G. Wistow, *Planning, Need and Scarcity*, London, Allen and Unwin, 1986.

36  H. Glennerster, *Paying for Welfare*, Oxford, Blackwell, 1985.

## Chapter 7   The Health Service

1   Central Statistical Office, *Social Trends 17*, London, HMSO, 1987, p. 135, table 7.39.

2   See the discussion in R. Robinson and K. Judge, *Public Expenditure and the NHS: Trends and Prospects*, London, King's Fund Institute, 1987.

3   *The Government's Expenditure Plans, 1987–1988 to 1989–1990* (see n. 3 in ch. 3), vol. II, p. 220.

4   D. Tuckett (ed.), *An Introduction to Medical Sociology*, London, Tavistock, 1976.

5   E. Friedson, *Professional Dominance*, Chicago, Aldine, 1970.

6   The British free service is compared with sytems in other countries in B. Abel-Smith, *Value for Money in Health Services*, London, Heinemann, 1976.

7   Report of the Royal Commission on the National Health Service, Cmnd 7615, London, HMSO, 1979, p. 353.

8   See T. Butcher and E. Randall, 'The Politics of Pay Beds: Labour Party Policy and Legislation', *Policy and Politics*, 9 (1981), pp. 273–93.

9   See P. Townsend and N. Davidson (eds), *Inequalities in Health: The Black Report*, Harmondsworth, Penguin, 1982.

10  Report of the Royal Commission (n. 7 above), p. 17.

11  Ibid., p. 15.

12  See DHSS, *Sharing Resources for Health in England*, London, HMSO, 1976.

13  See R. Klein and P. Hall, *Caring for Quality in the Caring Services*, London, Centre for Studies in Social Policy, 1975.

14 A. Lindsey, *Socialized Medicine in England and Wales*, Chapel Hill, University of North Carolina Press, 1962.
15 C. Ham, *Health Policy in Britain*, London, Macmillan, 1985.
16 R. Levitt and A. Wall, *The Reorganized National Health Service*, London, Croom Helm, 1984.
17 J. Allsop and A. May. *The Emperor's New Clothes*, London, King Edward's Hospital Fund, 1986.

## CHAPTER 8   EDUCATION

1 Department of Education and Science, *Grant Maintained Schools: A Consultative Paper*, London, HMSO, 1987, p. 1.
2 *Social Trends 17* (see n. 1 in ch. 7), p. 57, table 3.3.
3 J. Ford, *Social Class and the Comprehensive School*, London, Routledge and Kegan Paul, 1969.
4 Department of Education and Science, *Special Educational Needs* (Report of the Warnock Committee), London, HMSO, 1978.
5 *Social Trends 17*, p. 63, table 3.16.
6 See Sir F. Lincoln Ralphs, *The Role and Training of Education Welfare Officers*, London, Local Government Training Board, 1973.
7 *Social Trends 17*, p. 67, table 3.25.
8 Ibid., p. 60, table 3.9.
9 See M. Blaug, *An Introduction to the Economics of Education*, Harmondsworth, Penguin, 1970.
10 For a discussion of some of the legal issues in the central–local contest see M. Loughlin (n. 4 ch. 3), ch. 5.
11 Department of Education and Science and Welsh Office, *A New Partnership for our Schools*, London, HMSO, 1977.
12 See, in particular, J. W. B. Douglas, *The Home and the School*, London, MacGibbon and Kee, 1964; J. Floud, A. H. Halsey and F. M. Martin, *Social Class and Education Opportunity*, London, Heinemann, 1956; and B. Jackson and D. Marsden, *Education and the Working Class*, London, Routledge and Kegan Paul, 1962.
13 Douglas, *The Home and the School*; see also the Plowden Report (n. 28 in ch. 2)
14 See A. H. Halsey (ed.), *Educational Priority*, vol. 1, London, HMSO, 1972.
15 Plowden Report.
16 Department of Education and Science, *Education for All* (a brief guide by Lord Swann to the *Report of the Committee of Inquiry into the Education of Children from Ethnic Minority Groups*), London, HMSO, 1985, p. 9.
17 Ibid., p. 10.
18 J. Finch, *Education and Social Policy*, London, Longman, 1984.
19 D. E. Regan, *Local Government and Education*, London, Allen and Unwin, 1977.
20 M. Kogan, *The Politics of Educational Change*, Glasgow, Fontana, 1978.
21 M. Stone, *The Education of the Black Child in Britain*, Glasgow, Fontana, 1981.
22 J. Rex and S. Tomlinson, *Colonial Immigrants in a British City*, London, Routledge Kegan and Paul. 1979.

## CHAPTER 9   EMPLOYMENT SERVICES

1 *The Government's Expenditure Plans 1987–1988 to 1989–1990,* (see n. 3 in ch. 3), vol.II, p. 110.
2 Ibid., p. 122.
3 Ibid., p. 116.
4 Ibid.
5 Society of Civil and Public Servants, *Work for the Future – A New Strategy for Training and Employment*, London. SCPS, 1986, p. 15.
6 See Department of Employment, *People and Jobs*, London, HMSO, 1971.
7 Ibid., p. 5.
8 Quoted in House of Commons, *Seventh Report from the Expenditure Committee, Session 1976–77*, London, HMSO, 1977, p. 147.
9 See *Social Trends 17* (see n. 1 in ch. 7), p. 60, table 3.10.
10 See figures in *Unemployment Bulletin*, Issue 23, Spring 1987, London, Unemployment Unit, p. 14.

11  The figures in this paragraph are taken from *The Government's Expenditure Plans 1987–88 to 1989–90*, section 3.7.
12  J. Moon and J. Richardson, *Unemployment in the U.K.*, Aldershot, Gower, 1985.
13  A. Sinfield, *What Unemployment Means*, Oxford, Martin Robertson, 1981.
14  The Unemployment Unit is a voluntary research and campaigning organization based at 9 Poland Street, London, W1V 3DG.
15  D. Finn, *Training without Jobs*, London, Macmillan, 1987.

## CHAPTER 10   HOUSING

1  All these figures are taken from *Social Trends 17* (see n. 1 in ch. 7), p. 137.
2  *Housing Policy: A Consultative Document*, Cmnd 6851, London, HMSO, 1977, p. 14.
3  Ibid., p. 83.
4  M. Loughlin, *Local Government in the Modern State*, London, Sweet and Maxwell, 1986, p. 107. The data he quotes comes from S. Bailey, 'Absurd Framework', *Public Money*, 4 (1984).
5  *The Government's Expenditure Plans 1987–88 to 1989–90* (see n. 3 in ch. 3), vol. II, p. 157, table 3.9.20.
6  *Social Trends 17*, p. 143, table 8.12.
7  *Housing Policy: A Consultative Document*, p. 10.
8  *The Government's Expenditure Plans 1987–88 to 1989–90*, vol. II, p. 37, table 2.29.
9  Ninth report of the Housing Management Sub-Committee of the Central Housing Advisory Committee, *Council Housing Purposes, Procedures and Priorities* (the Cullingworth Report), London, HMSO, 1969.
10  *Housing Policy: A Consultative Document*, p. 79.
11  E. Burney, *Housing on Trial*, London, Oxford University Press, 1967, p. 71.
12  These are standards for local authority housing recommended by the Central Housing Advisory Committee, *Homes for Today and Tomorrow* (the Parker Morris Report), London, HMSO, 1961.
13  *Social Trends 17*, p. 145, table 8.16.
14  See, for a discussion of these studies, A. Murie, P.Niner and C. Watson, *Housing Policy and the Housing System*, London, Allen and Unwin, 1976.
15  D. V. Donnison and C. Ungerson, *Housing Policy*, Harmondsworth, Penguin, 1982.
16  S. Lansley, *Housing and Public Policy*, London, Croom Helm, 1979.
17  S. Merrett, *State Housing in Britain*, London, Routledge and Kegan Paul,1979.
18  P. Malpass and A. Murie, *Housing Policy and Practice*, London, Macmillan, 1982.
19  P. Malpass (ed.), *The Housing Crisis*, London, Croom Helm, 1986.

## CHAPTER 11   SOCIAL POLICY AND SOCIETY

1  Data taken from *Social Trends 17* (see n. 1 in ch. 7), p. 114, table 6.21.
2  *The Government's Expenditure Plans 1987–88 to 1989–90* (see n. 3 in ch. 3), p. 421.
3  See, for example, R. Harris and A. Seldon, *Overruled on Welfare*, London, Institute of Economic Affairs, 1979; and P. Minford, 'State Expenditure: a study in waste', *Economic Affairs*, 1984 (April–June).
4  See R. M. Titmuss, *Income Distribution and Social Change*, London, Allen and Unwin, 1962; and A. B. Atkinson, 'Income Distribution and Social Change Revisited', *Journal of Social Policy*, 4 (1975), pp. 57–68. Two useful more recent explorations of who gains from the Welfare State are J. Le Grand, *The Strategy of Equality*, London, Allen and Unwin, 1982; and V. George and P. Wilding, *The Impact of Social Policy*, London, Routledge and Kegan Paul, 1984.
5  B. Abel-Smith and P. Townsend, *The Poor and the Poorest*, London, Bell, 1965.
6  A review of the evidence is contained in Royal Commission on the Distribution of Income and Wealth, *Initial Report on the Standing Reference*, Cmnd 6171, London, HMSO, 1975.
7  See P. Townsend (ed.), *The Concept of Poverty*, London, Heinemann, 1970; R. Holman *Poverty*, London, Martin Robertson, 1978; Royal Commission on the Distribution of Income and Wealth, *Report No. 6: Low Incomes*, London, HMSO, 1978; P. Townsend, *Poverty in the United Kingdom*, Harmondsworth, Penguin, 1979; and J. Mack and S. Lansley, *Poor Britain*, London, Allen and Unwin, 1985.
8  R. Bacon and W. Ellis, *Britain's Economic Problem: Too Few Producers*, London, Macmillan,

1976. This argument, and the arguments about a 'crisis' of the welfare state coming from both Right and Left are evaluated in ch. 5 of M. Hill and G. Bramley, *Analysing Social Policy*, Oxford, Blackwell, 1986.

9 *Report of the Royal Commission on Local Government in England* (Redcliffe Maud Report), Cmnd 4040, London, HMSO, 1969.

10 *Policies for the Elderly*, London, HMSO, 1978.

11 See n. 4 ch. 6.

12 Home Office memo quoted in Higgins, *The Poverty Business* (n. 5 in ch. 1), p. 9.

13 See, in particular, J. Bennington, 'Strategies for Change at the Local Level: Some Reflections', in D. Jones and M. Mayo (eds), *Community Work One and Costs of Industrial Change*, London, CDP, 1977.

14 *Policies for the Inner Cities*, Cmnd 6845, London, HMSO, 1977.

15 Inner Area Studies, Department of the Environment, *Summaries of Consultants' Final Report*, London, HMSO, 1977.

16 M. J. Hill, *The State, Administration and the Individual*, Glasgow, Fontana, 1976, pp. 9–10.

17 *Report of the Committee on Administrative Tribunals and Enquiries*, Cmnd 218, London, HMSO, 1957.

18 For further discussion see J. Le Grand and R. Robinson (eds), *Privatisation and the Welfare State*, London, Allen and Unwin, 1984.

19 For further discussion see P. Hoggett and R. Hambleton, *Decentralisation and Democracy*, Bristol, SAUS, 1987; and J. Morphet, 'Local authority decentralisation – Tower Hamlets Goes All the Way', *Policy and Politics*, 15 (1987), pp. 119–26.

20 See n. 38 in ch. 2.

21 See n. 36 in ch. 2.

22 J. Higgins, N. Deakin, J. Edwards and M. Wicks, *Government and Urban Poverty*, Oxford, Blackwell, 1984.

23 R. E. Wraith and P.G Hutchesson, Administrative Tribunals, London, Allen and Unwin, 1973.

24 C. Harlow and R. Rawlings, *Law and Administration*, London, Weidenfeld and Nicolson, 1984.

# Index